# The Gloucestershire
Regiment

# The Gloucestershire Regiment

## A Definitive Account of the Most Decorated Infantry Regiment in British History

Matthew A. Holden

Pen & Sword

**MILITARY**

First published in Great Britain in 2026 by
Pen & Sword Military
An imprint of Pen & Sword Books Limited
Yorkshire – Philadelphia



ISBN 978 1 03619 285 3



Typeset by Mac Style
Printed in the UK by CPI Group (UK) Ltd, Croydon, CR0 4YY.

The Publisher's authorised representative in the EU for product
safety is Authorised Rep Compliance Ltd., Ground Floor,
71 Lower Baggot Street, Dublin D02 P593, Ireland.
www.arccompliance.com

For a complete list of Pen & Sword titles please contact

PEN & SWORD BOOKS LIMITED
47 Church Street, Barnsley, South Yorkshire, S70 2AS, England
E-mail: enquiries@pen-and-sword.co.uk
Website: www.pen-and-sword.co.uk
or
PEN AND SWORD BOOKS
1950 Lawrence Road, Havertown, PA 19083, USA
E-mail: uspen-and-sword@casematepublishers.com
Website: www.penandswordbooks.com

Dedicated to
266662 Bertram Holden
2/6th Battalion, Gloucestershire Regiment
KIA 19/07/1916
Fromelles
*"By Our Deeds We Are Known"*

# Contents

# A Forward by HRH the
# Duke of Gloucester KG, GCVO

We are all aware that acts of bravery on the battlefield are acknowledged by medals awarded to those who deserve it. There are other awards that are conferred on regiments, who were present on the battlefields, and these honours are embroidered on the regimental colours to recall battles won. Sadly, battles lost are not recorded, however well the regiment may have performed.

The Gloucestershire Regiment, during its 300 years of existence, happens to have participated in more victories than any other infantry regiment. During the First World War, the Gloucesters had 24 battalions and therefore took part in virtually every battle.

The interesting aspect of these Battle Honours is not just the number of them, but the fact that so frequently the Gloucesters played a key part in the battle. At the Battle of Alexandria in 1801, the Regiment fought back-to-back against Napoleonic troops, and for this they were awarded the famous Back Badge, becoming the only Regiment in the history of the British Army to be allowed to wear a badge on the back of their caps. More recently, during the Korean War, they managed to hold off a Division of Chinese troops long enough for a large part of the Commonwealth troops to escape to defend Seoul.

This book explains circumstances of each Battle Honour and is the first history to record the full story for those who should be impressed by these stories of service to this country by the people mostly from Gloucestershire.

# Introduction

Battle Honours began life as a way of recognising the achievements and legacy of military units in battles, wars and campaigns. They are usually awarded to units whose size is a battalion or larger. Although they have been around since the late 17th Century, the manner in which we recognise them began with the Siege of Gibraltar in 1779. Infantry regiments, such as our two protagonists, were entitled to display the name of battle honours, backed by a scroll, upon the Kings or Queens Colours and regimental colours.

Up until the First World War, every battle honour was entitled to be scribed upon the Colours. This meant that the Glosters had thirty-four by the end of the Boer War. However, after the First World War had ended almost every regiment had been involved in a vast number of battles. The Glosters alone had fought in excess of eighty battles and campaigns. Clearly, this is far too many to put on the Colours. Therefore, despite the great controversy that this decision caused, regiments were only entitled to select a maximum of ten honours to display on the Colours. This decision was once again made during the Second World War when only ten out of the twenty-two battle honours were entitled to be borne on the Colours. Further, in Korea, only a maximum of two battle honours could be displayed, despite the Glosters winning three.

The WWI honours also cause something of an additional anomaly. Ypres 1914, 1915, 1917 and the Somme 1916, 1918 are considered to be just two battle honours, not five. However, these were completely separate campaigns, operations and battles that are tenuously linked at best. As such, for the subject of this book, they shall be treated as individual honours.

Throughout the glorious history of the Gloucestershire Regiment, they have been awarded a total of 141 battle honours, with only sixty-one of these displayed upon the Colours. This makes the Regiment the most decorated infantry regiment in the history of the British Army and well worth recording within the pages of this book.

The main narrative for this work comes from documents discovered within the Regimental Archive held at the Soldiers of Gloucestershire Museum. There may be some elements of the work which differ from the now agreed upon history of events. However, this book examines the role of the Gloucestershire

Regiment and so it was deemed important to reflect the narrative found in their own archives.

It is helpful to have a short explanation of Regimental names used in this account. The Gloucestershire Regiment can trace its roots back to 1694 when regiments of infantry were named after the Colonel who raised them on behalf of the Crown. Usually this was in response to some grave national crisis. During the 17th Century, this way of naming regiments became rather confusing as the name changed to which ever Colonel took over from his predecessor.

As an example, the 28th (North Gloucestershire) Regiment of Foot started life as Gibson's Foot. Colonel John Gibson was warranted to raise a regiment in the city of Portsmouth. It consisted of thirteen companies of sixty soldiers in each plus three sergeants, three corporals and two drummers. After this, the Regiment was brought out by De Lalo, then Morduant, Windsor, Barrell and finally Bragg. It was eventually decided to rename regiments by the seniority in which they were raised, hence 28th Regiment of Foot.

During the Seven Years War, more men were needed. The Buffs (3rd Foot) raised a second battalion which after a few years became the 61st Regiment of Foot. Then in 1782 regiments were given counties to recruit from, the 61st were given Bristol and South Gloucestershire and the 28th Foot North Gloucestershire. For ease of following the paths of our two protagonists, the 28th (North Gloucestershire) Regiment of Foot and 61st (South Gloucestershire) Regiment of Foot are the names that will be used throughout the opening sections of the book.

In the Cardwell reforms of the 1880s it was decided to amalgamate certain regiments into one county regiment, hence the 28th became 1st Battalion, the Gloucestershire Regiment and the 61st became 2nd Battalion, the Gloucestershire Regiment. Both were regular battalions, one normally served as at home in UK while the other was abroad. Despite what the government wanted, both battalions were so proud of their individual histories that they continued to refer to themselves as 28th or 61st until further amalgamation in 1947 when they indeed became one.

In 1994, the Gloucestershire Regiment ceased to exist when they were amalgamated with the Duke of Edinburgh's Royal Regiment (the Berkshire and Wiltshire's) to become the Royal Gloucestershire, Berkshire and Wiltshire Regiment (RGBW). In 2007, further amalgamations were announced by the Government and the RGBW became part of the Rifles. Due to the vast amount of regiments that made up the Rifles they hold a combined 913 battle honours. Our story though will only follow that of the Gloucestershire Regiment, as they are the single infantry regiment that holds the distinction of having the most battle honours.

# The 18th Century

# 1. Ramillies

At the beginning of the campaigning season in 1706, the French general Villeroy marched from his defensive position at Leuven, Belgium. King Louis XIV of France had insisted on this move, as he wanted to avenge a recent previous defeat at Blenheim during the War of Spanish Succession. Villeroy saw that the Allied forces against him were dispersed, and he hoped to land the decisive blow before they had time to unite. Unfortunately for the French, their opponent would be arguably Britain's greatest every general, John Churchill, the Duke of Marlborough.

Marlborough instantly recognised the French error of leaving their defences and quickly concentrated the British, Dutch and Danish troops in his immediate vicinity. On Sunday 23rd May, the Allies found the French Army lined up either side of the village of Ramillies ready for battle. Marlborough realised that the French right flank could be turned, and so launched what would be an audacious plan.

The French left was based on high ground and centred on the two fortified villages of Offerz and Antrelize. At 10:00, Marlborough launched the entire British contingent, including the 28th (North Gloucestershire) Regiment of Foot, at the French left. The British, in two lines, marched to the top of the high ground where their iconic Redcoats were visible across the entire battlefield. Here they paused and moved back slightly to the crest of the hill.

The sight of the British caused Villeroy to panic and he immediately moved men from his right to cover the opposite flank. This was the exact mistake Marlborough had intended to provoke. For it was actually only the first line of Redcoats who remained on the high ground. Unbeknown to the French the entire second line, including the 28th, had moved back down the hill and were making their way towards the centre of the battle.

At 13:30 the cannon warmed up and then cavalry attacked the French right. Marlborough then sent in his infantry to attack the centre. The battle raged and did not go particularly well for the Allies until the second line of Redcoats arrived. The 28th along with the rest of these troops launched themselves into the fray and the French started to give way. At this point twenty-one squadrons of Danish cavalry managed to break through the crumbling French lines. They reformed in the enemy rear and then smashed into the centre. The French were broken.

The enemy were chased for six entire days resulting in total victory for Marlborough and the Allies. All of the French baggage was captured along with fifty-four out of sixty cannon. Within five days, Marlborough was riding into Brussels. Within two weeks the whole of Spanish Flanders had fallen. The 28th would be awarded their first ever battle honour and never before, or perhaps again, would a British general win such a resounding victory.

# 2. Louisburg

Although the factors behind the Seven Years War are wide ranging, it ultimately boiled down to the British and French attempting to construct an empire at the expense of the other. Conflict raged all over the globe, with the ports of France itself attacked along with other expeditions in Africa and India. Alongside this, the French had built a vast colonial holding in North America based around the St. Lawrence River, roughly the modern day boundary of the United States and Canada. Louisburg was the cork in the bottle of the St. Lawrence and its downfall would open up the entirety of French possessions to attack.

The city itself was built on a narrow headland resulting in water surrounding three sides and the addition of an excellent harbour. The landward side of the city was dominated by a sequence of hills making it vulnerable to a land assault. In February 1758, Admiral Boscawen's fleet of 157 ships arrived transporting General Amherst's army of 11,000 men.

The 28th (North Gloucestershire) Regiment of Foot would arrive later. Despite already being in Canada they were actually far south in Chignecto, Nova Scotia, and had to be transported to Louisburg by the bomb ketch 'Hawke'. Due to this fact, the army were already organised on arrival and the 28th were kept in reserve at first. On the 8th June, the British forces were ready to make their landing. The fighting was desperate, and only at the last moment was a bridgehead established.

The 28th did not take part in the landings. They were given perhaps an even more daunting task. The Glosters piled into small craft and sailed past the mouth of the harbour. These passed under the coastal batteries and feinted to make a landing at Lorambic. The hope was to distract the French from the true landing. The 28th were cannonaded by the coastal batteries but it remains unclear what effect this *ruse de guerre* had upon the French troops positioning.

The following day the 28th returned to the main force, and they began the onerous task of constructing roads through the camp so that the artillery could be transported to the battlefield. On the 1st July, the 28th along with the Highlanders and Light Infantry, marched out of camp and captured two small hills in front of Louisburg. Here, Amherst wanted to establish his batteries and the next few days were spent building redoubts and heading off French sorties. Once the redoubts were constructed, the artillery was moved up and fire opened on the city and its harbour.

On the 21st July, a French ship caught on fire after being pelted by the British artillery. The fire spread to several other ships in the harbour and this resulted in chaos. Two days later, another cannon shot set alight the 'Kings Bastion'. At this time, it was the largest building in North America. On the 24th July, one of the overworked gun batteries exploded resulting in several injuries for the 28th. Finally, the next day, the Royal Navy stormed the harbour and destroyed the remaining ships berthed there. This resulted in the city of Louisburg surrendering within 24 hours, along with 5,600 soldiers, two hundred cannon and a vast store of munitions.

On the 21st August, the 28th along with several other regiments embarked on ships and sailed off to the River Gaspie. Their goal was to destroy French fishing stations in the region. The British decided to reduce Louisburg to rubble using explosives. However, due to its vast size the operation took nearly a year.

# 3. Guadeloupe

In September 1758, the 61st (South Gloucestershire) Regiment of Foot were inspected by the Earl of Panmure at Chatham. He signed off on their inspection as *"a good Regiment, well-appointed and well disciplined"*. Although he did make a point of noting the men were of an unusually *"low size"*. This feedback was a positive for the regiment as they would soon be shipping out from Portsmouth to gain their first ever battle honour.

As it was, bad autumnal storms delayed the departure of the 61st, led by Lieutenant Colonel John Barlow, until the 12th November. In their party were six other regiments, along with eight hundred Royal Marines and five hundred artillerymen. The army crammed into sixty transports that were protected by eight ships of the line. Clearly, this was no small venture and the British certainly meant business in the Seven Years War by sending out such a strong force.

Major General Peregrine Hopson, previously Governor of Nova Scotia, was in overall command of operations. When the flotilla landed in Carlisle Bay, Barbados, on 3rd January 1759, two more ships of the line joined them. Commodore John Moore, who met them there, then took over control of the naval element of the expedition. The initial idea was to invade the island of Martinique. Yet, the defences and fortifications of Martinique proved to be far more advanced than intelligence suggested and they promptly left the island. Therefore, the large flotilla sailed for the secondary target of Guadeloupe.

Guadeloupe was a promising and important target for two reasons. Firstly, it was the main port for French privateers who mercilessly preyed upon British merchant shipping in the Caribbean. Secondly, it was the wealthiest of French colonial possessions in the West Indies, producing a rich yearly harvest of sugar and rum. Guadeloupe is actually two islands very close together. Guadeloupe to the west and Grand Terre to the east. These two land masses are separated by a narrow channel called the Salt River.

Arriving on 22nd January 1759, the island was found to be defended by three hundred French Marines and an artillery company, along with innumerable irregular units. At face value, the French were outnumbered yet one needs to consider that the rugged mountainous terrain and vast plantations full of dense, tall sugar cane was perfect for defence.

The British force arrived on the southern tip of Guadeloupe at a town called Basse-Terre. A large forty-seven gun fortress and another four coastal batteries, with a combined thirty-four cannon, defended the area. Immediately the Royal

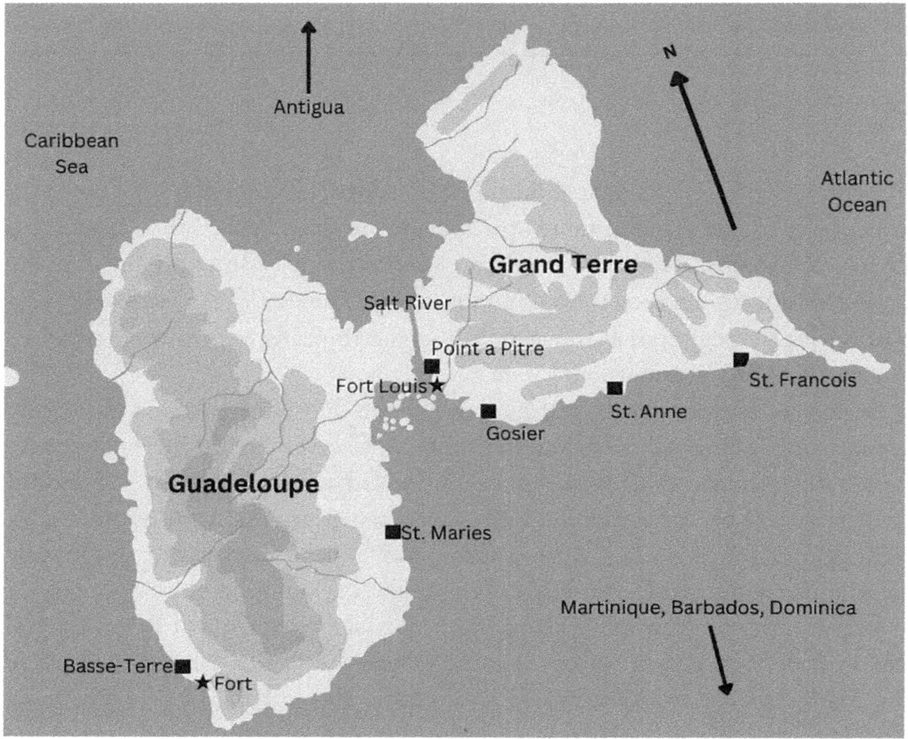


Navy swung into action and silenced the dangerous coastal batteries, whilst another three ships of the line attacked the fortress. Once safe enough, four bomb ketches moved close to the shoreline and began launching their deadly payload into the town. Suddenly, a huge explosion occurred as one of the shells hit the highly explosive rum and sugar harvest.

At 15:00 the next day, the first troops were landed a little way down the shoreline. The 61st were given orders to secure the town and fort, which they found to be abandoned. However, without realising it, these men were in mortal danger. The French had booby-trapped the forts magazine and it would explode imminently. Luckily though, the forts Genoese Chief Gunner had decided to desert his French paymaster and warned the 61st of their impending doom. They arrived at the magazine just as a drunken local, who had been well paid by the French, was staggering towards the explosives with a lit match in his hand.

After a few days, all the troops and supplies had been brought ashore when shots were heard at the picquets. It was learnt that the French were advancing and beginning to fortify a house close to where the army had landed. Hopson sent forward his grenadiers, amongst them, men of the 61st Regiment. A small skirmish occurred in which the French fled but a pursuit was impossible due to the thick jungle terrain.

The governor of Guadeloupe, Nadau du Treil, realised this strong enemy force would not be defeated in open battle, and so he led his men ten kilometres away into the impregnable mountains. The French now began something akin to a guerrilla warfare campaign. They would come down from the mountains, attack the advanced parties, and then disappear again before the British could arrive in greater numbers.

Growing tired of these incessant attacks by the French, on the 4th February, Hopson decided to send the 61st up into the mountains to attack one of their gun batteries. Unfortunately, Captain Barford of the 61st, leading the detachment, did little to distinguish himself. Firstly, he set off to attack the wrong battery and then en route he also naively set fire to native huts. The enemy were warned by these fires and a large French force hit the 61st in the flank. Despite this poor leadership by Barford, the men excelled themselves and within ten minutes, the enemy were withdrawing. The 61st lost eight men killed or wounded. The next day a deserter arrived and announced French losses of seventy killed and one hundred and thirty wounded.

Hopson then decided to extend his picquets out to a five-kilometre boundary, but by now, tropical disease had caught hold of the British. Just getting supplies to the outlying parties proved to be a superhuman effort. Within two weeks of landing on Guadeloupe 1500 men, almost a quarter of the army, had been struck down by illness. Six hundred dying men were loaded on board ships and carried off to Antigua in the hope that their lives might be saved in a more accommodating climate. Those who could work toiled away through the intensely humid atmosphere and beating sun, in their entirely inappropriate uniforms.

John Moore, Commodore of the Navy fleet, became exasperated by Hopson's inactivity. After landing at Basse-Terre, the army had not made any effort to advance inland. Luckily for Moore though, his command was independent of the land forces. The eastern isle, Grand Terre, was the most fertile and it was here that Moore decided to attack. The key to the entire island was a town called Pointe-a-Pitre that was guarded by Fort Louis. He battered the fortress and then installed three hundred men of the 42nd, along with a detachment of Marines.

The reason for Hopson's inactivity can be attributed to the fact that he was a dying man. Hopson was one of the first to succumb to tropical disease, and on the 27th February, he died. The situation on Guadeloupe now seemed completely hopeless. The army had made no inroads, over fifty percent of the men were now dead or dying, and their leader had passed away. Thankfully,

Colonel Barrington now stepped up into command and he proved to be an extraordinary soldier.

Barrington immediately jumped into action, he decided to leave Basse-Terre (except for the 63rd who were left as a garrison) and move all forces to Fort Louis. Upon arrival, the fort was found to have been badly damaged by Moore's bombardment, so eleven days were spent reinforcing the structure.

The positive start by Barrington was soon undermined, as on the 12th March news came that a vast French fleet had arrived in the Caribbean. Moore had no choice but to withdraw the British fleet to Dominica from where he could react to French movements. Before Moore left though, he begged Barrington for more men as the Navy too had suffered terribly from disease. Reluctantly, three hundred healthy troops boarded the ships and sailed off to Dominica. Another unfortunate side effect from this meant that the French privateers, previously held up in Guadeloupe, were able to escape. Over the next eleven weeks, they captured more than sixty British merchant vessels.

Unperturbed, Barrington read the military situation perfectly. Due to the terrain, the French had to split their forces multiple times to protect the various settlements and fortresses. By attacking these one at a time the British were guaranteed numerical superiority. The naval transports, which had remained at Guadeloupe, would be used to carry Barrington, Brigadier Byam Crump and Brigadier John Clavering to various points on the island where they could unleash their assault.

The first assault occurred on the 27th March, when six hundred men under Crump set off towards the south coast of Grande Terre to attack the towns of Sainte-Anne and Saint-Francois. Lieutenant Colonel Barlow was second in command of the operation, as many men were from the 61st. Whilst Crump headed towards Saint-Francois, Barlow and the 61st were tasked with attacking Sainte-Anne. After an initial assault, the French fled and the towns, along with their powerful batteries, were destroyed. These joint operations resulted in only one loss.

Meanwhile, Barrington ordered another three hundred men to attack Gosier. These men were the remainder of the 61st and so Major Teesdale was in command. The men of Gloucestershire, over four thousand miles from home, disembarked on the beach under heavy fire from shore batteries and trenches. They formed up in an orderly fashion on the beach and then advanced on the enemy, sending them fleeing in a panic. The town was then set on fire and the battery destroyed.

Barrington now decided to test the current balance of power. Surprisingly, rather than heading back to the boats, he sent orders for the 61st to march the twenty miles back to Fort Louis. This odyssey would take the 61st through thick jungle and over lofty mountains. On this journey, a newly constructed French fort was found to be blocking their path. It was well sited as it had a commanding view over Fort Louis. The 61st charged up the hill and entered the fort. The rather shocked French quickly surrendered, but not before the 61st had lost eight men and had another twelve wounded.

For a further two months, such operations continued in earnest until Barrington was ready to make his final assault on 18th April 1759. On the southeast of the western isle sat the French stronghold of Sainte Maries. All remaining French forces had gathered there and they were, as usual, well entrenched and had a good amount of cannon. The surrounding area was dense jungle and the French felt confident in their hide away. Unfortunately, they had not reckoned with the fact that the 61st Regiment of Foot were against them. These men would soon be well deserving of their first ever battle honour.

The French opened proceedings with a furious cannon fire. So confident were they in their "impenetrable" jungle surroundings, that they left all pathways completely unguarded. So, whilst the cannon boomed out, Barrington sent the 61st down one of these pathways. It brought them out immediately in the rear of the French entrenchments, which shocked their adversaries. The French, seeing the sudden appearance of the 61st, hurriedly abandoned their posts and fled to another line of trench works on the high ground surrounding Sainte Maries.

Barrington sent his entire army in pursuit, and a fierce battle commenced, with the jungle being desperately cleared along the way to make room for British artillery. The 61st, who were still wide out on the flank, ploughed on through the thick undergrowth. They came across some steep cliffs and began to climb. Reaching the top, they once again found themselves in the rear of the French trenches. Discovering that they had again been turned, the French now launched their entire force against the Glosters. Luckily, Brigadier Clavering had come up with his detachment and threw his men at the enemy. As Clavering describes below, the fighting was terrible but after a while, the French were finally beaten:

We pursued them as far as the heights of St Marie's, where we again formed our men for a fresh attack on the lines and batteries there.

Whilst the barricades were levelling for the artillery, we attempted a second time to pass the woods and precipices that covered the flanks of the enemy's lines; but, before we could get up our cannon, they perceived this movement, and began to quit their lines to oppose it, which made us resolve, without any further delay, to attack them immediately in front; and it was accordingly executed with the greatest vivacity, notwithstanding the constant firing both of their cannon and musketry. They abandoned here all their artillery, and went off in so much confusion, that they never afterwards appeared before us.

We took up our quarters at St Marie's that night, and the next day entered the Capesterre, which is the richest and most beautiful part of this or any other country in the West Indies.

On the 2nd May 1759, the French Governor, Nadau du Treil, signed the surrender documents. Ironically, the very next day, Admiral de Bompart arrived with the French fleet and vast reinforcements. It was too late though, and he had to respect the decision of submission and so he skulked off to make trouble elsewhere in the Caribbean.

The fate of Guadeloupe ended up causing quite a stir at home, in the press and in Parliament. Great men like Edmund Burke petitioned for the island to become a powerhouse of the British Empire economy in the Caribbean, whilst men like Benjamin Franklin argued for it to play a subordinate role to North America. As it was, the island was eventually ceded back to the French during the Treaty of Paris 1763.

# 4. Quebec

Back in North America, following success at Louisburg, Major General Wolfe landed his army of 9000 men at Ile d'Orleans, an island three miles downriver from Quebec, in June 1959. The 28th (North Gloucestershire) Regiment of Foot, 356 men strong, accompanied the army led by Lieutenant Colonel Hunt Walsh. What followed were weeks of failed attempts to gain a foothold on the mainland. The Glosters saw their first action on the 28th June, when a violent storm meant that the strong naval escort needed a new anchorage. The perfect spot was overlooked by French positions and so the 28th were sent in to clear the enemy. After a brief skirmish, the French fled and the fleet could safely harbour in its new location.

During July, the 28th foraged and took part in expeditions to other parts of the coastline. There were also hostile natives to contend with and two examples highlight how active this enemy were. At one point in the month, an advanced

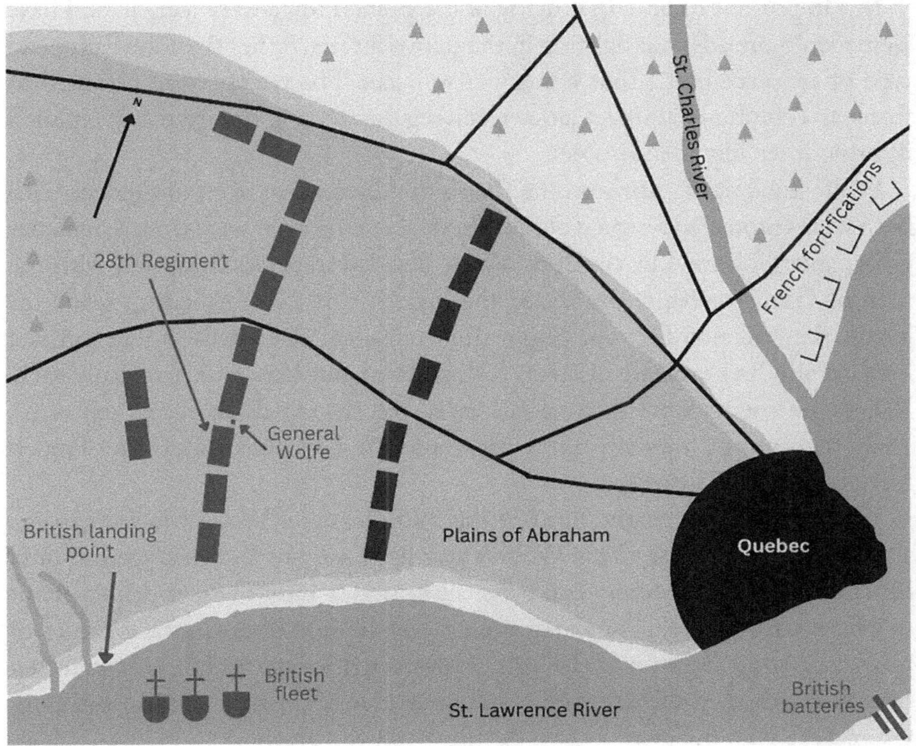

outpost up the St. Lawrence River was surrounded by five hundred natives. The 28th, who happened to be on hand, poured into the woods and fired upon the enemy. The natives had no intention of a standing battle with the British, and they fled. The Glosters returned with spoils of 150 horses, cattle and sheep. On another occasion, the Grenadier Company of the 28th were resting in a barn when they heard a commotion outside. The natives were attacking a party of Rangers, even scalping fourteen of the unfortunate souls. One-half of the Grenadier party rushed into action, whilst the other half swept around the flank and laid down a decisive enfilading fire.

Time was now running out in the campaigning season, and the French even believed that an attempt at landing would not come so late in the year. However, on the 13th September 1759, Wolfe loaded his army into boats and headed for a small beach where narrow and steep paths led to Quebec. Wolfe positioned himself in the lead craft whilst 320 men of the 28th took the honoured second position. Further behind them, another 1700 men swept silently through the night. The landing was made almost unopposed and immediately Wolfe and the 28th tore up the steep paths and attacked the few French at the top. They then silently formed up whilst the boats returned for the second wave. By dawn 4500 men had been successfully landed.

It is important to note that many of the French force were irregulars. These were men more adept at fighting in the native forests, rather than the European type of set piece battle that was about to occur. The enemy were not used to firing as a combined unit, let alone receiving devastating fire from a disciplined fighting force like the Glosters.

Wolfe lined up his army on the Plains of Abraham in front of Quebec with both wings protected by steep bluffs. On the extreme right were three Grenadier Companies, followed by the 28th. Wolfe decided to position himself with the men of Gloucestershire. By 09:00 the French had also formed up ready for battle, they opened fire and began their advance. The battle would not last long. Wolfe had ordered his men to load their muskets with two balls each. When the enemy were thirty yards away, the British discharged their arms. They then moved forward a few paces and fired another volley. The French force fled back to Quebec.

Whilst advancing at the head of the 28th, General Wolfe was shot in the abdomen and then the chest. Wolfe knew he was dying but managed to hold his last breathe until victory had been confirmed to him. There is debate about in whose arms he died. For a long time it was thought it was in the embrace of Captain Arthur Browne of the 28th. However, it is now widely accepted that he actually died in the arms of Lieutenant Henry Browne of the Louisburg Grenadiers who incidentally was Arthur Browne's brother.

Montcalm, the French commander, also died in the battle resulting in great confusion in Quebec. The French governor decided to abandon the city and march out with the remnants of his forces to link up with French troops elsewhere. He left a token garrison and this capitulated on the 18th September. The French would actually return in 1760 and defeat the British in another set battle; however, they failed to take the city itself. Expected French reinforcements never arrived after a great naval battle at Quiberon Bay, and the French colonial holdings in North America were no more. The 28th meanwhile, had left and were causing carnage in the Caribbean.

# 5. Martinique

On 24th December 1761, the 28th (North Gloucestershire) Regiment of Foot sailed from North America heading for the West Indies. En-route they linked up with more troops in Guadeloupe and Antigua. This force of thirteen thousand men were heading for the island of Martinique. The destination was reached on 7th January 1762, with the Royal Navy anchoring in several bays around the island to confuse the French.

Martinique's main bastion was Fort Royal and it was a daunting target. It sat on a vast rocky hilltop inside of a bay, well protected by gun batteries and surrounded by thick jungle. On the landward side of the bay sat a series of steep hills, including Morne Tortensson and Morne Grenier. Both had been strongly fortified by the French defenders. At first, the British landed troops to attack the gun batteries from the rear, but the jungle was found to be impenetrable. They tried elsewhere; yet again, the result was the same.

On the 14th January, the entire fleet anchored outside the bay where Fort Royal was situated and they continued to look for a landing place. The following day, a risky place was spotted five miles down the coast but this was defended by several batteries. Despite the risks, these batteries needed to be neutralised by the Royal Navy, and by midday on the 16th, the job had been finished. This allowed the 28th and the rest of the army to finally head ashore. Now began the march on Fort Royal.

This would be no victory procession. The terrain was awful with jungle, deep chasms and rising heights around every turn. The French had laid batteries on each and every vantage point and to neutralise them, the British had to erect their own batteries. This meant dragging cannon through the energy sapping topography. Finally on the 24th January, they reached their first objective, Morne Tortensson. Whilst the cannon pounded the slopes of the hill, a select force, including the 28th, marched along the coastline. They were covered by a thousand seamen in boats who rowed along the shore.

The British force attacked a series of redoubts, with the Light Company of the 28th being the first to make contact. A small party of men, led by Lieutenant Gilmer, stormed the first battery and turned two French guns on the enemy. When another force slipped down the right flank, the French panicked and fled. The battle took its toll on the British though with casualties amounting to 383.

The capture of Morne Tortensson gave the British a vantage point over Fort Royal itself, and the next day the cannon opened fire. This was immediately replied to with cannon fire from the next hill, Morne Grenier. It soon became clear that no attack on Fort Royal could occur until this obstacle had also been neutralised. On the 27th January, the British marched up the hill, when suddenly three French columns appeared. Fortuitously though, one of the columns exposed their flank to the Highlanders who immediately routed them, causing all of the French to flee. The 28th, along with the rest of the British forces, then charged after the enemy and spent the night driving the French away. After six hours draining work, the hilltop was secured with the loss of just a hundred casualties.

The British could now erect batteries just 370 metres from Fort Royal, and the French Governor retreated inland leaving just a token garrison to hold the fort. On 3rd February, the defenders of Fort Royal surrendered, handing over 170 cannon and huge quantities of ammunition. The fourteen ships that sat in the harbour were claimed by the Royal Navy. After another quick amphibious operation by the Marines, the French surrendered the entire island and Martinique became a British possession.

# 6. Havannah

Fresh from success at Martinique, the 28th (North Gloucestershire) Regiment of Foot sailed to Cuba with 378 troops. They arrived on 6th June 1762, knowing they had one specific target. Fort Morro, with its 154 guns and eleven mortars, was the key to Havannah, with Havannah the key to the whole of Cuba. The fortress overlooked the city, and could fire directly upon it, so taking this fearsome obstacle would put a huge dent in the Spanish empire.

The force that arrived in Cuba was arguably the largest the Americas had ever seen. Forty-five warships containing just shy of thirty thousand men prowled the coast looking for a perfect landing spot. On the 7th June, Admiral Sir George Pocock feinted a landing of marines four miles west of Havannah. Meanwhile, the Lieutenant General Lord Albemarle was landing his entire army ten miles further east. The army marched towards their intended target, but the Spanish put up resistance as they crossed the river Coximar. The enemy were quickly dispersed by fire from the accompanying naval vessels. The Spanish navy incidentally had extremely strong representation at Havannah. One third of their entire fleet was in the Cuban harbour. Upon the British arrival, the Spanish sunk three vessels across its mouth, to bar entry. Such was the fear of the Senior Service at this time.

On a hill behind the fortress of Morro, was a smaller fort called La Cabana. Were the Spanish to hold this for any length of time, then the British would find the venture quickly unravelling. Happily though, the Spanish holding La Cabana fled upon sight of the British reconnaissance force. On the 12th June, the siege train arrived and the erection of batteries at La Cabana began. This was back breaking work for the men of the 28th, as the ground was solid and water in short supply. Ten days later, twelve heavy guns and thirty-eight mortars began their bombardment of fort Morro. The fortress was well constructed and bristling with guns, so this would be no quick victory.

On 29th June, nearly a thousand Spaniards launched a sortie against the British batteries. Somehow, they managed to get around the rear and began to spike the guns. The British managed to push the attackers back swiftly and not much damage was caused. A few days later though, huge damage was done through a self-inflicted oversight. The batteries were manned by Royal Navy gunners who were far more proficient at firing than their Army brethren. The extreme rate of fire caused a gun to overheat and set several other batteries on fire. The resulting damage set the campaign back immensely.

Over a month into the siege, there had not been much progress so it was decided to begin a mine under the fortifications. Two days later, on 22nd July, almost fifteen hundred men sailed across the harbour from Havannah and attacked the siege works. The British were again quick to react and little damage was done. By the end of July, the mine underneath the right hand fortifications of Morro was ready to detonate. The British stormed the breach and the fortress was taken before the Spanish could regroup. Immediately, the British began constructing batteries facing Havannah.

On the 11th August, Albemarle ordered the Spanish to surrender but they refused. Forty-seven guns, ten mortars and five howitzers opened up a devastating barrage on the city. Within a few hours, every enemy cannon had been silenced and the Spanish had little choice but to surrender. This jewel in the Spanish empire contained rich pickings. Including the eleven men-of-war bottled up in the harbour, Albemarle received £12,500,000 (in equivalent modern currency) in prize money. Officers got £58,000, whilst the ordinary soldiers received £418, the equivalent of roughly forty days wages.

During the reduction of fort Morro, the 28th had lost eleven men and had a further seventeen wounded. They would remain in the Cuban capital for a year, but disease would strike them hard. A further 159 would die before they returned to New York for further duties.

# 7. St Lucia

In March 1778, France recognised the independence of the United States of America, once again bringing them into conflict with Britain. The 28th (North Gloucestershire) Regiment of Foot, along with nine other regiments, embarked at Staten Island, New York. The transport fleet, protected by twelve warships, appeared off the coast of St. Lucia on 13th December. The French holdings on the island were based around a thin strip of bays, headlands and inlets. It was here that the British would launch a three-pronged attack.

The first brigade, led by Brigadier-General Prescott, contained the 28th Regiment. They attacked a French outpost and took control of the heights at Morne Fortune. A second brigade, led by Brigadier-General Medows, made up of the flank companies (Light Company and Grenadiers) from nine regiments, including the 28th, landed at Vigie Peninsula to cover the left flank. The final brigade landed on the heights overlooking Cul de Sac Bay, the main harbour on the island.

The following day Medows Brigade, supported by Prescott's Brigade, assaulted the main fort and capital of the island, which were taken with surprising ease. The reason for this was that the French force of five thousand men had moved into the impenetrable jungle. Alongside this, they knew that a further force of nine thousand men were due to be landed on St. Lucia very soon. This force actually arrived with a strong naval escort within twenty-four hours, and they attacked the British fleet. The Royal Navy managed to repel their adversaries on several occasions, but the French still managed to land the infantry force.

On the 18th December, this army of nine thousand troops attacked Medows Brigade of 1400 men, who were back on the peninsula of Vigie. Despite being vastly outnumbered, Medows and the flank companies of the 28th had two major advantages. Firstly, they were the far more experienced warriors having just fought through the American War of Independence. Secondly, the French would have to march through an incredibly tight bottleneck entrance, only 150 yards wide, to gain access to Vigie Peninsula.

At 08:00, the French appeared out of the jungle and began their attack. As they marched through the entrance to Vigie, they were enfiladed by a British battery safely positioned on the other side of the bay. The tightly packed French fell in droves from this murderous fire, but their numbers told and they bravely continued their advance. Three times the enemy fell upon the British, and three times they were repulsed. The British readied themselves for the fourth attack, but they had run out of ammunition. Medows, realising the desperation of the situation, addressed the men with the now famous remark: *"Soldiers, as long as you have a bayonet to point against an enemy's breast, defend the colours."*

Yet the French did not come again. They had been comprehensively defeated, losing four hundred men killed and 1100 wounded. The British, by contrast, had lost twenty-five men and a further 255 wounded. The French attacked the other two British positions over the following days, but these were easily beaten back as the French had lost appetite for the fight. Within two weeks, they had evacuated the entire island. The ten-day campaign was over and for now, St. Lucia would be in British hands.

# Versus Napoleonic France

# 8. Egypt

On 8th March 1801, six thousand men landed at Aboukir Bay in an attempt to oust Napoleons Army of the East from Egypt. The 28th (North Gloucestershire) Regiment of Foot, leapt out of their boats and onto the shore under heavy French fire. These men drove up the beach and smashed into two French battalions also capturing several artillery pieces. After reforming, the men charged with bayonets towards another two 16-pounders that were causing much havoc on the beach.

Within twenty minutes of brief but furious action, the beachhead had been established. The men then settled down for a victory meal of cold boiled bacon and biscuits.

Within four days, the British Army led by General Sir Ralph Abercrombie, had brought all their men and supplies ashore. The advance on the historic

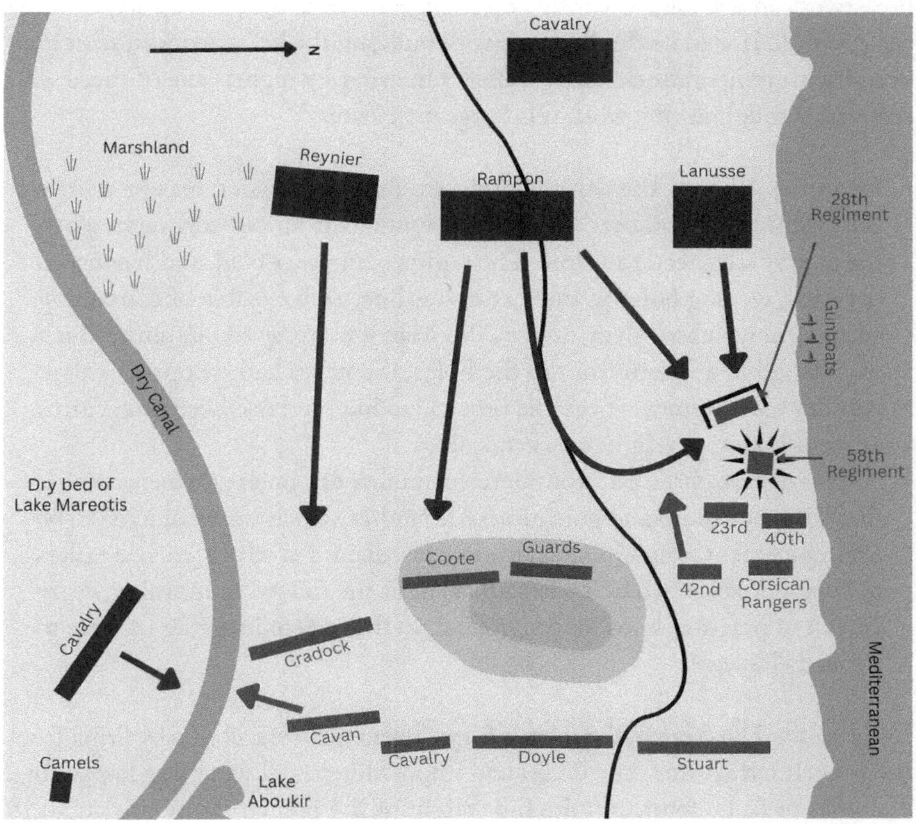

city of Alexandria now began. This would be no victory procession though, as six thousand Frenchmen with excellent cavalry and strong artillery blocked the route. Lieutenant Colonel Paget led the 28th on the right flank, and they were subject to horrendous artillery fire without being able to give anything in return. Eventually, the French were driven back to the walls of Alexandria and the advance, also known as the Battle of Mandora, had cost the Glosters thirty-five men.

Outside of Alexandria, preparations began in earnest for the final battle. The British line stretched a mile wide from the Mediterranean Sea on the right to Lake Mareotis on the left. The key to the entire position lay on the right flank, where a set of Roman Ruins lay atop a small ridge. This ridge was called Roman Camp, about 200 yards in front of this was a small rocky outcrop. General Moore was given responsibility for this sector and he placed the 58th (Rutlandshire) within the ruins and the 42nd Highlanders (Black Watch) on the left flank. The 28th were given the role of holding the isolated rocky outcrop.

Although isolated, the position of the 28th was completely necessary as it was of the upmost strategic importance. The 28th began to build a stone breastwork in a U-shape whilst two light guns were brought up to reinforce the position. It was, no doubt, hard work building the breastwork in scorching desert with temperatures falling close to freezing by night. One of those who suffered throughout the work was Sergeant Coates:

From the 13th to the 20th March, we remained quiet, except a little skirmishing with piquets and a few volunteers from our regiment, when the enemy advanced too close. The nights being very cold, and having no covering, we dug holes in the rear of our line, each capable of containing six men, in which we slept; on the 20th March we received our tents, which we pitched in a line in front of the holes. We never had stripped, or slept without accoutrements from the time of landing, and had been under arms an hour before day-light every morning.

This day we observed a considerable number of camels and men, coming from the southward and going into Alexandria, which we considered to be a reinforcement from Grand Cairo, in consequence of which, we had orders to be under arms two hours before daylight the following morning, every person of practical knowledge rejoicing in the idea of bringing matters to a speedy issue.

Early on the 21st March, the men of Gloucestershire were alerted by firing from the French left. It was only 03:30 and impossible to tell what was happening. This was in fact a feint, and the full weight of the French Army was about to descend upon the Glosters. This is made very clear in orders issued by General Menou, French Commander in Chief, the day before:

> The Army will attack the English tomorrow. The whole of the troops will in consequence be under arms at three o'clock precisely, without beat of drums or any kind of noise whatever, at two hundred paces in front of the present camp. The general attack will commence an hour and a half before daybreak, that is to say at half past four o'clock….
>
> The grand attack will be made by the left wing of the army under the command of General Lanusse, and by the centre, commanded by Generals Rampon and D'Estaing: they will advance to the redoubt in front of their position and carry it by the bayonet.

One brigade of General Lanusses Division were creeping up the Mediterranean coast, whilst Napoleons "Invincible Division" were making straight for the redoubt of the 28th. Due to still being nightfall, plus a generous topography, the two French columns were making their approach completely by surprise. Simultaneously, both flanks crashed into the redoubt and a furious firefight began. It was at this moment, commanding officer of the 28th, Paget, was shot in the neck and he was replaced by Lieutenant Colonel Chambers.

The 28th now found themselves practically surrounded. The French were swarming past their position, with the intention of dislodging the 58th Regiment from Roman Camp. The enemy had been promised a Louis d'Or, a sizeable amount of money, for every man that reached the ridge. Foolishly, the French ignoring the 28th Regiment was a huge mistake. They could easily fire into the rear of the enemy unimpeded, and this they did with some eagerness. The brigade of General Lanusses Division, which had crept along the shoreline, was dispatched in this fashion. They had no choice but to retreat to whence they had come.

A third brigade of Frenchmen now crept into action, with the intention of cutting off the 28th from the rest of the army. Unfortunately for them, they ran straight into the 42nd Highlanders who were advancing into action. The Black Watch ruthlessly dismantled their enemy to a man, not one escaped the battlefield.

A fourth French brigade now tried to repeat the same trick, and simultaneously catch the fearsome 42nd Highlanders whilst they were reforming. This action was almost achieved, but with the help of the 28th left flank, the enemy were once again driven off. Meanwhile at the front of the redoubt, the 28th held their lines and drove off repeated French infantry attacks. In their usual manner, the 28th would hold their fire until the last possible minute, and then unleash a devastating volley of fire.

Finally dawn had broken, and now the Glosters were more secure in their redoubt, at least by virtue of being able to see the enemy approaching. However, it was at this moment that General Menou decided to unleash his fearsome cavalry. The 3rd and 14th Dragoons had galloped up a valley on the left flank of the redoubt, smashing into the 42nd Highlanders who were still in disarray from the previous two victorious actions, and then straight into the rear of the 28th.

Luckily for the British, the French cavalry had ridden their horse straight into the sleeping holes that had been dug by Sergeant Coates and his men a few nights previous. The result was confusion and disorder, so a company of the 28th, led by Captain Gough, left the redoubt and mopped up the attackers. Fighting continued along the entire line, with French breakthroughs occurring and then being driven back. Yet it remained at the redoubt where the fighting was heaviest.

A multitude of French battalions now surrounded the redoubt, and it was at this moment that they decided to try another all-out attack. By this time though, Abercrombie had ordered the 23rd (Royal Welch Fusiliers) and 40th (2nd Somersetshire) up from the reserve to be positioned to the right of the ruins. They were ably assisted by three British gunboats who had sailed close to shore, and now unleashed a devastating fire upon the French attackers.

It was now time for one of the greatest moments in regimental history, possibly even in British Army history, to occur. Menou sent another squad of fresh cavalry down the flank. These 500 horsemen avoided the sleeping holes that had previously undone their brethren, and in three ranks with sabres drawn, they charged straight for the rear ranks of the 28th. Lieutenant Colonel Chambers noticed the precarious position, and gave the historic order *"Rear rank, 28th! Right About Face!"* The two lines of the Glosters were now fighting back to back, and with the cavalry at close quarters, the rear rank fired a shattering volley. Once the smoke cleared, a scene of carnage revealed itself. The cavalry were ripped to shreds and those who had survived were dealt with by the bayonet.

The rear rank of the 28th once again "about faced", and continued to fire upon the advancing French infantry to the front. Worryingly, much ammunition had been expended and the men began to assault their opponents by throwing stones. Abercrombie was then badly wounded and actually captured for a few moments. He was heroically freed by men of the 42nd Highlanders and he attempted to carry on leading the fight. Such efforts were in vain though, and he was soon carried off to one of the ships to convalesce. Sadly, Abercrombie would die from gangrene a few days later. Major General Hutchinson then took over command.

At this point, the French looked like they were retreating but instead they reformed some distance away, and began to pound the British with their superior artillery. Frustratingly, French sharpshooters also began to snipe with deadly accuracy from a distance. There was nothing to respond to this insult with as the British cannon had likewise expended all their ammo.

Perhaps fortuitously for the British, their enemy had no more stomach for the fight, and after an hour of long distance pounding, they marched off behind the walls of Alexandria. The day was won. Sixteen hundred Frenchmen lay dead on the battlefield, whilst the British had lost around 1100 killed and wounded. The majority of these were from the 42nd Highlanders, who had been caught in the open several times whilst supplying heroic support to their comrades of the 28th. The Glosters themselves had seventy-four men killed or wounded.

After a few days of recovery, the main units of the British Army moved to march on Cairo. A small force was left to watch over Alexandria, which eventually surrendered in September. The rest of Egypt soon fell, and Napoleons three-year occupation of Egypt had come to an end.

Great accolades followed the expulsion of the French Army from Egypt. All twenty-six British regiments who fought in the Egyptian Campaign were awarded the distinction of having a Sphinx within a laurel wreath incorporated into their badges. A special honour awaited the 28th Regiment though. They were allowed, uniquely amongst the entire British Army, to wear their regimental number on the back of their headdress. This 'back badge' was a reminder of the time that the men of Gloucestershire fought in two ranks, back to back simultaneously, at the Battle of Alexandria to defeat the enemy.

The 61st (South Gloucestershire) Regiment of Foot, also spent time in Egypt and were awarded the Sphinx. However, their experience was very different to that of their brethren from the 28th. At the beginning of 1801, they were stationed in South Africa. In late February, they secretly sailed for the island of Socotra in the Indian Ocean. Here they were to rendezvous with Major General Baird's expedition to Egypt.

They landed at Quseer with the intention of marching on Cairo, which was 377 miles away. The first task though, was to march 141 miles inland across the desert to find the Nile. From here, they would head north. Despite the unbearable heat of the day, freezing cold of the night and constant fatigue, the 61st had only lost one man, Drummer James Miles. Finally, Sergeant Pearson and the rest of his comrades arrived at Keneh on the banks of the Nile:

The moment we came in sight of the river a scene beggaring all description took place. All command was lost: in a moment as if in electric shock had passed through each of us, officers and men alike, burning with thirst, rushed off to get a draught off water. There was no respect of persons, and everyone drank his fill without asking the consent of his comrades.

On the 2nd August, the men were loaded on to boats and sailed 350 miles north, for news had reached them that Cairo had already fallen. Little time was spent in the capital before they sailed north again to Rosetta, where they went into camp at El Hamed. It was here that disease hit the regiment for the first time, with plague and ophthalmia (permanent blindness and agony) tearing through the ranks. Finally, after a few months, the diseases passed and the men made for Alexandria. Here they spent another year on garrison duty. One of their tasks was to remove Cleopatra's Needle and load it onto a ship. The Needle now sits in Westminster in the heart of London.

# 9. Maida

In 1806, the Kingdom of Naples declared against Napoleon so a French Army marched down the Italian peninsula. The Neapolitans had been promised assistance from the Third Coalition, but it never materialised. Instead, the British fell back to Sicily and the Russians fled to Corfu. The Neapolitans were crushed in battle, but a revolt against French rule then erupted in Calabria. The British decided to send an expeditionary force to help.

A British Army of just over five thousand men, led by Major-General John Stuart, sailed from Messina and landed at the Gulf of Sant'Eufemia on 30th June. Jean Reynier, whose II Corp were in Calabria putting down the revolt, marched to confront the British. Amongst the British forces were elements of the 61st (South Gloucestershire) Regiment of Foot. Most of the regiment were in Ireland on garrison duty. However, Stuarts personal bodyguard was formed by grenadiers of the 61st. Out on the flanks were brigades of Light Companies, which also included men of the 61st.

At dawn on the 4th July, the British broke camp and offered battle to their French foe. Stuart kept the River Lamato on his right flank, which is where Kempts Brigade, including the Light Company of the 61st, were positioned. The approach to the eventual battlefield saw the British marching through marshes and then across shrub land. This disrupted the order of battle, meaning the army arrived in an oblique line. Kempts Brigade emerged first on the right flank, and then the following brigades trailing behind until the extreme left arrived last.

The French marched to the battlefield in three columns and had to cross the Lamato River. This meant they also arrived in oblique order, with their first units taking the battlefield opposite Kempts Brigade. The British arranged themselves into two lines, and then when the enemy were 115 yards away they fired their first volley. The French continued their advance in column formation and Kempts men fired another volley at eighty yards. The French then quickened their pace and charged towards the British. At thirty yards, the British fired their final volley, attached bayonets and ran at their adversary. The combat was bloody but brief as the French soon fled.

Acland's Brigade on Kempts left had a similar tale to tell, but this time the French column only survived two volleys. Over on the extreme left of the battle, two further brigades pinned the final French column down whilst the 20th (East Devonshire) Regiment of Foot flanked the enemy and starting to fire enfilading volleys. The French began to withdraw en-masse, but there would be no chase as the British lacked the cavalry to do so. The men of the 61st would eventually move to Gibraltar ready to battle against the French in the Peninsula War.

It is worth a quick juncture at this point to study what happened in this battle in more detail. It is a pattern that will develop repeatedly throughout the battles against Napoleonic France, and be central to Britain's eventual victory. After great success in the French Revolution and then across Europe, attacking in column formation had become the norm. It made a lot of sense as a column could deploy swiftly and concentrate an attack. The British however, stuck to the old 18th Century method of deploying in line, which was seen as inferior.

The French column though, had rarely tested itself against men in line formation. Let alone the British line, which offered superior and devastating firepower. At Maida, Kempts Brigade was roughly 700 men strong and they got off three volleys before the French column reached them. That is 2100 rounds fired at an enemy who also had around 700 men. There could only really be one winner but for years, even until Waterloo, the French would keep faith in their column. John Fortescue in his seminal work "A History of the British Army" reinforces this situation:

The fight presents all the familiar features of the later battles in the Peninsula- a reckless dashing of a deep but narrow mass of bayonets against a shallow but broad front of muskets, with the inevitable result that the narrow front could not compete with the broad in development of fire, and that the columns were shattered to pieces in front and flank by bullets before the bayonets could come into play. The consequence which seems invariably to have followed was, psychologically, most curious. The head of the column, though staggering and wavering, still strove gallantly to advance, but the tail turned and ran; and the leading files finding themselves abandoned, broke at once before the charge of the victorious line.

# 10. Peninsula

The Peninsula battle honour covers all the battles of 1808–1814 in Portugal, Spain and southern France. Napoleonic Armies entered Spain in 1807 under the guise of a joint campaign against Portugal, a staunch British ally. Within a year, Napoleon had simply overthrown the Spanish monarchy and placed his own brother on the throne.

The Spanish of course did not take kindly to the overthrow of their Government and widespread uprisings were followed by a lengthy and successful guerrilla warfare campaign. They also became allied to Britain, paving the way for a protracted campaign involving Britain, Portugal and Spain against the French.

This chapter will not be used to examine the Peninsula War in detail as this battle honour can be seen as more of a 'campaign' award. The impending twelve chapters cover many of the major battles of the Peninsula War including Talavera, Salamanca and Toulouse. The narrative of the Peninsula War will be woven amongst these chapters giving a clear picture of the situation.

There are however two key points of the Peninsula campaign that should be considered further. Firstly, it was thought of by Napoleon as very much of secondary importance to his campaigns in the rest of Europe. Up until 1812, the forces of France achieved near unparalleled success outside of the peninsula. However, after the devastating decision to march on Moscow, the Peninsula campaign became a huge drain on Napoleons ability to rebuild his army. Over three hundred thousand French soldiers were in Spain and the vast majority could not be withdrawn because they had to fight Wellington, guard extensive supply lines and suppress Spanish revolts.

Secondly, although Napoleon was rarely present on the field in Spain and Portugal this had an interesting effect. In the first instance, it helped to slightly taper the pre-1812 image of Napoleonic Armies as near unbeatable. However, this also helped to shape the wider Allied strategy. There were always multiple Napoleonic Armies in the field but of course, only one could be led by Napoleon himself. The Peninsula campaign taught the wider European allies, such as Prussia, Austria and Russia, that they need not directly defeat Napoleon, as the destruction of his other armies could result in his final downfall.

Ultimately, Napoleons defeat at the Battle of Paris on 31st March 1814 saw his abdication a week later. This event also ended the Peninsula War and saw Napoleons exile to the island of Elba. Of course, Napoleon would return for one final tremendous roll of the dice the following year at Waterloo, with this battle covered in the final chapter of this section.

# 11. Corunna

The battle honour of Corunna specifically refers to the conflict that occurred on the 16th January 1809. However, one simply must examine the days that preceded this battle to understand the true glory of the 28th (North Gloucestershire) Regiment of Foot.

On the 2nd May 1908, the citizens of Madrid rose up against their French overlords. The rebellion was put down with an excessive use of force, but all this did was cause the patriotic fervour to spread outside the walls of Madrid. In July, the Spanish won a resounding victory over the French and the British Government saw an opportunity to cause a great hindrance to their cross Channel foe. Therefore in August, an army of twenty thousand, including the 28th (North Gloucestershire) Regiment of Foot, landed in Portugal.

The man in charge of the expedition was Sir John Moore, an old friend of the 28th having been their Divisional commander at the Battle of Alexandria (see Battle Honour 8). Moore led his army all the way to Salamanca, but upon arrival news came that Napoleon himself had arrived on the peninsula to assume personal command of the army. He had smashed the Spanish armies and then marched on Madrid.

This led to issues for Moore, who was there to cooperate with the Spanish allies. The British alone were not enough to defeat the 250,000 infantry and fifty thousand cavalry that the French had in the country. Realising the Spanish were defeated, Moore turned his attention to the nearby army of Marshal Soult. However, news then arrived that Napoleon was marching towards them from Madrid and so the great *retreat to Corunna* began on Christmas Eve 1808.

The port of Corunna was 240 miles away across mountainous terrain and the weather was abhorrent. Moore needed to form a solid reserve that would fight at the rear of the column, whilst the rest of the army retreated. This was considered a great post of honour and the 28th played a central role. Major General Paget was put in charge of this force, and he too knew the 28th well having been their commander in Egypt and having led them in Ireland.

The Reserve tangled with the pursuing army of Marshal Soult for the first time on the 29th December outside Benavente. On New Year's Day 1809, they marched through the town of Bembibre, where drunken soldiers were committing all sorts of deviance. The discipline of the Reserve, which became something of a badge of honour, allowed them to mop up the drunken and disorderly men who had dropped out of the retreating column. However, discipline was not always perfect amongst the 28th, and on the 3rd January, Paget had three soldiers strung up for disorderly conduct. Seconds before the men were to be dropped and their necks broken, news arrived that the French were just moments away. Paget said *"Soldiers! If you promise to behave well for the future, I will forgive these men– say yes, in an instant"*. He demanded their word three times before the men were cut down and the retreat continued.

Not all men continued the retreat though, as the Light Company of the 28th remained to guard a nearby bridge. The French cavalry, believing the British to be long gone, received a terrific barrage as they attempted to cross the obstacle. The French then brought up their infantry, and for the first time the two sides conducted one of many small infantry skirmishes. Fighting was often bayonet-on-bayonet. Only nightfall ended this first bloody encounter. Every bridge and defile through the mountainous retreat saw the Reserve stop and hold off the French until the last possible moment.

Conditions on the retreat became worse every day. Torrential rain, blizzards, sub-zero temperatures and snowstorms battered the men. Thin tracks, often only wide enough for one man, had to be navigated. Adding to this hazard was the fact that the march often continued deep into the night. The soles of boots quickly wore away, whilst clothing tore and became useless. Food and water was extremely scarce with the Reserve suffering particularly badly, as upon reaching a town or village they found it had already been pillaged clean by the rest of the army.

On the 5th January, the 28th arrived at the village of Nogales, and this proved to be a day of near constant action and excitement. Firstly, the oxen of the army treasury began to flounder and it was decided to throw the gold and silver over the edge of a cliff. Lieutenant Bennett of the 28th was ordered to stand guard with his revolver to make sure nobody tried to reclaim any of the treasure trove. Bennett must have been a very trustworthy man, as the amount at the bottom of the cliff amounted to £25,000 or £1.1 million in modern currency.

Morale was soon to receive a great boost, as further into Nogales the 28th happened upon a supply train bound for the Spanish Army. The Spanish had been defeated and the men of Gloucestershire were in dire need. Items such as clothing, boots and ammunition were, by this time, worth more to the men than the treasure sitting at the bottom of the nearby cliff. They fully replenished themselves and began to march off when suddenly the French appeared.

The 28th and 95th (Sherwood Foresters) held the line of a small stream, whilst the other battalions of the Reserve positioned themselves on a low hill towards the rear. More and more columns of Frenchmen started to arrive, but they were all warmly greeted with indomitable British firepower. Time and again, the scene was repeated and the Reserve desperately held on. Finally at

23:30, the British slipped away under the cover of darkness, and their adventures at Nogales were finally over.

Exhausted, the Reserve arrived at the next town, Lugo. The much anticipated rest had to wait though, as Moore had decided the time to stand and fight had arrived. Previous indiscipline of the retreating troops had dissipated, and the land was suitable for a defensive battle. Surprisingly though, Soult never offered battle and once again the British slipped away under the cover of darkness. This error would cost Soult a valuable twenty-four hours trying to catch up with his foe again. To compound this mistake, the British were arriving at Betanzos. Here they were met by a supply column from Corunna bringing much needed food, water and ammunition. Moore allowed his men a day's rest, and the weather even began to improve.

Upon leaving Betanzos, the British attempted to destroy the main bridge into town but it was only partly detonated. This meant that the Light and Grenadier Companies of the 28th had to once again cross the smouldering bridge and reset the demolition charges. Whilst doing so, they were attacked by an advanced party of French dragoons. These were given a good hiding though, and they escaped as quickly as they had appeared.

They had now reached the town of El-Burgo, the last stop before Corunna. Here again the bridge was demolished, but this time so much charge was used that it killed one man of the 28th Light Company and badly wounded four others. Finally though, on the 11th January 1809, the beleaguered column marched into Corunna. In just twelve days, Moore had marched fourteen thousand men across 240 miles of impossible terrain. The British Army was saved.

Except they were not! The harbour of Corunna was empty and the Royal Navy nowhere to be seen. For two days the Light Companies of the 28th and 95th were ordered to hold back the French Army at the El-Burgo crossing. Multiple skirmishes occurred as both sides fired across the narrow river channel. On the 13th January, Paget suddenly appeared and ordered the men to flee. This was very much out of character, but it soon became clear that the French had brought their cannon into positions and were moments away from obliterating the men of the 28th and 95th.

On the 14th January a most welcome sight appeared, the Royal Navy were sailing into the harbour. After a day of loading women, children and the wounded on board, the men of the Reserve were given the distinction of being the first fighting troops to leave Corunna. They proudly marched through Corunna ready to head back to England, when suddenly; they heard cannon fire in the distance. There was no need to tell Paget twice, he turned his men around and marched to the sound of the guns.

On the 16th January, the French had finally decided to give battle and twenty thousand men, with additional cavalry and artillery, marched on the port. The British though, had received fresh arms and ammunition whilst they also had the better position. After arriving at the battlefield, the Reserve found themselves in the centre. As the conflict raged, Moore decided to send them on a flanking manoeuvre and off they headed around the right. As they did so, they were delighted to bump into an entire French division trying the same trick. For this happened to be the division of Lahousaye, who had been the advanced force throughout the retreat. The men of Gloucestershire could finally show their foe what they were really made of.

The French fired the first volley but it fell short. The Reserve returned fire and did not miss their mark. Several more volleys were exchanged before bayonets were attached, and the men plunged into each other. The air was thick with insults, as these two adversaries had genuinely grown to dislike each other during the desperation of pursuit and retreat. The fighting was horrendous but a final bayonet charge from the Reserve forced their enemy into a retreat. The flanking manoeuvre continued, and eventually the entire French Army fell back in disarray.

During the battle, Moore had been struck in the breast by a cannonball. Much like General Wolfe at Quebec (see Battle Honour 4), he waited for news of final victory to reach him before allowing his life to ebb away. By 21:00 the 28th were embarked and, on the 26th January, they were landing at Portsmouth. It would not be long though until the 28th were back on the Peninsula, once again duelling with the legions of France.

# 12. Talavera

In early 1809, Arthur Wellesley (the future Duke of Wellington), had kicked the French out of Portugal and he now advanced into Spain linking up with the allies there. The 61st (South Gloucestershire) Regiment of Foot were not with the initial expeditionary force, but were ordered over from garrison duties in Gibraltar, where we left them after Maida (Battle Honour 9).

Once the 61st landed in Spain, they had a terrible time in locating Wellesley's fast moving army. For days on end, they marched through the searing heat and thick dust of the Spanish plains. Eventually after a 225-mile odyssey in eighteen days, they sighted the rear-guard of Wellesley's force. The 61st were immediately posted to General Cameron's Brigade in Sherbrook's 1st Division.

Wellesley was now in a difficult position as the supplies that had been long promised by his Spanish allies had yet to materialise. Water, food and ammunition were all running worryingly low, and so he had no choice but to stay rooted where he was, the town of Talavera. The Spanish however, buoyed by the arrival of their British allies and some recent successes, decided to march off themselves to fight the French invaders and so they disappeared off over the horizon.

Soon though, on the 26th July 1809, the Spanish returned. This time they were running at full speed whilst yelling and hollering. They claimed that the French were right on their tails. Indeed they were. Forty-six thousand men, amongst which were excellent cavalry and heavy artillery, were pursuing the Spanish Army down the road. Wellesley was trapped and had no choice but to stand and fight with his vastly outnumbered army of twenty thousand troops. He also had over thirty thousand Spaniards remaining, but had little faith in their abilities.

Wellesley has gone down in history as a legendary general, and one of his greatest abilities was in selecting a battlefield. Over the following chapters, a huge advantage shall be given to the British and their allies, purely on the ability of Wellesley to choose his ground so well. At Talavera he had already reconnoitred his chosen spot should battle be forced upon him, and this is where he set his army. The right flank of his forces rested upon the thick walls of Talavera itself, whilst a flanking manoeuvre against him would be doubly impossible here due to the path of the river Tagus. On his left sat the steep rising hill of Cerro de Medellin. To the front of his army, Wellesley had the almost dry bed of the River Portina. During the winter months, this river had cut away a steep sided ravine.

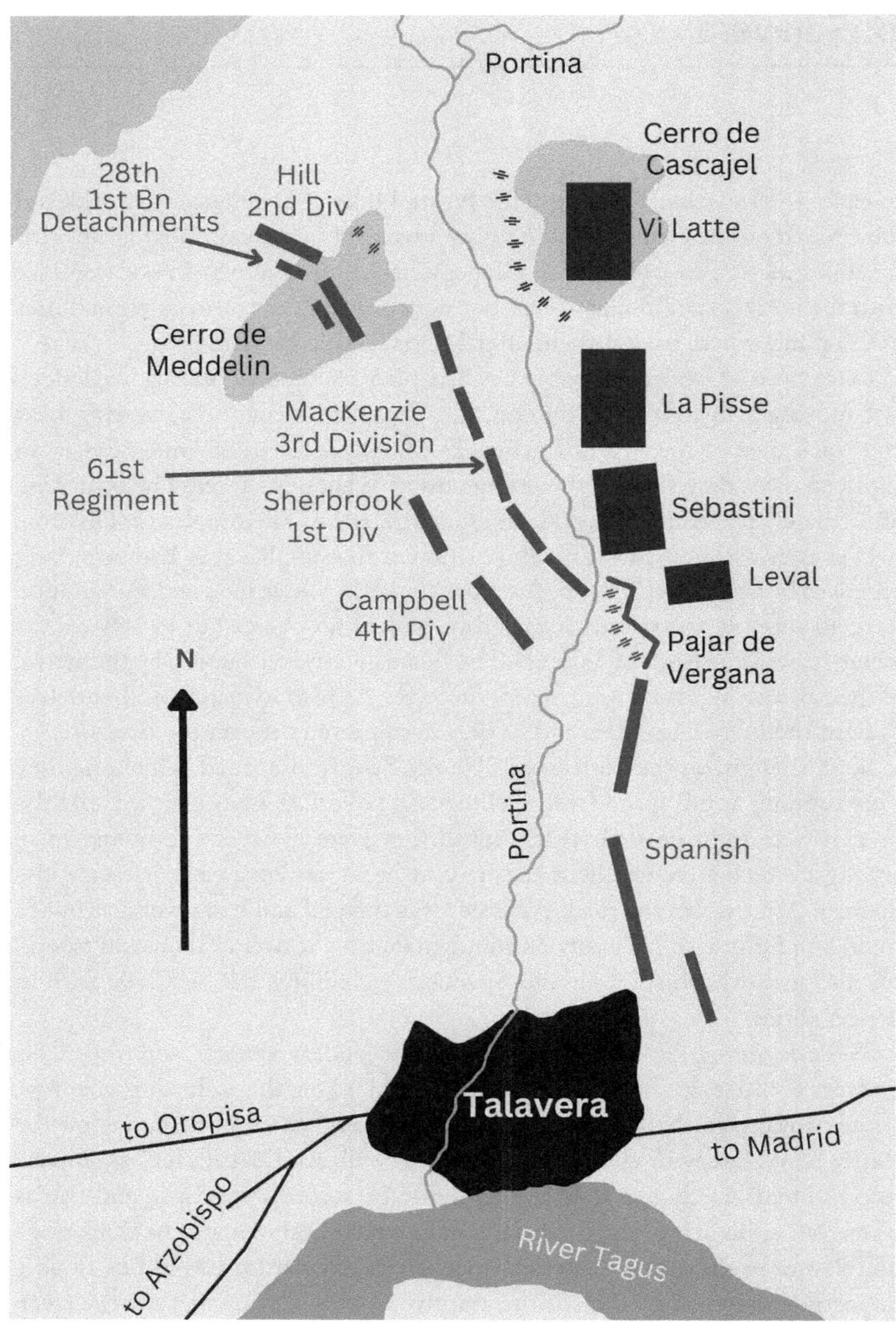
Portina
Cerro de Cascajel
Vi Latte
28th
1st Bn
Detachments
Hill
2nd Div
La Pisse
Cerro de
Meddelin
MacKenzie
3rd Division
Sebastini
61st
Regiment
Sherbrook
1st Div
Leval
Campbell
4th Div
Pajar de
Vergana
N
Portina
Spanish
to Oropisa
Talavera
to Madrid
to Arzobispo
River Tagus

On the 27th July, the Allied Army stretched out 2.5 miles long. The 61st were drawn up close to the centre in Cameron's Brigade, right up against the Portina. 1st Battalion of Detachments from the 28th (North Gloucestershire) Regiment of Foot were also present at the battle. They were posted on the reverse slopes of the Cerro de Medellin.

Due to communication issues, the majority of units who were supposed to be on Cerro de Medellin, a key feature of the battleground, found themselves elsewhere on the field. Marshal Victor, Commanding Officer of the French 1st Corp, noted this and launched an assault against the hill at 19:00. The opening salvo of the battle was from a cannon and unfortunately, it completely took off two men's heads of the 28th.

Fortuitously for the disorganised allies, night was quickly approaching and by the time Victor's first division arrived, they became lost on the hill. They stayed on Cerro de Medellin for the night though, and this caused all kinds of confusion. Rowland 'Daddy' Hill (his nickname was an affectionate moniker from the men due to his ruddy features and generous personality), one of Wellesley's most capable subordinates was on Cerro de Medellin reconnoitring the situation and barely escaped with his life.

Despite darkness, the hill was such an important feature that Brigadier General Stewart fired up his 3rd Brigade. This contained the men of the 28th along with the 29th (Worcestershire) and 48th (Northamptonshire) Regiments. An initial furious volley sent the French scrambling down the hill and over the Portina. Here they were cornered by further British troops and slaughtered. More confusion continued throughout the night as the 61st mistook some Cameron's on the advanced piquet for the enemy, and opened fire.

At 04:00, the sun eventually rose and illuminated the battlefield. Before the 61st stood an incredible sight, as the French were already lined up in battle formation. Two miles of French infantry stood in columns with a vast array of skirmishers lined up in front of them. Also to the front of the French Army sat eighty fearsome cannon. Off to the left of the 61st stood another huge body of infantry waiting in the Reserve. The French lined up not one single unit opposite the Spanish, and so the plan was clear. Destroy the British and win the Peninsula.

At 05:00, the entirety of the French artillery opened their deadly fire pouring it right onto Cerro de Medellin. The troops were ordered to lie down but it had little effect. The men of the 28th particularly, right in the centre, had great holes ripped open in their formation. Whilst the cannon were raging, the French sent in their first mass infantry attack and they headed straight up the slopes of Cerro de Medellin.

The French drove up the hill in column formation where they were met by the three battalions of Stewarts Brigade. The initial deadly volley unleashed at minimum yardage, shattered the first column. The French instantly retreated and ran back through other approaching columns causing chaos. Stewarts Brigade attached bayonets and charged into the enemy. Another brigade, stationed to the left of the hill, arrived to join in the pursuit and the French were soon back over the Portina. The British then reformed on the hill and once again, the French artillery opened up. The French had lost eleven thousand men in this first attack for the loss of just seven hundred British troops, two hundred of them from the 28th.

An oddity now occurred when the entire French Army sat down and enjoyed their breakfast. The British could only look on jealously as the supplies they were waiting for had still not arrived. The men did however head down to the babbling Portina, to quench their thirst in the heavily blood stained water. On the opposite side, the French were doing the same so pleasantries, and even handshakes, were exchanged. That is except for the 28th. Outraged by this geniality they started a mass hand-to-hand brawl, and the over powered French had to return to their lines.

At precisely 13:00, hostilities resumed with a French attack towards the Spanish troops stationed on the extreme right. This actually turned out to be a feint, but it was dealt with anyway by covering artillery and the questionable Spanish held their ground. The real attack would come at the centre of Allied lines and once again, a terrible artillery barrage was opened by the French. The 61st, who were only six hundred yards from the main batteries, suffered appallingly.

At 15:00, the French infantry began their march. Fifteen thousand men in huge columns 150 men wide were heading straight for the 778 men of the 61st Regiment. As always, the British line held its nerve and did not fire until the last possible moment. At fifty yards, the first volley was unleashed and the French staggered to a halt. Bayonets were then fixed and 1st Division drove their assailants back across the Portina once again.

As they had been ordered by Wellington, the 61st along with the rest of Cameron's Brigade halted on the other side of the ravine. The Guards and the German Legion who were with them, probably driven on by the sense of victory, continued the pursuit and they soon became isolated with the most deadly of consequences. They were badly mauled and came flooding back to Allied lines. Cameron's Brigade were now themselves isolated, as they were the only British troops on the French side of the Portina. A mass of French infantry attacked and they too fled back across the ravine.

After almost unlimited success, Wellesley was now in great jeopardy. The centre of his line had completely disintegrated and the hole was about to be plugged by the French. Luckily though, Wellesley had seen this coming the moment the Guards and German Legion had disobeyed their orders. Already he had sent the 48th (Northamptonshire) Regiment to fill the gap, but a terrible fight ensued. Against overwhelming odds, the 48th fell in great numbers.

After a while, Stewarts Brigade had reformed for they had merely pulled back with haste, they had not been beaten. Along with men of the 61st, they re-joined this most savage conflict and it raged for several more hours. Eventually though, at 19:00, the French were pushed back across the Portina for the final time. The entire French Army now began an orderly retreat and the day was won.

In this battle, the 61st would lose forty-six men killed, 205 wounded and a further sixteen missing. Just a few days after the battle, news arrived that Marshal Soult was approaching Talavera with a newly resupplied army. Wellesley had no choice but to fall back to the other side of the Tagus River.

# 13. Bussaco

By mid-1810, the road to Lisbon was clear for the French and they began to advance down it. Following his famous victory at Talavera, Wellesley now became the Duke of Wellington. He destroyed bridges on the road to Lisbon to delay the French, and to force them to march down a route of his choosing. Wellington needed to delay the enemy long enough for his grand defensive plan to protect Lisbon, the Lines of Torres Vedras, to be completed. This was a mountainous region where fortifications, redoubts and even flood plains were being constructed.

Time was ticking for Wellington, the French were moving too quickly despite his best efforts and their own supply problems. Therefore, Wellington had no choice but to meet the French in battle. Once again proving his aptitude at selecting battlefields, he chose Bussaco. This nine-mile long ridge rose up out of the plains to an average of 600ft. The River Mondego would cover the right flank whilst the hill itself was steep, rocky and covered in gorse. On the left flank ran the main road along which stood a convent. The hill had a gentle reverse slope, which would become another Wellington trademark.

The 61st (South Gloucestershire) Regiment of Foot were placed on the left flank close to the convent. The 28th (North Gloucestershire) Regiment of Foot were on the extreme right in 'Daddy' Hills 2nd Division, with the river Mondego to their front. At 05:30 on the 27th September 1810, the French began their attack just to the left of the 61st. Their infantry charged up the steep hill and by the time they reached the top, they were exhausted. After a brief but valiant fight, the French were scampering back down again.

Wellington then realised that 2nd Division, including the 28th, were useless way out on the right flank. The French could not attack them anyway as they were prevented by the river. Wellington ordered the entire division to march around the rear of his army, and take their place in the centre as a reserve.

Marshal Ney now sent his Corp up the steep hill, but they were ambushed by well-concealed men of the Light Division. A horrendous attack occurred on the French flank, and 1200 men fell for the loss of just twenty-one British soldiers. During this period, Ney also sent his voltigeurs (skirmishers) up the hill to engage the division in which the 61st resided. This was to stop them from giving assistance to the soon to be ambushed Corp. This long range sniping between the voltigeurs and 61st lasted the entire morning, but caused very few casualties.

By 14:00, the French accepted that they would not be able to make a push on Lisbon without huge losses against the British on their well chosen ground. One of the main advantages Wellington had was that the hillside was so steep the French could not bring their superior cannon into play. Later, the French Army wheeled around and tried to unsuccessfully outflank Wellington. The Allies then made an easy and slow retreat back to the Lines of Torres Vedras.

The 28th saw no fighting in this conflict, and the 61st were only involved in the skirmishing with voltigeurs. So perhaps the highlight of the day for the regiments of Gloucestershire was Sergeant Pearson of the 61st being grabbed by the collar from behind. He angrily spun around, ready to pummel who ever had accosted him. It was Wellington himself stood there. He told Pearson to hold his horse whilst he surveyed the battlefield for a moment.

# 14. Barossa

The Battle of Barossa is very much a quirk amongst these chapters, as it is a sideshow from the main Peninsula campaign involving Wellington. The city of Cadiz was a major Allied harbour, and the de facto seat of Spanish political power since the French had conquered Madrid. It had been besieged by the French under Marshal Victor since early in 1810. In January 1811, Marshal Soult ordered Victor to send him a third of his army so that he could finish the siege of Badajoz. This gave the Allies a great opportunity to lift the siege and a cunning plan was put together.

Four thousand British troops under General Graham and eight thousand Spanish under General Lapena would sail out of Cadiz, and land a little way down the coast at Tarifa. They would then stealthily move back towards Cadiz and fall on the besiegers from the rear. On the 21st February 1811, the British task force landed at Tarifa where they found the 28th (North Gloucestershire) Regiment of Foot under Colonel Belson, who had been disrupting the French supply lines. These men were soon enrolled into the expedition and a few days later the Spanish arrived.

Alongside the British units was something of an anomaly. Colonel Browne of the 28th had been in charge of the regiment when they were garrisoned at Gibraltar (whilst Colonel Belson was on sick leave), just twenty-five miles away. He had made a real impression on the people of the Rock, and he was affectionately nicknamed Commandante Loco (Mad) for his eccentric antics. The Governor of Gibraltar insisted that Colonel Browne be in charge of his own battalion, and so he was given two companies of the 28th, along with the grenadiers and light companies of the 9th (East Norfolk) and 82nd (Prince of Wales Volunteers) Regiments.

Despite strict orders from Wellington himself, to the contrary General Graham felt it best to put himself under Spanish command. The march started well as a French garrison numbering three thousand at the town of Medina Sidonia was eradicated. Just down the road at the monastery of Casa Vieja, two companies of French were also chased off by the 28th. Yet despite these early successes, it was at Medina Sidonia that things began to take a strange turn.

The Spanish commander General Lapena clearly began to lose his nerve. He announced that from now on the men would only march at night. If this was not bad enough, he decided he would choose the worst terrain possible to march over so that the French would not be able to catch them. On the 3rd

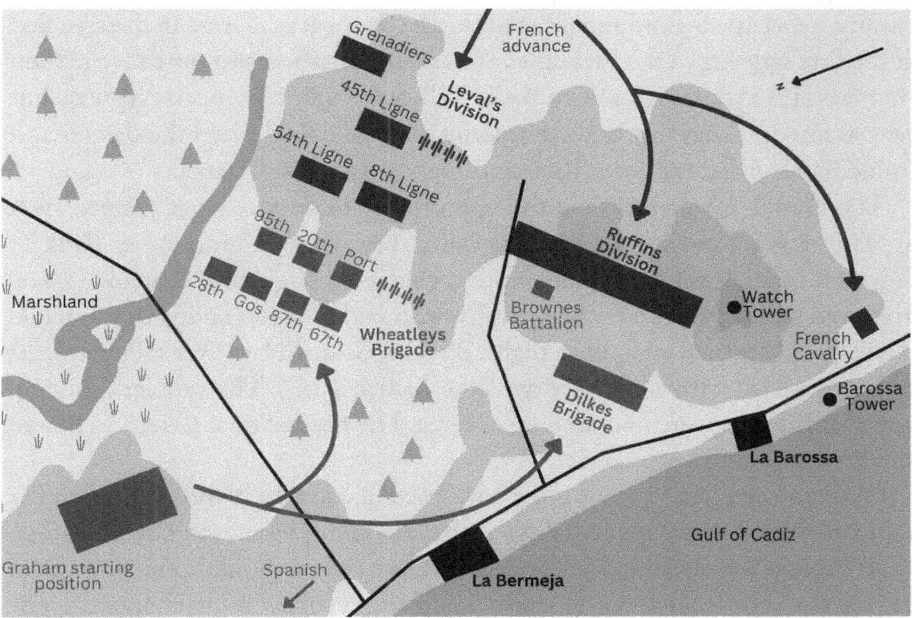


March, they reached the flooded river of Barbate. The Spaniards refused to cross, eventually only relenting when General Graham himself waded across to prove it was possible. This day they covered just twelve miles in fifteen hours.

Due to the now bizarre antics of the "secret" task force, Marshal Victor was all too aware of the situation. He knew the routes they were taking presented ample opportunity for an ambush, and so he awaited his moment. At dawn on the 5th March, the task force had been marching for fifteen hours. The Spanish pushed on and successfully dislodged the French from the next major obstacle, Santi Petri bridgehead. By now, the army was strung out over many miles with the British just passing a hill known locally as Cerro de Puerco. The British named it Barossa Hill due to it being the name of a nearby watchtower.

The British decided the time had come for a well-earned breakfast. The valuable baggage train was miles in the rear and Graham needed to wait for it to catch up. He waited at Barossa Hill in case anything went wrong, as he identified it as a solid defensive position. Eventually though, enough men caught up and General Lapena ordered them onwards. Graham left Colonel Browne's Battalion on the western slopes of Barossa waiting for stragglers. Marshal Victor had been personally watching all this unfold from a distance. He was confused by what was actually happening, as the movements he saw defied good military sense, but he knew this was his opportunity to attack.

Victor believed that Barossa Hill was now empty. He could not see Browne's Battalion from his position, so sent a whole division, 2500 men and five hundred cavalry, to occupy the prominent feature. The Spanish who were in the area fled at the first sighting of the French, so the cavalry smashed into the baggage train that was still making its way up the line. Browne may have been eccentric but he was also unbelievably brave, bordering on suicidal. He read the danger and immediately faced the three thousand French with his 470 men.

The French cavalry relished the opportunity to destroy what seemed such an easy target. Leaving the baggage train, they wheeled onto either flank of Browne's men. At the exact moment they charged though, the German Hussars appeared and it was the French cavalry who ended up being hit in the flank. They quickly turned and put to flight. By now, Graham had hurriedly returned to Barossa Hill with the majority of the British Army. The problem though, was that his men were in marching order and he needed time to reform before the French infantry attacked.

Graham then issued what must have been an extremely difficult order. He told Browne to throw his battalion at the oncoming French to buy him some time. Browne was delighted at this near certain death order, and cheerily ordered his men on. He decided not to waste time firing a volley, but to charge straight in with the bayonet. Sadly, the French cannon had just summited the hill and eight deadly pieces were ready to fire. The first volley dropped two hundred men. The second volley fifty. The battalion had been obliterated, but Browne, still riding around on his huge Spanish charger, implored his few remaining boys to try for a third and final push. They refused and took shelter behind whatever cover they could find.

The sacrificial act had brought Graham the time he needed. The Guards Brigade were ordered up the hill whilst Wheatley's Brigade, containing the 28th, tackled another French division that was advancing across the plain below Barossa. The Guards, after a furious firefight, succeeded in establishing themselves on top of Barossa, but down in the plain going was far more difficult.

Wheatley's Brigade had to form up through a wooded area, all the while under terrible cannon fire. The British line, 2600 strong, then attacked the French column, which was four thousand strong. The 28th found themselves on the left flank, so Colonel Belson ordered them to fire from centre to flank at the French who were approaching from an angle. All shots were to be aimed at the legs of the enemy. After the first few volleys, bayonets were fixed and they plunged into the French masses. Sheer weight of numbers against them forced them back. Again, the British tried and again they were pushed back. The deadly battle raged for two hours, as casualties mounted up on both sides. Finally, the men of Wheatley's Brigade made one more charge and the enemy broke.

Whilst this engagement was taking place, the 87th (Royal Irish Fusiliers) had the great honour of capturing a French Eagle. This symbol of French martial power was the first to be captured during the Peninsula campaign. The 28th lost forty-three men killed and incurred a further 171 casualties. So disgusted was Graham by the Spanish, who had remained idle during the conflict, that he split his men off and marched back to Cadiz.

# 15. Albuera

In early 1811, Wellington was tied up fighting Massena at Cuidad Rodrigo, whilst Sir William Beresford was besieging the town of Badajoz. In May, Marshal Soult marched out of Sevilla with 24,000 men intending to relieve the siege of Badajoz. Beresford decided he would meet Soult in battle and he headed to a battleground that had previously been selected by Wellington.

As always, Wellington had chosen well. Albuera was a low ridge that reached a maximum height of 150ft. To the front of the ridge was a low stream and in front of this was a thick olive grove. The 28th (North Gloucestershire) Regiment of Foot were present at the battle, and fought with Stewarts 2nd Division in Abercrombies 2nd Brigade. Abercrombie was the son of the hero who had led the army at the Battle of Alexandria (Battle Honour 8) a decade earlier.

The town of Albuera was actually a total ruin having previously been sacked and burnt by marauding French troops. However, the two roads that ran through the area were still essential to any army so this is where Beresford placed his best troops, the 2nd Division. On his right he placed the Spanish troops, whilst on the left his Portuguese allies.

At 08:00 on the 16th May 1811, the Allies were sat down to a hearty breakfast when suddenly the French attack began. As Beresford expected, Soult came marching straight down the main roads and 2nd Division, including the 28th, were immediately into action. However, this attack was a mere feint by Soult and whilst Beresford's best troops were occupied, he sent two divisions and two cavalry brigades down his left on a wide flanking manoeuvre.

At 09:00, the flanking move came to fruition and the French smashed into the Spanish stationed on Beresford's right. A third of the Spanish fell almost instantly and the rest ran for their lives. By now, the feint attack down the centre had subsided and Beresford was able to extricate 2nd Division and ordered them to march to assist the Spanish. Colebourne's 1st Brigade arrived on the scene first, but suddenly another 1200 enemy cavalry appeared on the wing and crashed into them. In seven minutes, 1600 men were dead or wounded. 1st Brigade had ceased to exist. The Allies were on the verge of a terrifying defeat.

Abercrombie's 2nd Brigade now arrived on the scene along with the men of the 28th. What they saw before them was a scene of absolute chaos. Everywhere their allies were being slaughtered or running for their lives. Such an action in battle is rare, but there was only one way to restore order. 2nd Brigade formed into line and indiscriminately opened fire. Many Allied soldiers fell from friendly fire but most importantly, the marauding French cavalry retreated.

The men of 2nd Brigade felt they had secured the day and three cheers were given in unison down the entire line. At that exact moment, a breeze swept across the battlefield and momentarily cleared away the smoke, haze and driving rain. What this breeze revealed was the entire French V Corp and a host of cannon just fifty yards to their front. Eight thousand French infantry stood before the three thousand men of 2nd and 3rd Brigade (who had now come up to join the action). In true British fashion, despite coming under a murderous fire from the French cannon, the lines calmly reformed and returned fire.

The French cannon particularly did terrible slaughter, as the Allies had nothing to answer them with on this part of the field. For half hour, the two masses of infantry exchanged volley after volley and the casualties mounted up every minute. Finally, without orders from Beresford, General Cole of 4th Division marched his men to the sound of the guns. He appeared on the right flank of 3rd Brigade and the battle finally began to sway in favour of the Allies. Soult still had his reserves though and at this critical moment, he threw them into the melee.

For another thirty minutes the butchery continued. Somehow, Abercrombie managed to remove his men from combat and suddenly they appeared on the right flank of the French V Corp. Finally, the battle swung the Allies way once and for all. The French, still advancing on the field in column formation, could do nothing to combat being attacked on three sides by the deadly British line formation.

The French broke but carried out a very orderly withdraw. The British could not chase down their adversary as the retreat was still covered by the numerous French cannon. During the battle the 28th had 164 men killed or wounded, just over a quarter of their strength. The figures elsewhere were far more appalling though, especially amongst 1st Brigade and the Spanish. Over two thirds of the Allied Army would be killed or wounded on this day.

Both armies remained in the area and reformed for battle the next day. Yet neither had the audacity to offer battle again after such a bloody encounter. Marshal Soult is said to have been furious that Beresford refused to retreat, as he believed he had won the Battle of Albuera. Beresford agreed that he had lost the battle despite holding the field at the end of the day. Wellington arrived two days later and made Beresford change his report to reflect an Allied victory. His reasoning was that the public back at home needed a morale boost.

# 16. Salamanca

After successfully completing the bloody siege of Badajoz in early 1812, Wellington marched back into Portugal to face French forces who had invaded once again. A series of marches and counter marches now took place with the Allied Army of Wellington, and the French Armies of Soult and Marmont trying to outmanoeuvre each other. At one point, the armies of Wellington and Marmont were marching in parallel with just fifty yards distance apart. The rivers that criss-cross this area of central eastern Spain almost proved the undoing of the Allies on several occasions.

On the 22nd July 1812, the usual marches began and Marmont spied the rear guard of Wellington's Army up in the distance, and so began his pursuit. However, this was in fact Wellingtons advanced guard and by pursuing, Marmont's Army found themselves spread thinly over the plain of Salamanca, ripe for the taking. After weeks of marching, the first true error had been made and Wellington would seize his chance with aplomb.

Marmont's centre was particularly weak and it was passing right next to the Allied Army. Quick as a flash, Wellington ordered three entire divisions to smash into the enemy, and this they did. In just forty minutes, 40,000 Frenchmen were either dead, wounded or fleeing from the field in despair. Just as quickly as they had taken the ascendancy though, the Allies soon found themselves in trouble. 4th Division, one of those who had routed their foe in the centre, were at the village of Los Arapiles on top of a small hill. They were attacked by a mass of French infantry who had come to the assistance of their compatriots. As 4th Division fell back, a large contingent of French cavalry had by now wheeled around and fallen upon their flank.

Meanwhile, Clintons 6th Division had moved up to some cornfields in support of the attack upon the French centre. Amongst them in Hulse's Brigade, were the 61st (South Gloucestershire) Regiment of Foot, led by Lieutenant Colonel Barlow. At 18:30, the 6th Division were ordered to retake the village of Los Arapiles and it was captured after a brief fight.

On the other side of the village, the 61st had to stop their firing as before them the men of 4th Division were still mixed up fighting with their French counterparts. Eventually though, the French defeated their foe and moved onto their next target. This was to be Hulse's Brigade and nine French battalions faced just the four from Britain. A long combat now began, with volleys being unleashed by both sides from close range. After a period of time, the British

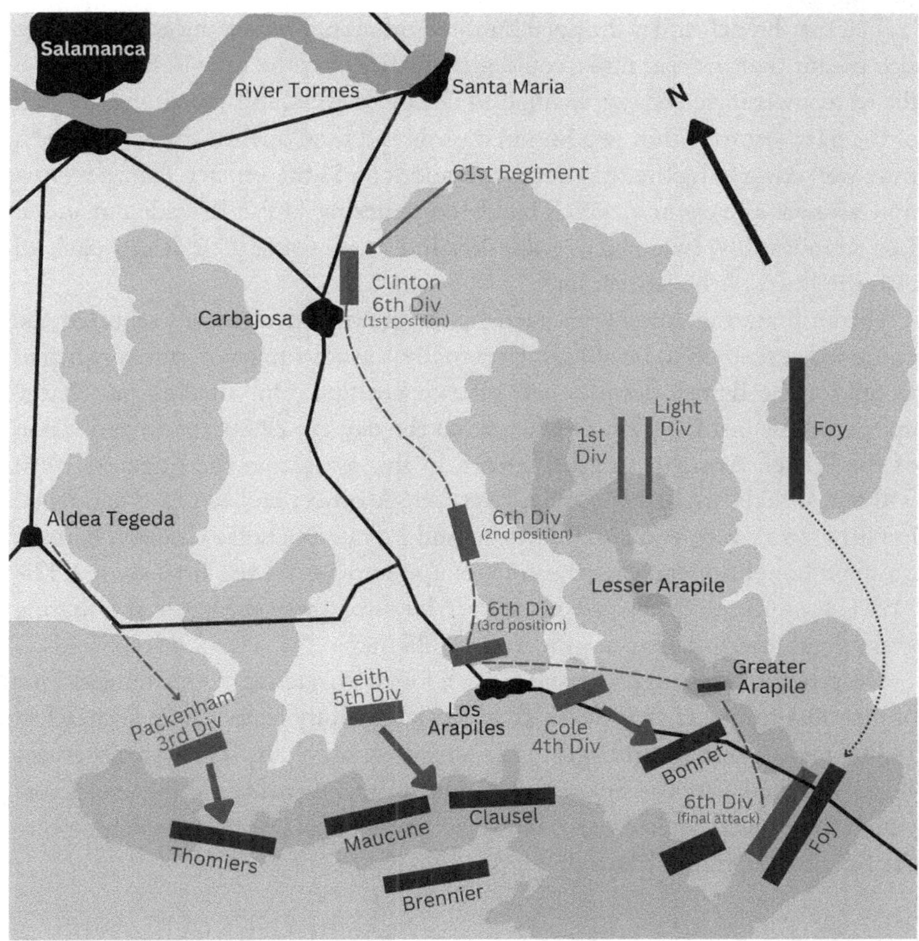


started to gain the upper hand but during the conflict the 61st lost their Commanding Officer, Lieutenant Colonel Barlow.

Once the French began to pull back, the men of Hulse's Brigade halted as they had been previously ordered to. They immediately came under heavy fire from a battery of twelve guns up on the hillside. These were joined by an immense amount of sharpshooters and the casualties started to mount up. Hulse ordered his men to sit on the ground to reduce losses. This was coupled with the fact that darkness was closing in and the battle would soon be over.

Incredibly though, the battle was only just beginning for the 61st. As the French Army fell back, they left one of their untouched reserve divisions on top of a steep and heavily wooded ridge to cover themselves. Clinton decided that 6th Division would remove this obstacle, and so in an instant the men were scrambling up the hill to duel with this last French effort.

The first French volley dropped hundreds of men. The steepness of the ridge also meant that the rear ranks could actually fire over the man in front, and so their firepower increased exponentially. The 6th Division, still containing the men of the 61st, got to within two hundred yards and then opened fire. The French were well covered by the terrain though and it had little impact. Another issue now arose as the cannon, which had been pestering Hulse Brigade outside of Los Arapiles, now switched to grapeshot and began firing their deadly payload into the heart of the British line.

For an hour, the adversaries exchanged volleys and witnesses reported the entire ridge seemed to be ablaze. Eventually, the advantage of numbers began to tell for the British despite their inferior position. One final all out charge up the hill by 6th Division finally carried the day. By 22:00, the final division of the French Army was in full retreat. In this assault up the ridge, 61st lost 340 out of their original 516 men. Every single officer and sergeant had fallen in battle, so Private William Crawford and Private Nicholas Coulson had the ultimate honour of carrying the colours up the ridge for the final charge. The 11th (Devonshire), the neighbour of the 61st throughout the battle and sharing every great feat, lost sixteen officers and 325 men.

Despite the heavy fighting and British losses on the ridge, this remains one of the most complete victories in all of British military history. The French lost 14,000 men, two Imperial Eagles and six regimental colours. The victory became slightly tainted after the Spanish abandoned the only bridge in the area across which the French could escape. However, Wellington was soon marching into the Spanish capital of Madrid.

# 17. Vittoria

Between Salamanca and the Battle of Vittoria, a series of great advances and retreats occurred across the Iberian Peninsula. The winter of 1812 found Wellington all the way back in Portugal with the French on his tail. The season allowed some respite, and for the two foes to resupply with men and arms. For the start of the campaigning season, the French expected the Allies to take their usual advance into Spain and so lay in wait. Wellington though, did something quite unexpected and the French soon received news that the Allies were marching through the mountains of northern Spain. It was now their turn to beat a hasty retreat across the peninsula.

During this period, the 28th (North Gloucestershire) Regiment of Foot, found themselves in Hills Corp once more. They were stationed in Stewarts 2nd Division and O'Callaghans 3rd Brigade. The men of Hills Corp eventually reached close to the town of Vittoria along with the rest of the allies. Vittoria lies in a rugged basin hemmed in on all sides by the Pyrenees Mountains. Three French armies had united in the basin, but Wellingtons plan was simple. Hill would go down the right flank whilst Wellington himself led through the centre.

At 05:00 on 21st June 1813, the 28th were called to arms and they marched across the river Zadorra. They met with little resistance until they wheeled into the basin and ahead in the distance stood the entire Army of the South under General Gazan. Immediately before them though was the village of Subijana de Alava, which had been identified as a key position on the French advanced front. 3rd Brigade, with the 28th leading the charge as senior regiment, assaulted the village. They were hassled by a fourteen-gun battery en-route, but to their surprise, they found the village empty.

The village was indeed a key position for the French and they had in fact not abandoned it. Just behind Subijana de Alava, was an area thickly wooded with olive trees and interspersed with rocky ravines. It was here that the French would make their stand. By now, 1st Brigade had occupied the higher ground above 3rd Brigade and they both agreed to send two battalions to flush out the French. Surprisingly, given how early it was in the battle, the 28th were already out of ammo. They had to stand and wait under heavy fire for supplies to be brought up.

Removing the initial French defenders from their well defended hiding place, proved an easy task. In response, Gazan sent in three divisions to eradicate the British battalions who had now assumed a defensive position. After a stubborn

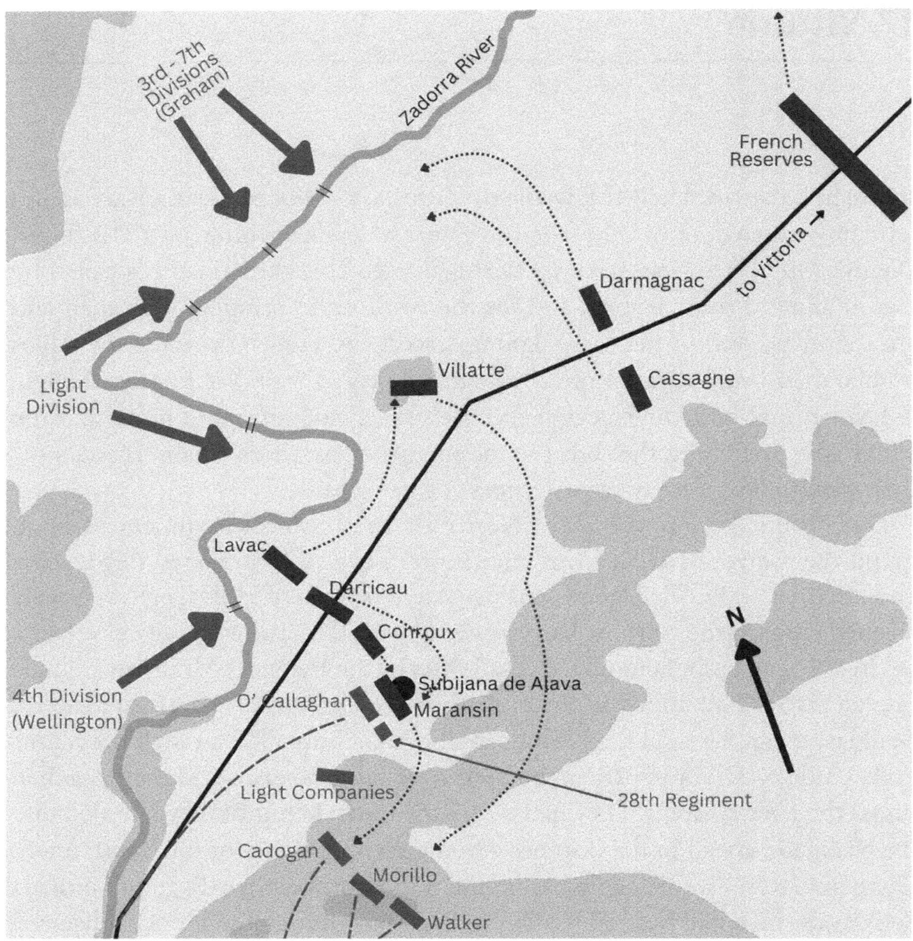


fight, the French slowly pulled back. However, they had made a serious error of judgement. They very wrongly assumed that Hills Corp was the entire Allied Army but of course, they were not.

To French surprise, men were spotted streaming into the basin at 13:00. It turned out that this was in fact Wellington leading the main force into battle. Things now turned from bad to worse for the French. An hour later firing was heard from the northeast. This was General Graham advancing with yet another Corp. He had taken a circuitous route to reach the battle, obtaining the element of surprise that Wellington had wanted.

At this point panic took over the French, and they began to retreat en-masse. Wellington's plan had worked perfectly. Hills Corp had pinned the French on their left, whilst two manoeuvres crushed the centre and then turned the right wing. The 28th counted sixteen men killed and a further 192 wounded.

Graham had blocked the road out of the basin towards Bayonne, so the French streamed down the narrow road towards Pamplona. Amongst them were King Joseph (Napoleons brother), his entire court, the remnants of three French armies, thousands of civilians, the baggage train and five years of booty. Many French souls and much loot never made it the sixty-five miles to Pamplona.

# 18. Pyrenees

After retreating from Vittoria, the French forces eventually made their way to Pamplona. From here, they managed to escape across the Pyrenees and make contact with Bayonne, which had much needed supplies and reinforcements waiting. Leaving Pamplona in his rear was not an option for Wellington, so the 28th (North Gloucestershire) Regiment of Foot and 61st (South Gloucestershire) Regiment of Foot began to lay siege to the town. Wellington though, would soon withdraw the 28th as he had other ideas and on the 2nd July 1813, he led his army into the Pyrenees.

D'Erlon had been left to screen any potential routes through the Pyrenees mountains and on the 5th July the 28th, still in O'Callaghans Brigade of the 2nd Division in Hills Corp, formed up to smash through the French defenders. The French pulled back once they saw their adversaries and it was not until the 7th July that contact was made. At the pass of Maya, Wellington sent the Portuguese to pin the French centre, whilst O'Callaghans Brigade went along the right flank. This meant a steep and sheer two-hour climb to reach the pinnacle called the Rock of Aretesque.

Finally reaching the Rock of Aretesque, the British found the French waiting for them. Volleys were exchanged between the two sides but the French had the advantage of easily being able to send in more and more men. Soon O'Callaghans Brigade were greatly outnumbered, and the situation looked desperate as the only path of escape was down the rocky precipice they had just climbed. As is often the case in mountainous regions, a sudden heavy fog descended on the battlefield and fighting ground to a standstill. The 28th spent a freezing cold night camped on the spot, but were no doubt heartened by the fact that the Command-in-Chief himself decided to share in these hardships.

The British rose before dawn ready to carry on the previous day's battle. They were quite shocked to find the French had retreated overnight, despite having an advantage in position and numbers. On the 14th July, the bulk of the Spanish Army arrived at Pamplona, which allowed the remaining British contingents, including the 61st, to march into the Pyrenees.

Meanwhile, Marshal Soult had taken control of all French forces in the south. He now came up with an audacious plan to win the war with one swift move. He would smash through the Allied right flank, relieve Pamplona and come up in Wellington's rear, forcing him to surrender. The French had always lived off the land in Spain, which certainly did not endear them to the local populace.

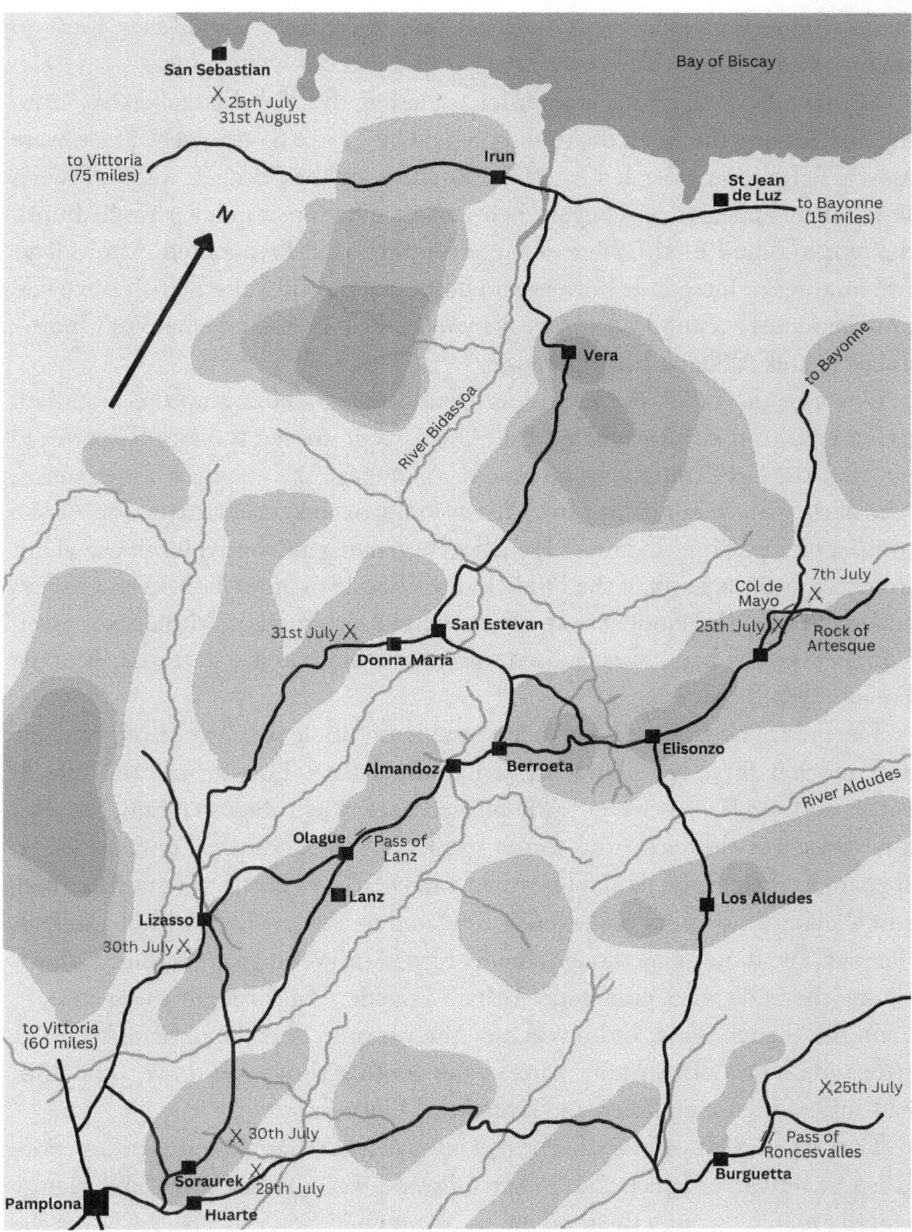


Here Soult did not have that luxury in the mountains, so his plan was to capture the supplies of the army he was intending to destroy.

Two French strongholds remained in Wellingtons rear, one being Pamplona the other being San Sebastian. The latter was attacked unsuccessfully on the 25th July, which the 61st could audibly hear in the distance. Later that day, they heard gunfire from a different direction, one where there should have been no enemy. Soult's daring offensive through the Pyrenees had begun.

Meanwhile Wellington's main force, including the 28th, had fallen back into the line, leaving the Rock of Aretesque held by a force of 400 men. These were mostly light companies led by Major Bradbey of the 28th. At 11:00, French skirmishers appeared and began their assault. The forces quickly swelled until the four hundred British were facing seven thousand Frenchmen. After forty-five minutes of incredible bravery and desperate fighting, the British force had to surrender. Two hundred and sixty men lay dead including a hero of Oporto, Talavera and Albuera, Major Bradbey.

Down in the valley, the main force had been scrambling up the mountain to lend aid to their beleaguered colleagues, yet it arrived too late. They could not save the light companies but could still engage the enemy who remained. The 28th, who were furthest from the scene, arrived at the battle to see a huge conflict raging. More and more French were arriving and one column was about to smash into the flank of the Highlanders. The 28th unleashed several volleys and saved the Highlanders from almost certain destruction. Morale was given a further boost when it was realised the enemy they had just defeated, were the French 28th Regiment.

The French however, seemed to have an inexhaustible supply of reinforcements and another three regiments arrived on the scene. This turned the tide of battle, and the British were slowly pushed back down the mountain. Disaster now struck as the retreating forces suddenly saw an entire French division appear on their right flank. They had marched into battle via another road, and Wellington's forces now rapidly retreated to a defensive position a mile in the rear. The mountains though, finally turned in Wellington's favour, as down yet another side track emerged a British brigade. This brought them straight upon the French flank, and it was now their turn to beat the retreat. At 20:00, after nine hours of constant combat, the conflict simmered down. The 28th had suffered ten men killed and a further 149 wounded.

That evening Hill arrived, for he had been absent so far, and ordered his entire Corp to retreat fifteen miles. What followed was a treacherous, and energy sapping march through the mountains. Meanwhile, Soult had been leading the advance on another front with little success. Shockingly though, the entire Allied force suddenly began to retreat en-masse in front him and they were pushed almost all the way out of the Pyrenees. Finally, just two miles from Pamplona, Thomas Picton found his courage again and ordered a halt. On hearing of the retreat, a furious Wellington ordered 6th Division, including the 61st, to march into reserve on the flank.

Wellington had been with the 28th when news of the retreat reached him. In a daring and truly dangerous act, he galloped through the mountains all alone to reach the scene of the developing crisis. He then sent a message to 6th Division, asking them to up their speed at all costs and join him at the village of Sorauren. Seeing their arrival on the 28th July, the French launched an immediate assault.

The first French column marched through a valley just as the 61st had arrived on one of the upwards slopes, whilst the Portuguese were stationed on the other side. The French walked straight into a trap and faced volleys of fire from both flanks. Soult then threw his men against the Allied centre and a battle brewed up along the entire line. After two hours of bloody combat, the French withdrew unimpeded. Soult then pushed his forces against the right wing, but as usual, Wellington had chosen his ground well. The French, who had to climb steep slopes before they could engage their foe, were pushed back.

At 16:30, the light companies of 6th Division were ordered to attack the village of Sorauren. They were met by a furious French fire and made no progress. The men of the 61st managed to find cover behind an earth wall and from this spot, they kept the French pinned down until nightfall. This battle was over but the British were ready at dawn to attack again. What waited for them was a great surprise. Soult had gambled on relieving Pamplona and gaining the British supplies there with haste. Wellington now firmly stood in his way and the French Army were literally starving to death. Soult now came up with a plan that was almost as audacious, to get back to France. What occurred was a disastrous nine-day march, which resulted in no less than ten battles, mostly fought on mountaintops with bayonets fixed.

At dawn on the 30th, Wellington quickly realised the French were on the run. Soult had left three divisions behind to cover his retreat but these were almost instantly eradicated. Wellington merely manoeuvred his men to completely surround the French, and then they were attacked from all directions. As an example of its one-sidedness, the 61st suffered just fourteen casualties. Meanwhile, Hills isolated Corp still had to deal with D'Erlon's eighteen thousand men that stood in their way. Near the village of Lizasso, the conflict heated up once again. The light companies, now commanded by Captain Harman of the 28th, held the right flank whilst the rest of the 28th were placed in support of the main line.

D'Erlon wanted to attack the left but started with a feint on the right flank. This saw the start of nearly seven uninterrupted hours of battle for the light companies. The action then became general along the entire line and after a few hours, the Portuguese began to give way. The 28th came up from the reserve and jumped straight into the battle, filling the hole and pushing the

French straight back down the mountain. After the Portuguese reformed, the 28th went back into reserve but later on, more Portuguese became isolated and greatly outnumbered by their opponents at the hamlet of El Ariba. Nineteen men from the 28th went to their aid, including a beast of a man, Lance Corporal Tank. He began impaling Frenchmen on his bayonet, lifting them into the air and then throwing them over a cliff. This sight was enough for the French and they beat a hasty retreat.

By evening, D'Erlon had finally turned the British left flank but Hill simply ordered his men to pull back to a prominent ridge in their rear. The French had no chance of shifting the British from this position and so later that night, D'Erlon joined Soult on the retreat. On the 2nd August, having reached the French border, the 61st came into contact with the rear guard. This would be the last action in the Pyrenees for either of our protagonists. The conflict continued to rage elsewhere and by the time the French were safe, half the number who had marched into the Pyrenees had perished. Many thousands fell in battle but many more also died of starvation on their desperate retreat.

# 19. Nivelle

By the winter of 1813, Napoleons stranglehold on Europe was fast diminishing. He had been defeated at the Battle of the Nations, the largest single conflict the world had ever witnessed. Meanwhile, Wellington waited in the Pyrenees poised to invade France itself. This was of course, no easy task. The French held a line sixteen miles long across the hilly southern banks of the river Nivelle. They reinforced their positions with redoubts, trenches and many cannon. Alongside this, the French would have the added advantage that inspires soldiers to such great deeds, fighting on home soil.

Soult did not have enough men to hold the lines and so his army was thinly spread. Wellington knew that if he concentrated his forces at a particular point he could break through. This battle featured both the regiments of Gloucestershire on the field, with firstly the 28th (North Gloucestershire) Regiment of Foot, 733 men strong, in the 2nd Division of Hills Corp. The 61st (South Gloucestershire) Regiment of Foot, 578 men strong, were in the 6th Division, also in Hills Corp.

Hills Corp were instructed to attack the left flank of the enemy where D'Erlon had two lines of fortifications to hold. 6th Division, with men of the 61st, would attack the fortifications which included five redoubts bristling with artillery. These were interconnected by a series of trenches. The fortifications protected an essential crossing point, the bridge at Amotz. The Portuguese allies attacked the centre of D'Erlons lines, whilst the 28th and the rest of 2nd Division went on a wide flanking manoeuvre.

At 07:00, all the troops were in position and the battle commenced. The first line of defences, being the weaker, were easily overcome despite the majority of French cannon fire being directed at them. The next line of defences would not so easily fall. The 61st, along with the 11th (Devonshire) and 36th (Herefordshire), formed the leading parties of the assault. Under heavy fire from grape, shell and musketry they waded across the waist high Amotz. Forming up on the other side, they then began their ascent of the steep hill. They first took a small breastwork and then leapt into the Harismendia Redoubt, their primary target. At this moment, the French fled. So much for the advantage of fighting in your own backyard.

2nd Division meanwhile, completed their march around the flank and fell on the Finodetta Redoubt. The 28th were reduced to a mere supporting role, and had to watch as furious fighting developed in front of them. The battle would see the 61st lose seven men and have forty-two casualties, whilst the 28th only had three casualties all day.

# 20. Nive

After defeat at Nivelle, Marshal Soult retreated to the strongly fortified port of Bayonne. To protect this manoeuvre he left three strong divisions on the far bank of the River Nive. Wellington's first task then, was to deal with these troops before he could safely advance on Bayonne. He sent Hills Corp down the right flank with the 28th (North Gloucestershire) Regiment of Foot, whilst the 61st (South Gloucestershire) Regiment of Foot accompanied them in Beresford Corp. Wellington would take the rest of his army and head for Bayonne itself.

At daybreak on the 9th December 1813, a huge bonfire was lit on one of the nearby hills. This was the signal to attack, and so the 28th waded through the waist high Nive, despite coming under heavy fire. They reached the far bank and drove off the French picquets to allow the rest of their Corp to cross safely. Hill was now able to turn his Corp towards Bayonne and began his march on the port. However, Soult sent out his reserve to seize the high ground in front of Hills Corp and their path was now blocked.

During the night of 8th/9th December, Beresford's Corp had secretly laid pontoon bridging across the River Nive. 6th Division, the men of the 61st amongst them, charged across the pontoons and chased the enemy out of a nearby wood. Their advance continued until they reached the village of Villefranque, where they met heavy French resistance. Wellington then arrived on the scene, threw his Portuguese troops into the village and they fought a hard battle to secure it. No sooner had they caught their breath, Soult ordered a counter attack and the village was once again in French hands.

The 61st were ordered to accompany the reformed Portuguese troops and they once again pushed into the village. Taking the village proved a success for one momentous reason. Just before the push, Hills Corp began to arrive on the scene. Together, men of the 61st and the 28th fought shoulder to shoulder to secure the victory. This would be the first, and only, time in the history of our two storied Gloucestershire regiments that they fought side by side.

We now reach a juncture over which historians still debate. The taking of Villefranque by our two protagonists officially ended the Battle of Nive, but actually hostilities continued for several more days. Although some may refer to the following events as the Battle of St. Pierre, it is worth exploring further because of the mighty role played by the 28th.

An issue had developed for Wellington, in that his army was now firmly split in two by the river Nive. This was not lost on Soult, and he repeatedly attacked the main body of troops for several days. 6th Division and the men of the 61st, were withdrawn to the rear so they could provide support should the French break through. Hill meanwhile, moved his Corp to a more defensive position anchoring himself on the Chateau Larralde, which was held by the 28th.

On the 12th December, the Allies prepared for another day of aggressive assault by the French. Marshal Soult though had changed tact and instead of attacking the main body, he decided to hit the isolated men of Hills Corp. That morning, seven French divisions along with thirty cannon, headed straight for the Chateau Larralde. At 08:00, the first French columns appeared out of the mist, yet were incredibly held back by a hail of bullets from the 28th outposts.

General Darricau, in charge of this operation, decided to throw more men at the 28th and the outposts withdrew to the main line. For seven hours, the French hoards came time and again at the chateau with often nothing standing between them and victory, except for the thin red line of the 28th. By midday, the men of Gloucestershire were in real trouble, but some quick thinking saw the right of their line swing around. They were now firing directly into the flanks of the enemy and once again, the French fell back.

By 15:00, Hill thought the French had been worn down enough and he ordered a general advance along his entire line. The 28th, fuelled by rage and blood lust, chased their foes almost to the walls of Bayonne. Only by being physically held back by their brethren did they survive. Each man of the 28th had fired a minimum of 170 rounds over the duration of the battle, equating to roughly one shot every two and a half minutes of this seven-hour conflict. This is a great rarity for such a lengthy battle. Often in the warfare of this period, there are prolonged lulls in the action as unit's reform or different areas of the line are attacked.

The 61st played a small role in this battle. They had been moving back to cover off this assault by the French, but the pontoons they had used so well days earlier had been damaged by a sudden water rise in the Nive. They spent the day desperately repairing the pontoons so they could come to the aid of Hills Corp. As it was, they arrived just in time to take part in the final chase to the walls of Bayonne.

The 28th amazingly, only lost six men killed at the Battle of St. Pierre and had ninety-six wounded. The French saw three thousand men fall on the battlefield. Terrible winter weather would see the next few months being generally inactive. Wellington left a body of men to besiege Bayonne, whilst he headed off with the 28th, 61st and the rest of his army to pursue the forces of Marshal Soult.

# 21. Orthes

After the battle at Nive, operations died down for a while as the winter weather hit both armies hard. During this time, Marshal Soult was forced to send many of his best men, over ten thousand in total, to reinforce Napoleon who was trying to hold back nearly half a million men who had crossed the Rhine to assault his forces. Soult rested the right flank of his army on the city of Bayonne and held the line of two rivers, the Adour and Gave de Pau.

Wellington began to make his move when on the 23rd February 1814, he sent Sir John Hope across the Adour with strong naval support. This forced Soult to realign his forces and to move back to hold just the Gave de Pau. Wellington crossed the river and Soult was forced back yet further, to hold high ground overlooking the Orthes-Dax road.

At dawn on the 27th February, the 61st (South Gloucestershire) Regiment of Foot crossed the Gave de Pau on pontoon bridges and joined four entire divisions ready to give battle. At 08:00, Wellington sent the 6th Division, along with the 61st, forward as reserve to a feint attack on the French right flank by the 3rd Division. The main attack by Wellington would actually come in the centre of the French position. This assault would rapidly bog down under intense fire, so Wellington quickly made the decision to turn the feint attack into the main assault.

3rd Division, despite coming under severe cannon fire, managed to secure the pinnacle of the hill. General Foy, commander of the French flank, was wounded and confusion quickly began to set in. The 6th Division then arrived to mop up the remaining enemy and then Wellington threw more men at the centre. Meanwhile, Hills Corp, including the 28th (North Gloucestershire) Regiment of Foot, had been some way off on the opposite flank when they were ordered to advance.

The 28th did not have the luxury of pontoon bridges like their comrades from the 61st. This found them wading through the Gave de Pau with icy waters lapping up to their chests. As the leading elements of Hills Corp came into contact with the French, they began to flee from the battlefield. The French would regroup at the next river crossing but the Battle of Orthes was lost. The men of Gloucestershire suffered no fatalities, but the 61st did have eleven men wounded.

# 22. Toulouse

Defeat at Orthes was followed by further French losses in March, so Marshal Soult now retreated to the town of Toulouse, sited on the far bank of the River Garonne. Toulouse was well situated for a defensive action as it had a thick inner ring of medieval walls, yet it was not in the town that Soult would make his stand. To the rear of Toulouse ran the Royal Canal, which was a hundred yards wide. Behind this lay Mont Rave, a three hundred foot high hill overlooking the town. This is where Marshal Soult would position his army.

Throughout these pages so far, Wellington has been given great credit for the various victories and rightly so. However, here at Toulouse his strategy and tactics can be found lacking, starting with a comedy of errors whilst trying to cross the Garonne. Pontoon bridges were laid across the river and the men massed ready to charge across and do battle with the enemy. It was soon discovered that the bridges were too short and so the men stood down. On the 20th March 1814, the 28th (North Gloucestershire) Regiment of Foot marched down river in Hills Corp with 2nd Division, alongside other battalions in Pringles Brigade. Finally, they managed to cross the river but it was found that their path was obstructed by flooding. Therefore the next day, they marched back over the river and returned to their previous position.

Soult had been watching these failures and remained content to stick with his original plan, fortifying Mont Rave. A series of redoubts were built along the top of the hill and trench works were thrown up on its steep slopes. Toulouse was the main arsenal for south-eastern France meaning they had a mass of high quality, high calibre artillery, with which to furnish their defences.

A third attempt to cross the Garonne was now made by Beresford's Corp. The 61st (South Gloucestershire) Regiment of Foot were with them in Clintons 6th Division, alongside Lamberts Brigade. This time, the pontoon bridges were long enough and the entire Corp crossed the river. During the night though, floodwaters swept away the bridges and Beresford's men became dangerously isolated. Surprisingly, Soult did not attempt to attack them. He must have been supremely confident to turn down this opportunity of wiping out over ten thousand men. As it was, after being stranded for four days, Beresford's Corp managed to get back across the Garonne.

Finally, after much delay, the battle began on Sunday 10th April 1814, Easter Day. One suburb of Toulouse, St. Cyprien, lay on Wellington's side of the Garonne but it was well fortified. The job of taking this area was given to 2nd

Division and the men of the 28th. They first pushed back the outposts and then launched themselves against the mill of Bourassol. Upon approaching, it was discovered that the mill was surrounded by a ten-foot high wall. This provided excellent cover for the French and they began to drop the attackers in droves. Only a piece of quick thinking, and quite unbelievable bravery, could rectify the situation. Luckily, the 28th had just the man.

Lieutenant Irwin, already noted amongst the men for his strength and initiative, charged through a hail of bullets and leapt over the mill wall. All alone, he began to personally deconstruct the obstacle with his bare hands. Somehow, he survived and made a gap large enough for the Grenadier Company to swarm through. This is all the French needed to witness and they fled from the wall and the mill itself.

The fighting now developed into fearsome house-to-house combat. As the French abandoned a house, they would set it ablaze and then entrench themselves in the next dwelling. Each street had cannon covering it, but eventually St. Cyprien was taken. The men of 2nd Division were a long way from the main action though. Carrying on the attack to Toulouse itself would have been suicidal, so they spent the rest of the day on top of houses, watching their brethren in action on Mont Rave.

As previously mentioned, the geography of Toulouse made it a dangerous place to attack and Wellington came up with an extreme plan. He would send his main body down the left flank, wheel to the right and march through the thin strip of land between Mont Rave and the River Hars to the rear. This would expose his men to a lethal flanking fire from the redoubts on top of the hill. The 61st led the entire division on this deadly march, and as they passed Mas Augustins redoubt at the centre of the hill, the very first cannon shot that rang out lifted a man clean of his feet and tore him to pieces. The going would be hard this day.

The Spanish had already started their attack on the northern end of Mont Rave, and it was not going well. Finally, after marching the entire length of the foot of the hill, the 61st reached their destination to the south, the Sypiere redoubt. The time was noon when the attack of 6th Division began with the 61st in the centre. They began their ascent of the hill under the watchful eye of Marshal Soult. He had been monitoring the brave, yet surprising, march of 6th Division for some time. He now thought the time was right for a formidable counter attack.

As the men of 6th Division marched up the hill, the redoubts opened a terrifying cannonade upon them. Almost five thousand men leapt out of their trenches and cavalry smashed into the flank. But now, something incredible occurred. General Taupin, commander of this assault, perhaps remembering how often a French column had been defeated by the British line, called his men to a halt. He ordered them to switch from column formation to that of a line. The 61st watched on in astonishment, and moments later unleashed a horrendous volley of their own. General Taupin fell instantly, and then the 61st charged up the hill and smashed into the still reforming Frenchmen. The enemy fled in panic, but there was still much fighting to be done.

The original target of the 61st, Sypiere redoubt, still needed to be taken. They charged the enemy alongside the 36th (Herefordshire) and broke into the redoubt. The enemy were strong here, and the men were mown down in great numbers. The attackers were just about to fall back, when a Grenadier Company from the 91st (Argyllshire Highlander) suddenly appeared and poured on their fire. The redoubt was taken but in this glorious scene Colonel Coghlan, Commanding Officer of the 61st, fell at the head of his men.

Soult now ordered his troops back to a secondary line of works, but these were not as well fortified as the first line that had just been broken through. Despite this, a pause in the action occurred as 6th Division carried out the laborious task of dragging cannon up Mont Rave. After a long lull in the combat, Wellington ordered the entire army to attack at once. The 6th Division charged at the remaining Calvinet and Augustins redoubts, but the badly mauled 61st were ordered to remain in support.

This supporting role did not last long however. The Highland Brigade had successfully taken Calvinet redoubt when a huge French counter attack smashed them to pieces. The 61st, now only 250 men strong, reinforced the few remaining men of the Highland Brigade and they somehow held onto Calvinet. Mont Rave was now almost cleared, except for the Grand Redoubt, which the Spanish had failed to take despite repeated attacks.

At 16:00, yet another huge counter attack by the French looked as though it might swing the tide of battle at the last moment. The French marched out in their usual column formation and headed straight for the 61st. The Light Company hurried to the front of the line and began an expert sniping of the enemy. One man managed to drop the Colonel leading the counter attack and at this sight, the French turned and ran.

Finally, after a gargantuan effort, the artillery had reached the top of the hill. They opened fire on the remaining obstacle, the Grand Redoubt, at this point the French knew the day was lost. At 17:00, the firing died down and soon Soult was retiring behind Toulouse thick walls. The 6th Division had lost 1204 men with 180 of these coming from the 61st. Only the Adjutant and two ensigns remained on the field for the men of Gloucestershire. The 61st Regiment were undoubtedly the heroes of the day, and forever carry the moniker "the Flower of Toulouse".

On the 12th April, Wellington began preparations to take Toulouse itself. During the night though, Soult escaped with the remnants of his army. The 28th and 61st were soon back on the chase. Before the pursuit could begin, Wellington dwelled in Toulouse for a few days so that Colonel Coghlan, who had so valiantly led his men on that deadly march across the thin strip of land between Mont Rave and the River Hars, could have a huge public funeral.

The following day staggering news arrived. Napoleon had signed the Treaty of Fontainebleau, agreeing to abdicate and go into exile on the island of Elba. After eleven years of near perpetual warfare and almost six million deaths, the war was finally over… at least for a few months.

# 23. Waterloo

In March 1915, the 28th (North Gloucestershire) Regiment of Foot, were embarking onto ships for garrison duty on the island of Bermuda. The early spring weather had delayed them for a few days, and this was enough time to bring the startling news that Napoleon had escaped from Elba. Two months later, the regiment instead found itself in Brussels, once again, under the command of Lord Wellington.

Napoleon had collected a vast army and was marching on Brussels with 124,000 men and 370 guns. Standing directly in his way, was Wellingtons army of 120,000 allies along with Bluchers 83,000 Prussians further east. Napoleon decided to split his forces. He personally led 65,000 men to knock the Prussians out of the contest, whilst Marshal Ney would check Wellington with the remaining 59,000.

Wellington decided to meet Ney at the crossroads of Quatre Bras, some eighteen miles south of Brussels. Blucher took up position just six miles to the east, so the two armies could provide mutual support. At 04:00 on the 16th June 1815, Lieutenant Colonel Nixon led the 28th out of Brussels heading towards Quatre Bras along with the rest of Picton's 5th Division.

Napoleon ordered both battles to begin concurrently at 14:00 but by this time, Wellington had only seven thousand infantry in place. The rest of the hundred thousand men were strung out along the eighteen-mile road to Brussels, including the 28th. The French repeatedly smashed into the Allies, but Wellington would form line or square admirably, depending on whether he faced infantry or cavalry. Throughout the day, more and more men arrived to be thrown into the battle. Napoleon was victorious against the Prussians but by 20:00, the Quatre Bras crossroads were still controlled by the Allies. Wellington had been so impressed by the actions of the 28th, who lost 92 men on this day, that he chose to mention them in dispatches.

Nevertheless, the following day Wellington was forced to withdraw to maintain contact with the retreating Prussians who had been beaten but not defeated. He decided to stop at a little village called Waterloo. This site was of course, extremely well chosen. Wellington set himself up on a ridge called Mont St. Jean, where to his front he had a fairly steep slope, whilst to the rear there was a gentle incline. This allowed for easy manoeuvring, but also kept his cavalry and reserve units hidden from cannon fire and from Napoleons sight.

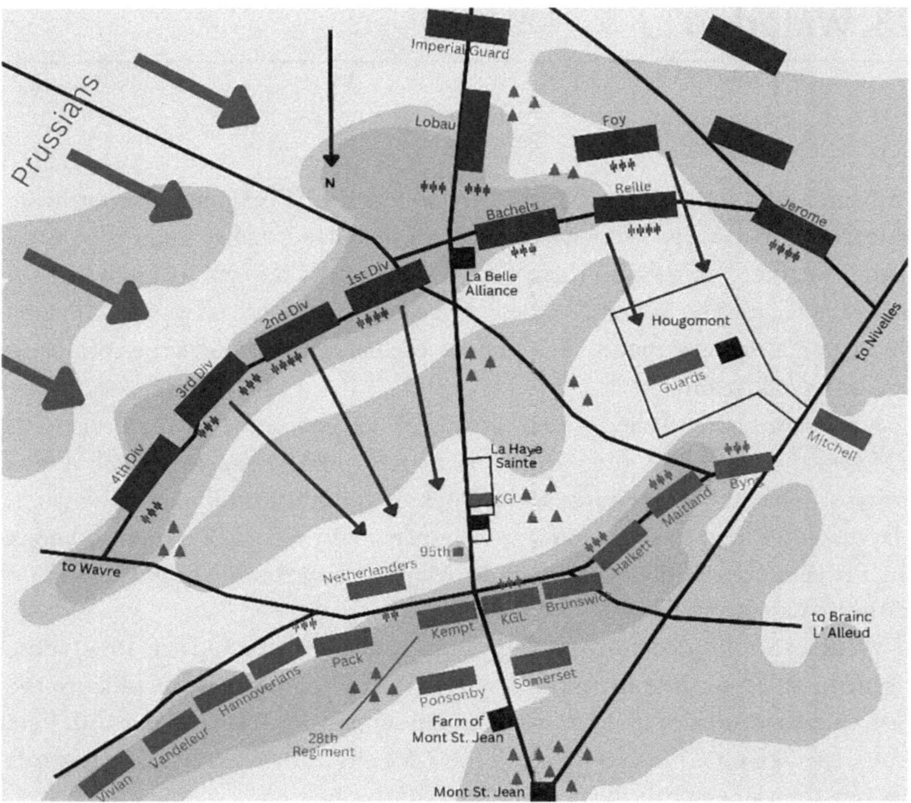


On the 18th June 1815, both sides began to form up for battle. The 537 men
of the 28th Regiment were posted, along with the rest of Picton's 5th Division,
to the centre of the line, just behind the farmhouse of La Haye Sainte. The 28th
were in Kempts 9th Brigade, so had the 32nd (Cornwall) on their right and
the 95th Rifles on a sandy knoll just to their immediate front. To their left they
had Packs Brigade, so the 1st (Royal Scots) were the regiment on their flank
but some distance away. The reason for this gap was that the Netherlanders
had misunderstood Wellington's orders, and instead formed up alongside the
skirmishers further to the front. La Haye Sainte itself was held by battalions
of the Kings German Legion.

Napoleon lined his army up on the opposite ridge called La Belle Alliance.
It was higher than Mont St. Jean, offering a better position for his superior
cannon. The two armies stretched 5000 yards and were split by a shallow valley
several hundred yards wide. Straight through the middle of the battlefield ran
the Charleroi to Brussels highway. It was on this key element that the 28th sat
awaiting the battle.

Napoleon now had 74,000 men and 250 guns, whilst Wellington could muster 66,000 men and 156 guns. His plan was to wait out the day and hope the Prussians would arrive. Napoleon himself also had a simple strategy, which was to smash straight down the Brussels road through La Haye Sainte, brush aside Kempts Brigade and capture the village of Mont St. Jean. This would effectively split the Allied Army and the day would be won.

At 11:00, news reached the 28th that Blucher and the Prussians were on their way to help them. This sent the men into a wild frenzy. There was of course, no way they could have actually known this but the news had a greatly positive effect upon the men's morale. Napoleon had delayed starting the battle, as he wanted the ground to dry a little to benefit his cannon and cavalry. Eventually though, at 11:30 the first shots rang out.

Napoleons first move was to attack the farmhouse at Hougoumont, which anchored the Allied right flank. This was actually a feint to get Wellington to weaken his centre by sending men to help the right. Wellington though remained steadfast and Napoleon actually wasted two French divisions with this diversionary assault. The farmhouse was held by the Guards Division and they gave the French a real battering there.

At noon, the 28th could see roughly eighty cannon being rolled into position directly opposite them atop La Belle Alliance ridge. By 13:30, these cannon were in position and Napoleon gave word for the main attack to begin. The eighty cannon roared into life and this was replied to with much gusto by the Allied artillery. Kempt ordered his brigade to lie down so the 28th avoided the worst of the carnage. Consequently, this barrage also sent the Netherlanders scampering back into their rightful position in the line alongside the 28th.

Whilst all this was occurring, D'Erlon's Corps was rolling into action. Four fine divisions of Frenchmen marched in columns towards Picton's Division. In excess of 16,000 men, in ranks of twenty-four, marched through the valley with their eagles glistening in the early afternoon sun. A fearsome sight they must have been. Elements of the First Division soon broke off, and attacked La Haye Sainte but the remaining three wheeled towards Kempts Brigade and the Netherlanders. Meanwhile, the 95th had to pull back from the sandy knoll in the face of overwhelming numbers.

French sharpshooters came in advance of the columns and starting taking pot shots at their enemy. This though, was too much for the Netherlanders who suddenly turned and fled the battlefield. The 28th jeered whilst the Grenadiers had to be physically restrained by their officers to prevent them from shooting the fleeing men. The result of all this was that the gaping hole had reopened between the 28th and the Royal Scots.

At this point, the 28th were ordered to stand up (they had still been led flat on the ground to avoid cannon fire), but were surprised to find the French Second Division forming up directly opposite them. Unperturbed, they unleashed a murderous volley at forty paces and then fixed bayonets and charged right into the enemy. This tactic shook the French but they remained steadfast. To add further to French difficulties, the reformed 95th and elements of the Kings German Legion began to fire into their flanks.

The reason the French managed to stand this crazed onslaught was because they only actually faced half of the 28th Regiment. When the initial bayonet charge took place, they were horrified to discover the entire French Third Division had occupied the place of the Netherlanders on their direct left. Nixon, quick wittedly, ordered the 28th Grenadiers and left wing to wheel round and pour fire upon the enemies flank. The brigade that the French were attacking, Packs, had suffered badly at Quatre Bras and so only fielded 1400 men. The French Third Division were carrying the day.

Much to French surprise though, the Union Brigade of Heavy Dragoons and Lord Somerset's Household Brigade of Cavalry, suddenly came flying over the crest of Mont St. Jean from their previously hidden position. They smashed into the exposed flank of First and Second French Divisions right in front of Kempts Division. The enemy fled in sheer panic from the cavalry, who pursued them right up the slopes of La Belle Alliance. Sadly though, overwhelmed by the might of victory, the cavalry had gone too far. Napoleon sent his Polish Lancers into the attack and these brave men were decimated.

On a slightly odd note, Lieutenant Deares of the 28th was so overcome with relief and excitement of the lifesaving cavalry charge that he decided to also pursue the French on foot, all by himself. He did a good job of cutting down five of his opponents, before he was over powered and taken prisoner. Luckily for him, he was released to re-join his regiment the very next day, although the French had stripped him of all belongings except for his pantaloons.

The remaining French Division (it will be remembered that four attacked), were repulsed by a light cavalry charge. The confused retreat worried the attackers at La Haye Sainte so much that they too broke off their assault by 15:00. During all this action, Picton had been killed and so Kempt took over the Division. This meant that Sir Philip Belson was now in charge of the brigade containing the 28th. Kempt reformed his division to close the gap caused by the Netherlanders flight, so that now the 28th and Royal Scots were alongside each other, and the 95th retook their position on the sandy knoll. 6th Brigade, who had only just arrived on the battlefield, were brought up to the rear of the centre to provide support. All units were now roughly where they had started the battle and Napoleons plan was in tatters.

At 15:30, a slight lull in the action was interrupted by more French marching down the Brussels Road. The most intact brigade from the previous retreat, attacked La Haye Sainte whilst a brigade from Second Division attacked Belson's Brigade in skirmish order. This was to prevent them from helping their comrades at the farmhouse. At the same time, the French also dramatically increased their cannon numbers opposite Kempts Division. This soon opened up a murderous fire, but the various Allied regiments, once again, pulled back slightly behind the ridge to hide from the worst of it. The infantry attack on the farmhouse, much less ruthless than the first, quickly dissolved.

Having failed in his attacks on the right and centre of the Allied line, Napoleon now turned his attention to the left wing. He sent a mass of his cavalry tearing across the valley and into the divisions stationed there. In good order, these men fell back slightly and then formed square. Of course, cavalry alone could not break these fortresses of men and so they were ripped to shreds by the supporting Allied cannon.

At 16:30, two Prussian officers suddenly appeared upon the battlefield and rode into view of the 28th. The Prussians were looking for Wellington and their presence was met by an almighty roar all along the line. At the same time, Napoleon once again attacked La Haye Sainte and once again, the Kings German Legion held firm.

An hour and a half later, the 28th began to hear an ever increasing noise (instantly recognisable as the sound of battle), two miles to their front left. The field was alive with excitement. Had the Prussians finally arrived? Either way, Napoleon decided that he simply must break the Allied centre. So the battered First and Second Divisions, this time supported by Cuirassiers, attacked La Haye Sainte for the umpteenth time.

Amazingly, the French finally succeeded but not because of martial superiority. Somehow, the wagon carrying rifle ammunition had been lost during the battle and the defenders of the farmhouse had run of bullets. Napoleon seized on this stroke of luck by immediately occupying La Haye Sainte and bringing up two cannon. These instantly began to shower Belson's Brigade with terrifying grape shot. The French also took control of the sandy knoll, previously occupied by the 95th and once again, the dangerous sharpshooters came into play. At this point, Lieutenant Colonel Nixon fell and so Captain Kelly became Commanding Officer of the 28th.

With the advantage of La Haye Sainte, the French made repeated attacks upon the 28th and their comrades but they continued to hold firm. The Kings German Legion though, who had so valiantly held the farmhouse for so long, were now ruined. Most of their officers had been killed and they still had little ammo. Incredibly, for men who had fought so hardily, they now decided to merely leave the battlefield. So many men streamed away that Bluchers scouts reported to him that the whole of Wellingtons Army was fleeing. Once again, a huge hole opened up in the centre, this time on the right of the 28th.

Kempt kept his cool though, and reformed the division and placed them directly across the Brussels road. The remaining gap was plugged by the Light Cavalry Brigade, who quite impressively did this on their own initiative having travelled all the way from the right wing. During this period, Captain Kelly fell and so Captain Teulon now became the Commanding Officer of the 28th. Kempts Division had been in the thick of the action all day. The 28th had started with just over 500 men, and now the line covering the Brussels road was a single one in skirmish order.

At 19:00, having checked the Prussian advance, Napoleon decided the vital moment of the battle had come. He would drive the Old Guard straight down the Brussels road and smash Wellingtons beleaguered troops to pieces. Ney led the Old Guard in person, but he made a series of bizarre errors. Firstly, he travelled obliquely down the La Belle Alliance ridge, thus exposing the cream of French fighting power to Allied artillery. Then instead of appearing in the centre, he led the Old Guard to the Allied left flank, which had recently been reinforced. At the same time as this was happening, the remains of the Second and Third French Divisions made their final onslaught against their old foes of Belson's Brigade.

The legendary Old Guard were beaten back by the Allies, whilst at the same time the men of the Second and Third Division realised they had been lied to. Over on their right were not French reinforcements but in fact the Prussian enemy. A general panic spread like wildfire through the French ranks and they began to flee in droves. Wellington rode along the entire line with his hat aloft. This was the signal for a general advance up La Belle Alliance.

The French Army was broken, but the brave and fearsome souls of the Old Guard had formed three squares. They fought heroically, but were eventually overwhelmed by Belson's Brigade and the men of the 28th. Wellington and Blucher met at the top of the ridge, and it was decided that the fresher Prussians would continue the pursuit, whilst the British halted in their current positions. For the 28th, eleven hours of carnage had come to an end. The 28th Regiment had twenty-six men killed and a further 133 wounded. The Battle of Waterloo had been won, and an old and most worthy enemy defeated once and for all.

# Mid–Late 19th Century

# 24. Punjab, 25. Chillianwallah, 26. Goojerat

**Punjab** lands were centred around the delta of five rivers, in an area stretching through modern day Kashmir. They reached from the Indus River in the West to the River Sutlej in the east. The Sikhs took advantage of declining Afghan control to forge their own Empire. Founded in the early 1800's, they soon came into conflict with the East India Company.

After the death of powerful ruler Ranjit Singh, the fledgling empire quickly began to disintegrate with infighting over leadership and an expensive army to maintain. The British looked to gain from this and in late 1845, war was officially declared. The British triumphed and peace ensued for a short time before war broke out again in 1848 after the murder of two British agents.

The 61st (South Gloucestershire) Regiment of Foot were three years into a fourteen-year tour of India. They were on garrison duty in the town of Jullundur led by Lieutenant Colonel McLeod. When news of the renewed conflict reached the 61st they hurried to join Lord Gough, commander of the Army of the Punjab.

Leaving Jullundur on the 23rd September 1848, it was soon realised that the Sikhs had taken control of a small nearby fort called Rungur Nunglo. They reached the fort on 13th October, finding it strongly constructed of mud and with a deep moat but fortunately, no artillery. The bombardment opened up at 06:30 and stopped again at 10:00, as the Europeans had to shelter from the oppressive sun. In the afternoon, the 61st were ordered to prepare batteries to move within 300 yards of the enemy. Several men were killed in this duty. When the cannon started again at 16:00, the forts doors were blown off, however, it was considered too late in the day to assault.

The next morning, the 61st readied themselves for the attack but it was soon discovered that the Sikhs had made their escape through subterranean tunnels or by lowering themselves from ropes down the ramparts. The fort was then blown up and the march continued. A few days later, the 61st approached Fort Murree but the enemy fled on sighting the British and, once again, the fort was demolished. Without tents, and now dwindling rations, they continued to march towards the friendly Army of the Punjab.

An unfortunate event occurred on the 26th October when the 61st discovered they were a man down. They assumed locals had kidnapped him and they threatened to burn the village down unless their comrade was returned. The man was not found and the 61st remained true to their word. In the battles that followed weeks later, this man actually surfaced fighting for the Sikhs. The deserter was killed by the 61st but this was probably little comfort to the people whose village lay in ashes. Finally, after nearly two months marching, the Army of the Punjab was sighted.

Lord Gough was attempting to cross the River Chenab so he could engage the vast Sikh Army. On the 22nd November, at the Battle of Ramnagar, Gough attempted to cross the river. Opposing the British were masses of Sikh artillery but these remained out of range. The British artillery was moved to the front and an awesome artillery duel took place. The 61st were given the task of protecting the artillery and moved to the front, pushing back the Sikh advanced posts. The battle was ultimately a stalemate, as no way could be found over the Chenab and for several days the adversaries eyed each other across the river.

On the 1st December, the 61st joined 8th Brigade in 3rd Division, under Sir Colin Campbell. The entire division, eight thousand men strong, marched out of camp determined to force a passage twelve miles downriver. They reached the ford at Ranikan but it was strongly held by the enemy. The only way to get across the Chenab was to outpace the Sikhs and this is what they did. 3rd Division marched forty-two miles in twenty-seven hours with only a few breaks to catch their breath. Finally reaching Wazirabad, they found an unprotected crossing.

The infantry crossed the river in seventeen large boats whilst the artillery dragged their cannon, which completely submerged under the water, through the river. The cavalry element also marched through and several troopers were dragged away by the strong current. Another lightening march back down river was now needed to catch the Sikhs off-guard. The British arrived at the Sikh camp on the 3rd December.

The 61st sat down to a breakfast of turnips and then readied themselves for the Battle of Sadulpur. The Sikhs formed a line and opened fire with their forty cannon. The British infantry had to pull back a hundred yards under such a terrific pummelling and they then lay on the ground. The British artillery finally warmed up and a two hour duel now began. Both sides attempted to turn their opponents flank with cavalry but neither was successful. For three and a half hours, the 61st lay face down in the dirt, until nightfall came and the action died down. The regiment had lost four men killed and eight wounded. The Sikhs had mistaken 3rd Division for the entire army, thus underestimating their own great numerical advantage. Had they attacked wholeheartedly then the result might have been catastrophic for the British.

The Sikh Army withdrew overnight, and so the British began their pursuit. Eventually the enemy managed to slip away through dense jungle and the Army of Punjab halted the chase. On the 9th January 1849, after a week's break, they once again hunted their adversaries. On January 13th, Goughs columns came

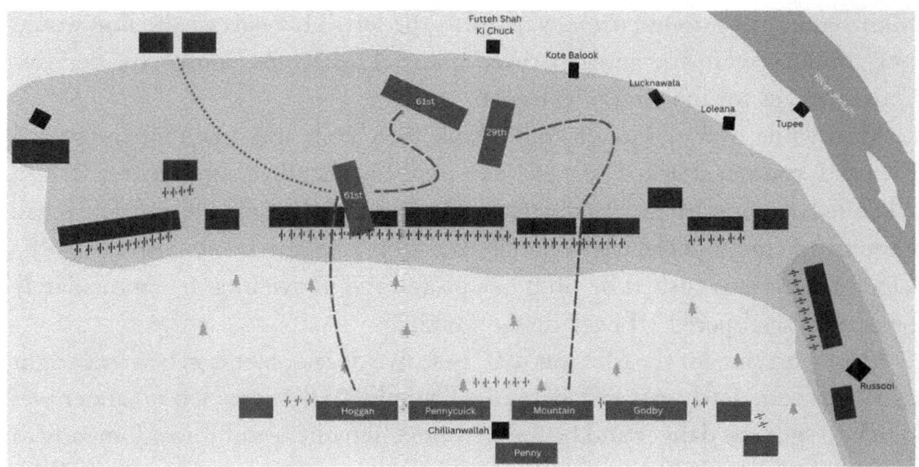


under sustained fire from a mound near the village of **Chillianwallah**. The Sikhs had decided to make their stand.

Gough formed his men into a standard formation, which was a line of infantry with his flanks protected by cavalry, and his cannon interspersed along the line. The 61st found themselves on the left of this line with friendly native infantry on either flank. The day was getting late and in the European tradition, they were expecting to make camp, as it would soon be too dark to fight. Suddenly though, the 61st heard the ferocious sound of countless cannon roaring out from their opposite wing.

The Deputy Assistant Adjutant General, Major Tucker, appeared on horseback with a message from Gough. The 61st would be heading straight into the jungle before them to clear the enemy. Therefore, they loaded their weapons and began the advance. The jungle itself was not overly dense and allowed for a view of around 250 yards. The task was to prove an easy one anyway, as only light skirmishing occurred, and the jungle area was quickly cleared. Once the 61st had cleared through the jungle though, a frightening sight awaited them.

On top of a ridge were the Sikh Army, with so many cannons that they disappeared off in to the distance. No man was able to count how many there actually were. Still, the 61st pushed on and charged up the ridge towards their formidable foe. Despite facing a murderous fire and charging up hill, the Glosters were soon amongst the cannon. A quick but fierce fight developed when the 61st overpowered the cannon and sent the supporting infantry retreating in fear. This area of the battlefield had been swiftly cleared and all seemed to be going well.

The Glosters left flank was supposed to be watched by a brigade of cavalry under Sir J. Thackwell, along with elements of the 18th Horse Artillery. However, a zealous young staff officer arrived and reissued orders for them to attack a

Sikh Battery positioned some way off to the left. This part of the line would not connect again for another three hours. This would soon have decisive consequences for the men of the 61st.

Meanwhile, over on Goughs right flank, the picture was much the same until they were counter attacked by matchlock men. Five hundred and eighteen British fell killed or wounded in a mere matter of minutes. Alongside this setback, it will be remembered that the 61st were flanked by two regiments of native infantry. One of these was rushed by Sikh troops and the native infantry immediately broke and scampered off back down the hill.

Most worrying for the 61st was that these two developments meant their right flank was completely exposed. Brigadier Campbell, Divisional Commander, was quick to spot the danger and he ordered the Grenadiers and First Company to form right. Campbell then personally led them in a daring raid on three Sikh guns that were enfilading the Glosters. These were quickly dealt with, and McLeod brought up the remaining men of the regiment. Lieutenant Hudson tells the story in more detail:

> At this moment a number of Sikh Regular troops, about two Regiments, with a number of Irregulars led by seventeen or eighteen fanatics (akalis) rushed down upon the right flank of the brigade shouting their war cry and beating their drums. The right Regiment, the 36th N.I., gave way and in spite of gallant efforts of their officers bolted to a man down the rear of the 61st.
>
> General Campbell seeing this galloped up to the grenadiers and with half No 1 (composed partly of grenadiers) wheeled them back on their left and ordered them to fire a volley. The enemy were checked by this when within 80 yards, and when after firing for half a minute the General gave the word to charge we went at them with a will. They broke and fled in every direction leaving two guns in our possession.

The actions of the 61st meant they were now entirely facing right and could see the whole Sikh Army lined up before them. A glorious march began as the 61st started to merely mop up the enemy, hitting each unit in the flank with every attack. The day was advancing well for the men of Gloucestershire, and the battle would soon be won. Suddenly though, a large body of enemy cavalry appeared in their rear and continued their charge. The previous disappearance of the cavalry support on the Glosters left flank now spelt huge trouble. The 61st, much like their brethren of the 28th at Alexandria nearly fifty years hence (see battle honour 8), found themselves in the most perilous of situations.

Brigadier Campbell bellowed the order "61st, right about face!" and with no time remaining, the Glosters managed to unleash a mighty volley that stopped the attacking horsemen in their tracks. As if this was not enough, another cavalry charge was suddenly spied towards, what was now, the regiment's rear. The rear rank turned about face once more and the result was much the same. The 61st fighting back to back in line formation, against standard military convention, had fought off two charges from feared enemy cavalry.

This fine action was just a mere interruption to the regiment though. Instead of taking stock of the glorious deed that they had just accomplished, the 61st continued with their rolling up of the Sikh Army. After more vicious fighting, the Glosters suddenly came face to face with the 29th (Worcestershire) Regiment, who had been working their way over from the opposite flank. Oddly, both armies maintained their position on the battlefield and both claimed victory. Gough's 'full frontal' attack on an entrenched position with numerous cannon was seen as foolhardy back home in Britain and he was roundly criticised.

One hundred and fourteen men of the regiment were killed or wounded at the Battle of Chillianwallah but this would not be their last. The 14th January was spent collecting the wounded and burying the dead. The Glosters actually found very few wounded, and the dead men they discovered had been stripped completely naked by the Sikhs. That evening, some men of the 61st, including Sergeant Halliday, found themselves on piquet duty during a terrible storm:

The night of the 14th my Company was on outlying Piquet, the dead Sikhs were still lying about in all directions unburied, The rain fell in torrents. The wind howled dismally through the low jungle of the Battle Field. The night was pitch dark, all these things combined rendered scene more dreary The roar of Artillery and the Rattle of Musketry was still ringing in my ears, the noise and uproar, the groans of the dying and the Wounded, the immense number of the enemy and the determined manner they Fought, for on several occasions I saw them after having the Bayonet through their bodies to the muzzle of the piece, when they could do no more, catch the Bayonet with both hands and try to wrench it off the Muzzle of the piece and even when almost drawing their last breath they would spit at you as you passed.

The rest of the month was spent fortifying the camp and skirmishing with Sikh outposts. The 61st were charged with building a small fort, which protected the camps right flank. On the 14th February, the Sikhs suddenly broke camp and marched off into the distance. Their destination was the city of **Goojerat**. The Army of the Punjab pursued them, and covered thirty-eight miles in four days through thick jungle. Another area of the Punjab was also being assaulted by the British at Multan. On the 20th February, Gough was given a great morale boost when General Whish arrived with three fresh brigades, having successfully quelled the Multan rebellion.

At 07:00 the next day, the Army of the Punjab fell in knowing that they were about to face what would be the final battle of the campaign. The destruction of either army meant ultimate victory. The men of the 61st marched three miles through waist high cornfields before they saw the city walls. The Sikh Army was spread out in front of them with their fifty-nine cannon and masses of cavalry on either wing. To the front of the Sikh line, they had fortified several small villages. Gough's two wings were separated by the dry riverbed of the Dwara and the 61st found themselves in the reserve on the left flank.

The Battle of Goojerat opened up with the now customary artillery duel. However, for the first time the Army of the Punjab had the advantage, as their gunners were more skilled. After quickly winning the artillery battle and some cavalry manoeuvring on the flanks, Gough pushed forward his right flank. The first fortified village, Bara Kalra, was taken after a vicious infantry battle. The fighting was close, but Gough brought up his artillery and grapeshot made the difference.

The next fortified village, Chota Kalra, now fell with superior artillery once again making the difference. Meanwhile on the left flank, the artillery protected by the 61st, cleared three villages to their front. This meant the entire bulk of the infantry were able to advance unopposed up to the Sikh line. They then wheeled right and unleashed the campaign winning enfilade into the enemy line. A final Sikh cavalry charge tried to save the situation but the artillery, again supported by the 61st, saw them off. The Sikh Army collapsed and the men fled.

On the 22nd February, the main force of Gough's Army pursued the enemy whilst the 3rd Division, including the 61st, went on a different route to try and cut off the fleeing Sikhs. All they could find were three abandoned cannon, and so after several days they returned to Goojerat. On the 2nd March, the 61st and 53rd (Shropshire) Regiments left camp with some native infantry and cannon. They were ordered to catch up with an advanced force, who had already left with the expectation of accepting the Sikh surrender. To everyone's surprise, Gough now suddenly appeared and it was thought that he intended to lead the column. However, he had caught the men up so he could give the following speech:

Soldiers of Her Majesty's 61st Regiment I could not let the opportunity pass without coming to say goodbye, and address a few words to you with regard your conduct on the 13th of January [Chillianwallah] when you defeated with comparatively small loss a great number of all arms of the enemy.

I have in the course of my military life witnessed many glorious feats of arms, but the likes of yours is without parallel. You, the 61st, I am proud to say you are a credit to the army, and an ornament to the professionalism to which you belong, and during the remainder of my life I shall think of the 61st with feelings of admiration and respect, and as your conduct has been so exemplary in the field, I shall not fail to represent your conduct to his Grace the Duke of Wellington, in order that it be laid before the Queen.

This address was met with great cheer by the 61st. Although Goughs full frontal tactics were unpopular and misunderstood back in Britain, the men had grown to love him. The following day saw the Glosters march back through the battlefield of Chillianwallah. On the 9th March, the entire day was spent crossing fast flowing rivers and thirteen different streams. Several days later, they marched into the entirely destroyed village of Pukha Sarai. The Sikhs had accidentally blown up the village whilst attempting to destroy their store of ammunition. On the 16th March, they reached Rawalpundi where the Sikh Army lay. They had surrendered two days earlier and after a few more days, the entire province of Punjab was annexed.

# 27. Alma, 28. Inkerman, 29. Sevastopol

The 28th (North Gloucestershire) Regiment of Foot, embarked on the troop ship Niagara at Liverpool in February 1854. Huge crowds lined the streets to wave off their heroes whilst the night before departure, the officers had dined with the Mayor of Liverpool. National excitement about the possibility of a European continental conflict for the first time since the Napoleonic era was reaching fever pitch. The destination for the 28th was the Allied docking areas on the Gallipoli Peninsula, over four thousand miles away. For now, Turkish controlled Gallipoli was actually friendly with Britain. The 28th were sailing out to do battle with a new foe, the Russians.

When leaving Liverpool, the regiment were a thousand men strong. The 28th spent two months in the tented city that was springing up all over Gallipoli, and they consumed their time digging trenches and building forts. From here the regiment moved by steamer to Varna. Despite having seen no action, their numbers had reduced to 720 men with nearly three hundred being lost to Cholera in the infamous staging camps. By the 14th September, the 28th Regiment had crossed the Black Sea and landed at the port of Eupatoria, just north of Sevastopol on the Crimean Peninsula. The 28th found themselves in the 3rd Division under Sir Richard English.

The first big battle of the Crimean War took place on the River **Alma**. This would set the tone for the rest of the campaign as the French, British and Turkish allies worked together appallingly. French Commander, Jacques Arnaud, sent his brave troops up a sheer cliff and turned the Russian wing. The British commander, Lord Raglan, refused to do battle until he saw that the French had succeeded. Eventually the British would turn their wing of the battlefield and the Russians retreated towards the city of Sevastopol. Although present on the battlefield, the 28th saw very little action. This was mainly due to the Russians destroying a vital bridge that crossed the battlefield. By the time enough men had traversed the river, the Russians were in full retreat.

Immediately following their defeat at Alma on 20th September 1854, the Russians sank several warships in the mouth of Sevastopol harbour. This instantly neutralised a huge Allied advantage in naval supremacy. The Allied land forces meanwhile prevaricated and decided against making a direct assault on Sevastopol. Instead they laboriously crossed the Tchernaya River and over the Fedioukine Hills to arrive on the cities southern flank.

Tactics and strategy now began to take shape for the first time, which would dominate global warfare for the next half a century. On 9th October, the French started to break ground on their series of trenches and the British quickly followed suit the next evening. Less than a week later the city was encircled by a ring of trench works and the Allies brought up their 126 big guns. The Russians meanwhile, began to place their 318 guns in defensive positions. At 06:30 on 17th October 1854, the great bombardment of **Sevastopol** began.

The Russians commander, Prince Menshikoff, decided to empty Sevastopol of all non-combatants. This left a garrison of just over 35,000 men with twenty thousand of them being navy personnel. This meant that defence of the city had fallen to Admiral Kornilov, but he fell during the opening salvos on the 17th October. This left overall control of defending the city in the hands of Chief Engineer Lieutenant Colonel Todleben.

To bring supplies onto the peninsula the French selected a small port called Kamiesh towards the southwest, whilst the British used the fishing harbour at Balaclava roughly eight miles to the south. It was these overextended supply lines that the Russians unsuccessfully attacked on 25th October. The Battle of Balaclava, in which the 28th Regiment were not involved, resulted in a stalemate. This however, allowed the Russians to continue hampering British supply lines, which would soon have a devastating effect.

The building of trench works around Sevastopol continued until early November as they became more and more intricate. A pattern now developed as the Russians would suddenly come charging out of the city, attack the trenches and attempt to neutralise them. The Allies would counter attack and drive the Russians off. However, on the 5th November, these reciprocal actions developed into a much larger conflict.

A hundred Glosters along with eight thousand other Allied troops were on monotonous trench digging duty when suddenly sixty thousand Russians appeared and stormed the Allied lines. The Glosters grabbed their weapons and charged to the right flank, where they held their ground despite being outnumbered by nearly 8:1. The fighting was desperate and the Russians charged repeatedly. When the 28th Regiment men ran out of ammunition, they began to use Russian ammo that was taken from their fallen enemies. Eventually, during one Russian charge, the French cavalry appeared on the wing and chose their moment perfectly. They rolled up the Russian flank and their foes retreated back to their lines.

The Battle of **Inkerman** had taught the Russians a valuable lesson. Their enemy, superior in training, experience and firepower, could not be defeated on the field of battle. Instead, the Russians turned their attention to holding out the siege. They now somehow infiltrated a vast portion of their army back into the city of Sevastopol. They had seen off countless invaders over the centuries and knew that an unstoppable force was on its way to lend assistance.

Like Charles XII of Sweden and Napoleon before them, the Allies quickly found out that *General Winter* would be no friend to them. Soon after the Battle of Inkerman, Russian autumn turned to the unbearable Russian winter. On the 14th November *the Great Hurricane* struck. This destroyed twenty large French and British ships holding supplies off the coast. Perhaps even worse, almost all of the newly supplied tents that the men were bivouacked in were torn to shreds. Once the hurricane had subsided, the snows began to fall. In a letter home to his cousin, Major Williams paints the scene of chaos:

We have had a most fearful storm since my last. Loss at sea very great- 15 of our Transports, the French Liner "Henri IV", 120 guns, and a Turkish Liner have been lost. The scene in camp was miserably ridiculous- a sudden gust of wind, about 5 A.M. blew every Tent down. I was in bed at the time with everything on but shoes, when away went the tent, bed, everything. Shoeless I was blown right across the lines, and though drenched to the skin could not help laughing at the sight of so many fellows being blown about in various stages of nudity. My servant brought my shoes which were put on over the wet socks, and my Great Coat over my wet clothes and in that state I had to pass twenty-four hours in a field on Outlying Picquet.

Uncles' Chamois leather shirt, which has been most useful, was too wet to be worn. What a terrible next night I passed, to cold to sleep, walk or sit down. Never had I known cold before.

But only fancy the poor men, if their officer was so bad, they were ten times worse. Worse clad, more wet, and nothing to eat for twenty mortal hours. A great number died that day from sheer cold. One poor fellow of the 4th was found under the lea of a wall where he had gone for shelter, stiff, cold and dead- his hands on his knees supporting his head. People had passed him several times thinking he was resting there.

The Allies, like many before them, were ill prepared for a Russian winter. They had little or no equipment suitable for such extremes of temperature. Although not as bad as central Russia, temperatures on the southern coast of Crimea can hover around freezing point for weeks on end. The siege quickly turned into a nightmare for the attackers. Along with the harsh weather, overstretched supply lines brought the men of the 28th to the brink of starvation. Dead men, horses and mules littered the ground. Men would fall to sleep at night never to awaken again.

Despite all this hardship, the war continued in earnest. Small skirmishes and engagements at least kept the survivors alert. Frustratingly though, the Allies would see their artillery breach the walls of Sevastopol and the evening would be spent planning an attack. By daybreak the next morning, the hardy Russians had repaired the breach and no attack would be possible. In February 1855, the Russians sank another series of large ships in Sevastopol harbour to further frustrate the Allied effort.

Sharpshooters became a strong feature of the siege on both sides. A man would go out before dawn and select some cover from where he could snipe the enemy for the day, before returning to safety after nightfall. Casualty rates were high and it must have been a nerve wracking and lonely affair. The 28th Regiment were heavily involved in these activities, with Captain Maunsell leading the 3rd Division of Sharpshooters, containing a handful of picked men from the 28th and other regiments. Below he tells of what a "typical morning" involved:

I led my party, therefore, while it was yet night, in front of the Green Hill trenches, and posted them as required; and when day came, and the firing began, our men, as expected, were enabled to do no little execution amongst the Russian gunners, and very effectually aided in silencing their fire, though at no slight loss to themselves.

On the second or third day of our duty I took thirty sharp- shooters to within two hundred yards of the Redan, and posted them there, while I myself, with ten more, took up our positions on the left, overlooking the Woronzoff Road, for I felt certain the Russians would attack us from that quarter. We were then a thousand yards ahead of the trenches, which had advanced 1,200 yards from the Redan. As soon as daylight appeared I could see the enemy had observed us, and soon a party of infantry in skirmishing order were coming down the Woronzoff Road to dislodge us. My ten men kept up a well-directed fire, however, and in a short time the Russians, though doing their best to advance under any cover they could find, were effectually checked. The big guns in the batteries then fired canister, which peppered and whizzed about us, happily, as we had fair cover, without doing much harm. It was somewhat of an ordeal for the nerves, however, and before long I observed three of my men growing fidgety, and whispering suspiciously among themselves. Presently, just as I was directing the firing on the enemy's sharpshooters, my Sergeant cried: Look, sir, at those men running away! Shall I fire at them?' 'No,' I said. 'Give me your rifle,' and shouting to the men, and at the same time pointing the weapon at them, I warned them that if they did not immediately return I would fire. They saw I was in earnest, and, very much ashamed and crestfallen, they slunk back.

After this the Russians, seeing they had failed to dislodge us so far, sent a body of infantry against our right, which was a manoeuvre I had been secretly hoping all along they would omit to make. They attacked us suddenly, and one of my men, who was a little separated from the rest of us, found himself surrounded by four of the enemy. He was a fine, powerful man of my regiment, and he ran one of his assailants through with his bayonet: but in trying to escape from the other three he was forced to jump down a precipice, where he hurt himself severely and smashed his rifle, but yet managed to limp away. This time there was clearly nothing to be done but shift position, which we accordingly did, to the other side of the Woronzoff Road, where we were not only undisturbed, but found ourselves still better placed for firing into the embrasures.

This was a typical morning's duty with the sharpshooters.

Captain Maunsell would lead his Divisional Sharpshooters for seventy-six days, and be one of the few remaining 'originals' who had not fallen or been badly wounded. Sadly though, his luck ran out when a bullet from a Russian sharpshooter shattered his left arm. Maunsell would survive the ordeal, ship back to England, and then retire years later on the pension of a Major-General.

Finally, as the weeks turned into months, the sun began to shine and the temperature started to climb. By springtime, the men of the 28th Regiment found themselves billeted in huts that had sprung up all over the Uplands. Cold weather gear, although slightly too late, began to arrive in droves. The supply situation also completely turned, as a railway system was built from the British controlled port of Balaclava right up to the siege line. Further rejoicing was had, when in early May an army from Sardinia, fifteen thousand strong, arrived to help replenish some of the losses experienced over the winter. Despite such positivity, the Glosters Commanding Officer, Lieutenant Colonel Frank Adams, still felt they faced an uphill struggle as he recounts to his brother in the letter below:

The business of the men is a very bad one: we have no Army to do any good with. The men are dying horribly, I have only 100 men fit for duty that arrived in the Crimea when we first started. The Reservists die as fast as they come out: they are such young things.

The winter is just coming to its last legs: we have some cold lately, but when it is fine the sun has power. The huts are getting very numerous now about camp. The railway progressing fast and will be at Lord Raglan's by the end of the month, and it will then be within 40 minutes march from my camp. But we have managed very well lately for all sorts of supplies.

The country has got so nice and dry. My men have had vegetables issues
to them for 3 weeks and upwards now every day. But a tent life is beastly
and no mistake.

The Russians are getting stronger every day. Their batteries rise like a
mushroom. The place (Sevastopol) now is impregnable. We must have
150,000 more men if we think we can lick them. It would be a blessing
to have peace, for Alma & Inkerman are nothing to what we shall have
to go through…

We are at war with the wiliest race of warriors in the world.

Finally by 18th June 1855, the Allies felt strong enough again to launch a full
scale attack upon Sevastopol. The plan was for an all-out attack on the Russian
centre. At the same time a strong Russian position on the Allied left, Picket
House Ravine, which contained a cemetery and reinforced houses, would be
attacked. This is where the 28th would find themselves with General Eyre in
overall command. Despite the vast majority of troops being concentrated on the
centre, it was actually Picket House Ravine that would see the fiercest fighting.

The division in which the 28th were based managed to take control of
the ravine and they held the position all day under heavy Russian artillery
bombardment. This area was then reinforced by the Royal Engineers and it
became part of the Allied lines. The 28th were ready and poised to continue the
attack onto the streets of Sevastopol itself, as long as the main attack succeeded.
However, it did not.

Confusion between the French and British over what shape the initial
bombardment would take proved disastrous. The French decided upon having
no bombardment at all and so immediately fell into difficulty. So much so, that
the British had to delay their own attack to lend support. By the time the main
British assault came, the Russians were ready and repulsed their enemy with
ease. General Eyre was wounded in the fighting at Picket House Ravine, along
with six hundred of his men, sixty-seven of them from the Glosters. The 28th
had done their job exceptionally on the day but it proved a small footnote in
the overall picture. Lieutenant Colonel Frank was proud of his men on this day:

Our Brigade did their work well on the 18th. Eyre was wounded and all
my seniors. I was in command of the Brigade from 4 p.m. and I had all
the arrangements to make to bring them out of action, and I am happy
to say with satisfaction we brought all our wounded with us - the Grape,
Cannister and shells were pouring upon us all day long - 32 officers - 602
men killed and wounded out of one Brigade – 5 officers, (and) 62 men
(of the) 28th Regt.

It was a cruel hot day, and it was God's Mercy any of us were spared – the men behaved admirably – and my young fellows I was much pleased with; they are as brave as lions, and will make excellent soldiers. They are daily under fire and care not the least for it – the only thing to guard them from is exposing themselves too much.

By the 8th September 1855, the Allies were ready to try another attack. The French successfully stormed and occupied the Malakhov Redoubt that loomed over the city. A general attack was ordered and the 28th stood ready. However, with the loss of the Malakhov Redoubt, the Russians knew the game was up. They retreated from the city leaving it in flames. There was relatively little action seen during the coming winter and, by March 1856, the 28th were sailing back to Malta as a peace had been signed with the Russians.

It is believed that 20,000 British soldiers lost their life during this campaign, over eighty percent of them from disease. The Russians meanwhile, lost 100,000 men alone in defence of Sevastopol.

# 30. Delhi 1857

Following the end of the Second Anglo-Sikh War (see Battle Honour 26), the 61st (South Gloucestershire) Regiment of Foot remained in northeast India. They took part in a variety of expeditions and garrisoned numerous towns. In 1856, they arrived at Ferozepore seven hundred men strong. A year later, in May 1857, the Indian Mutiny erupted. There is a variety of reasons for this, but what ignited everything were rumours that the cartridges for the new Enfield rifles were greased with animal fats that were offensive to both Hindus and Muslims.

At Ferozepore, two regiments of Native infantry and one of Native cavalry joined with the mutineers. After initial troubles, the Glosters seized the town's main arsenal and two mutineers were hung. This seemed to quell any discontent, and in June the 61st were ordered to Delhi. It was here that the mutineers were joining forces from all over the country, and they even brought the old Mogul King out of retirement to be their figurehead.

In two columns, the 61st marched 250 miles under the hot Indian sun. This season can also be very wet on the sub-continent and the men marched in treacherous conditions. Almost inevitably, the group picked up deadly cholera on their long travel and by the end of the campaign, 246 men would have died. When they finally reached Delhi on the 1st July, many men promptly made their way to the infirmary. John Edward Wharton Rotton was Chaplain during the Siege of Delhi:

> Cholera was committing sad devastation in the two European Regts. In 3rd Bgde. I allude to the 8th and 61st Foot.
>
> It required strong nerves to withstand the sickening sights of these 2 infirmaries. The patients constantly retching, made the place very offensive. The flies almost as innumerable as the sand on the sea shore, alighted on your face and head and crawled down your back….
>
> Happily cholera was not general throughout the camp. It was principally confined to these two regts., and the cause of its prevalence among them some medical authorities connected with the fatigues of a long march in the height of the rains.

The city of Delhi was seven miles in perimeter with its eastern walls protected by the river Jamma. As it was, the British only had enough men to invest the northern side of the city and so during the early months of the siege, thousands

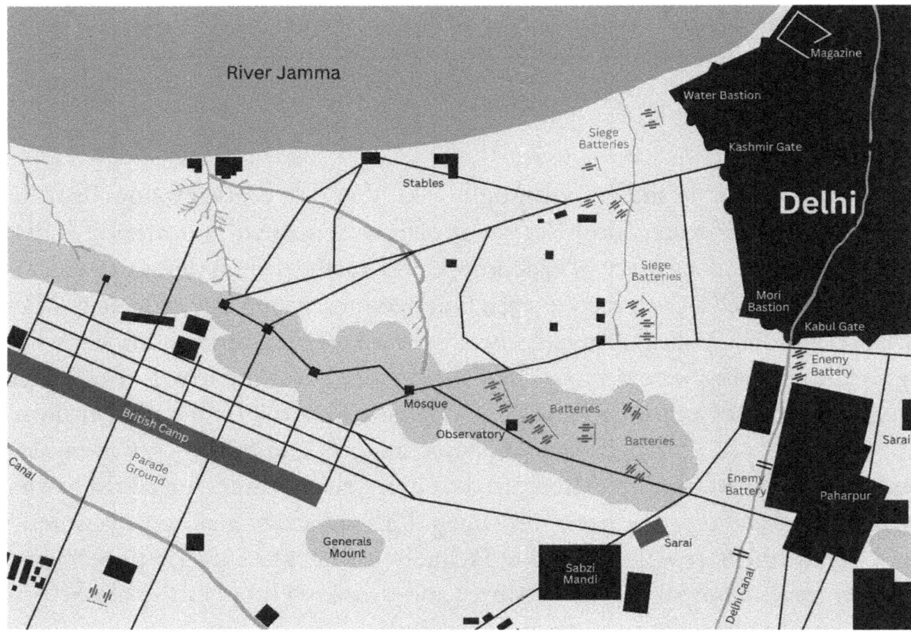


of mutineers streamed into the city. The British camped behind reinforced high ground but were already running seriously low on supplies. The shot fired from Delhi was collected up to be used by the British cannon. The goal was to await reinforcements and a large siege train, whilst the mutineers contented themselves with a plan to reduce the enemy by constant sorties.

On the 4th July, a rebel force left Delhi and began plundering to the rear of British lines. The 61st joined a column that were ordered to chase them down. The interception was made but the mutineers simply ran back into the safe arms of Delhi after a small engagement. The horrendous conditions continued to wear down the besiegers though, as six men of the 61st died of heat exhaustion on this mission alone. The men's morale picked back up when a convoy of elephants arrived to carry them back into the camp.

The situation was constantly tense, as one never really knew who was friend or foe. For example on the 9th July, a 'friendly' regiment of Native cavalry marched through camp but on the way out suddenly attacked the picquets. The 61st, who happened to be nearby, quickly formed up. Many of the men were without uniform but speed was of the essence. They charged the cavalry and saved the men and guns of the picquets.

In early July, another rebel force marched out of the besieged city and took control of a close by village. The men of 3rd Brigade, including the 61st, were sent to rectify this situation. Three hundred men of the 61st drove the rebels out and chased them until they happened upon a heavily fortified serai. These were a feature of colonial India during this period, and were just a walled or enclosed area for trade caravans to meet or rest. The serai was stormed and 3rd Brigade chased the mutineers, leaving the 61st as a temporary garrison. As soon as their brethren had left, another three hundred mutineers appeared and surrounded the serai. The 61st desperately held on until 3rd Brigade returned to cut them out. The mutineers lost five hundred men in this engagement, whilst the British had thirty-one killed and two hundred wounded.

These kinds of operations and patrols continued throughout the month of July until, at last, the siege train arrived containing thirty heavy guns. Along with the much needed siege train, many reinforcements and supplies poured into the British camp. They began to get their guns in position for assaulting the walls, until on the 25th August, the 61st were once again called into action as another huge sortie had left Delhi.

The mutineers plan was to outflank the besiegers and hit them in the rear, but the British knew this and managed to intercept them at a place called Nujjufghur. The mutineers had fortified another serai and their strong position was helped by having rivers to their north and east. The British managed to cross one of these rivers under fire from heavy grapeshot, and formed up for the attack. Twenty yards from the serai, they unleashed a volley and then charged. The enemy cannon were overwhelmed and then the 61st supported another attack on the neighbouring village. By this time, the enemy had seen enough and headed back towards Delhi. Despite being outnumbered 3–1, the British suffered sixty wounded, compared to eight hundred losses for the mutineers.

By the 13th September, the British guns had opened up on the walls of Delhi and the next day the breaches were large enough to consider an attack. There were two promising breaches, with the one near Waters Bastion being attacked by men of the 2nd Column, featuring the men of Gloucestershire. Just as they were about to set off, they foolishly realised they did not have the necessary scaling ladders. These took a long time to locate, but luckily, the delay did no harm. The breach was quickly secured and then the column swept right and captured further ramparts. The only trouble came from Sepoys hidden in adjacent houses and trees, but these were quickly dealt with.

The 4th Column, who had a more difficult task of blasting through one of the city gates, were not faring so well. Fortuitously, the men of 2nd Column brought up some guns they had captured within the city and turned them on the forces facing 4th Column. Even so, the 61st and their comrades were the only ones to taste real success on the day, and by nightfall, the British began establishing their lines along the area 2nd Column had captured. The following two days were dominated by heavy street fighting, which did not see the British advancing far but yielded huge casualty numbers amongst the mutineers.

One moment that did stand out during these few days of heavy fighting was the award of the Gloucestershire Regiments first ever Victoria Cross.

During the siege of Delhi, on September 14th, 1857, while Surgeon Reade was attending to the wounded at the end of one of the streets of the city, a party of rebels from the direction of the Bank, having established themselves in the houses in the street, commenced firing from the roofs. The wounded were thus in very great danger, and would have fallen into the hands of the enemy, had not Surgeon Reade drawn his sword, and calling upon the few soldiers who were near to follow succeeded, under a very heavy fire, in dislodging the rebels from their position. Surgeon Reade's party consisted of about ten men in all, of whom two were killed and five or six wounded.

At this point, a breach was made in the wall near to the mutineer's main magazine, and on the 16th September, the Glosters were selected to lead the attack. This would be no easy task as the mutineers had positioned six 32-pounder cannon in the breach. The 61st though used incredible speed, not always a feature of European style warfare in this period, to reach the cannon before they had even fired a shot. Surgeon Reade VC was one of the first into the breach and he assisted a sergeant in spiking one of the guns.

The mutineer's magazine was then quickly captured, and the 61st locked themselves inside awaiting reinforcements. After a few hours, the enemy began massing outside of the magazine and fired volleys at the Glosters. A few well-placed grenades dispersed any potential trouble though. The 61st then took stock of the situation, and counted 186 captured guns and much beer. Plenty of which was missing by the next day according to Sergeant-Major Baker:

The Regiment was formed up before daybreak on the 16th September 1857 in quarter column; the Grenadier Company in front. We formed up outside the Church and marched in silence along the College wall in the shade. On arrival near the breach Colonel Deacon gave the word "Charge!" Then the breach was soon mounted and we cleared the Magazine of all Sepoys and thieves, and after a short time closed the gates. But they gave us little peace for in about two hours time they returned in force outside the walls and gave us a good peppering; but we warmed the rascals outside with hand-grenades, so when they found they could not dislodge us they retired and left us quiet.

The breach was defended by six heavy guns-32 pounders-loaded with grape-shot and facing the entrance to the breach; but the rush of our men was too sudden to permit them to be fired-we captured 186 guns, a very large number of cases of bottled beer, and plenty of rum in bheestie-bags. We remained a few days in the Magazine and found the beer very acceptable, we afterwards moved to the Ajmere gate and then to the College.

The house-to-house street fight had not been going well, but now the British adopted a novel method to reduce casualties. Once a house had been captured, a hole was blown in the wall attached to the neighbouring house. The men then poured through the hole and captured it. Using this method, they had taken a quarter of the vast city by nightfall. The following day the entire western wall was seized, and that evening the mutineers scrambled to leave the city.

On the 21st September, the 61st were amongst those selected to pursue the remaining rebels. Numbers though had dwindled so low, through casualties and even more so from cholera, that they simple could not continue. They had lost nine killed, 142 wounded and had four men missing during the battle. The next few months were spent on garrison duty within the city itself.

One final exceptional moment occurred within the 61st Regiment to really distinguish these men above all others. After the successful completion of the siege, it was determined that every regiment would receive two Victoria Crosses. The actual recipients would be decided by vote of the soldiers themselves. The bawarchi were native Indians who carried water, prepared food and kept the camp in a pleasant condition for the British. Out of admiration for the incredible work of these men, the 61st voted to give their allotment of VC's to the bawarchi. Due to the unforgiving policy of the British Government at this time, an Indian could not receive such an accolade. The 61st nevertheless stood firm and refused to vote again. The VC's were taken back, yet the soldiers of Gloucestershire had proven themselves to be of outstanding character.

# 31. South Africa 1899–1902, 32. Defence of Ladysmith, 33. Paardeberg, 34. Relief of Kimberley

In 1881, the Boers decisively defeated the British at the Battle of Majuba and won independence for their territories of Orange Free State and Transvaal. Frictions continued for a host of reasons, but predominantly due to the vast mineral resources that can be found on the southern tip of Africa. In October 1899, war was once again inevitably declared with the 28th (North Gloucestershire) Regiment of Foot arriving just two days after it had become official.

Upon their arrival from Calcutta, the 28th were immediately dispatched to join General White's forces, which had concentrated in Natal around the town of Ladysmith. White was a great hero of the age, had fought in the Indian Mutiny and then been awarded the Victoria Cross in the Second Afghan War. However, he was now a much older gentleman and warfare had developed somewhat beyond his understanding, as the following tales will show. It is also

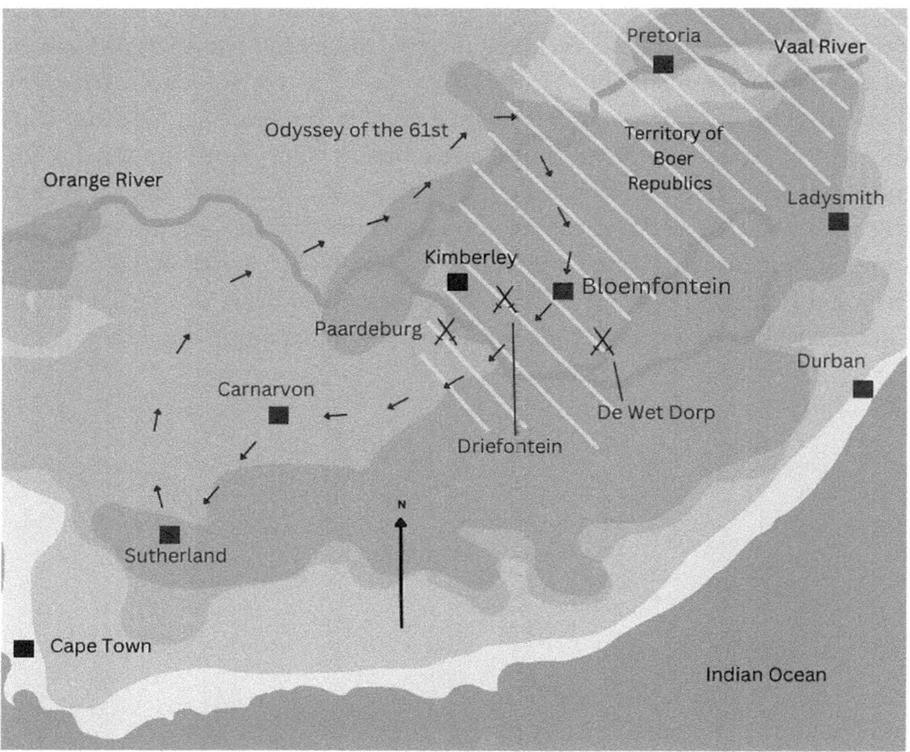

important to remember that the Pax Britannia, a prolonged period of peace brought on by British global domination, was in full swing and so the British Army had hardly seen combat for forty years. The troops and their leaders were incredibly green.

When the 28th reached White's Army, he was planning to pin down gathering Boer forces so that other Allied troops in the area had a clear path into the town of Ladysmith. White set off with a column five thousand strong, including four infantry battalions, three artillery batteries and some cavalry. Seven miles into their advance the column came under heavy fire from a hill range near the town of Rietfontein. What happened next is still hotly disputed. Most sources sympathetic to the Glosters state that confused orders were received, whilst many others claim that Lieutenant Colonel Wilford, the Commanding Officer of the 28th, charged without orders.

Either way, on the 24th October 1899, the Glosters did indeed charge towards the enemy ridge. They managed to chase some of the Boer from their position. The 28th then suddenly found themselves halted and were instantly pinned down by intense Boer fire. Frustratingly for the British, the Boer fought in a fashion unfamiliar to the large European armies. The 28th could not see their adversary, yet the evidence of their presence was pinging all around their heads. After several hours, the Glosters finally managed to withdraw but not before they had lost Wilford himself, along with six men dead and a further fifty-eight wounded. Sergeant Averies describes the scene in more detail:

On Tuesday last (the 24th) we were in action for the first time marched away from camp about 4.15 a.m. We had proceeded about 7 miles along the road when we were ordered to attack the enemy who were holding a strong position behind a very high hill off the road to our left. My company was about the first to leave leading the way across some open fields. We had not got very far across some open fields before we were fired on by the enemy's artillery. The first shell dropped only a few yards away but luckily for us it did not explode. As we got nearer their position the bullets fell around us like a shower of hailstones.

I will not attempt to describe the fight, it is to horrible no one can form any idea of the battle field unless he has experienced it. We lost our Colonel and about 10 men killed and 54 wounded (in my own Regiment) and yet there we were, smoking our pipes and cool as ever not knowing but the next shot would carry us off. We were under fire for 5 hours. Then we retired & marched back to camp fairly done up.

On the 29th October, two thirds of the battalion marched out of Ladysmith once again and headed for a feature called Nicholson's Nek. This force under Lieutenant Colonel Carleton was to hold a position seven miles north of Ladysmith. They would protect the main forces left flank (another much larger group was marching out of Ladysmith under General White), and hold a passage open for harassing cavalry to come and go.

The 28th rode out along with the Royal Irish Fusiliers and No. 10 Mountain Battery. Major Humphrey was now in command of the 28th and they set off at nightfall. Disaster occurred almost immediately as something spooked the mules of No. 10 Battery and they stampeded, taking with them the all the guns and the majority of the columns ammunition. Each man was left with just twenty rounds each. To make matters worse, the main attack column under General White suffered a bad defeat and now the men of Carleton's column were dangerously exposed.

General White returned to Ladysmith and immediately messaged the column at Nicholson's Nek to return to the town. Carleton sent a man to receive the message and he was immediately shot dead. He then sent another and then another. Both were shot dead. The Boer had arrived. Carleton then panicked and decided to move position even though it was still nightfall. The Fusiliers scurried up the neighbouring Kainguba Heights, only to come fleeing back down again crying that the Boer cavalry were there. Nevertheless, the entire column ascended the Heights and stayed there for the rest of the night.

Dawn instantly highlighted Carleton's mistake. Kainguba Heights was the lowest hill in the area and all the surrounding hills were crawling with Boer warriors. Once again, they could not prove this fact with their own eyes. The only evidence came from a flurry of shots sounding from every direction. The Boer had again adapted a fighting style that would cause European style armies much issue. The British would form up in line, march towards the Boer and unleash a volley. The Boer though, would simply fall back out of range and then when the British were reloading they charged in and picked off a few men before retreating again. Time after time, this pattern would be repeated from dawn until 14:30. Slowly the Boer started to claim Kainguba Heights as the British pulled back towards the southern slopes.

What occurred next is a comedy of errors that, much like Rietfontein, is still highly controversial. In the afternoon, a group of roughly twelve Glosters positioned themselves in a Kraal, a tiny, fenced settlement. They gave covering fire to the rest of the regiment so that they could fall back a little way. The men in the Kraal became cut off and were being slaughtered, so they raised the white flag. The Boers, thinking this was the general surrender, began to let out a thunderous cheer throughout their entire army. The rest of the 28th believed this cheering truly did signal the general surrender and began fleeing from the field. Upon seeing the Glosters leaving the battlefield in a panic, Carleton actually did surrender his entire force. Nearly a thousand men lay down their arms, whilst the rest managed to retreat to Ladysmith. Eleven Glosters were killed at Nicholson's Nek, whilst a further fifty-one were wounded.

If one was to discount the often needless slaughter of WWI, then this weeklong period must mark the worst, and certainly most embarrassing, period in regimental history. Of course, a number of factors must be taken into consideration. The men and their leaders were all inexperienced, with none having ever fought in a major conflict before. Communications at both battles were poor and the leadership of High Command left much to be desired. The Boer too were a fearsome enemy, using tactics that had never been experienced. Despite their inexperience, there is never any doubt that the Glosters fought bravely. That alone, is enough to keep the history and spirit of the regiment intact.

Within three days of Nicholson's Nek, the Boer forces had invested **Ladysmith**. The entire Army of Natal was trapped and so the whole of Natal Colony lay open. It is at this point a Boer weakness rises to the fore. Their forces were built to defend and to use guerrilla warfare tactics. They never invaded the Colony and these factors would cause them issue at the forth coming siege.

The fourteen-mile perimeter of Ladysmith was divided into four sectors, and the much diminished 28th held an area on Junction Hill overlooking the railway line that headed north out of the town. General White was now a beaten man; he spent most of the siege languishing in his Headquarters. Thankfully for the 28th, the northern area was controlled by Colonel Knox who ordered them to fortify the lines. Those in the south were not so blessed and their leaders took no action against potential assault.

Due to the large civilian population, the ration situation soon became desperate with food cut to an absolute minimum. The Boer were not well equipped for a siege, but they still made an attempt on Ladysmith on the 9th November 1899. They stormed a position south of the Glosters location (Kings Post) and simultaneously another to the east (Caesars Camp). After some fierce fighting the Boer were driven back.

The Boer had little artillery with which to besiege a town, but they did have the feared Long Tom. This was a Creusot 155mm gun, with a shell weighing 43kg and a range of nearly 10,000 metres. On December 22nd, as the men of the 28th were settling down to breakfast, Long Tom zeroed in on them. The gigantic shell exploded in their midst, instantly killing nine and wounding a further nine. After this, a series of whistle blows were put in place to warn the besieged of when Long Tom was firing and what its target was. 2nd Lieutenant Theobold was one of those who was in Long Toms sights:

We had a "look-out" in camp with a telescope fixed on a tripod and every time Long Tom was fired the N.C.O. on duty gave warning with a whistle. If it was fired in the direction of Waggon Hill, one blast, if in direction of Town, two blasts, and if in our direction, three blasts, when everyone took cover, from the sight of puff of smoke till the shell reached its billet, several seconds elapsed, which allowed time to take cover.

On December 22nd, 1899, Long Tom put one over causing 17 casualties…One day I was detailed to get 8 men and go to the Town Hall Hospital for the task of burying one of our men who had died (4151 J. Pickett). This time we received a "Salute" from Long Tom, just as the Chaplain had finished the Service, before he had taken off his Surplice a shell came over and went in the grave, I said to the Chaplain, one would think they would let the dead R.I.P., it was a narrow escape for all 10 of us, they well knew what they were doing.

General Buller was on his was with a force to relieve Ladysmith, and the Boer had to remove men from the siege to face this new threat. Before they did this, they wanted one more attempt on the town. Therefore, on the 6th January 1900, the Boer launched their attack. The northern sector, including Junction Hill, held firm behind their newly constructed fortifications. On the southern side, it was a different story though, as they had still not bothered improving their position. The fighting was hard and only a last minute charge by men of the Devonshire Regiment turned the day.

The siege was finally lifted on the 28th February, the survivors were immediately sent to Durban for recuperation and picking up reinforcements. A morale boost was received when the men who had been captured at Nicholson's Nek were found just outside Pretoria. They had been well treated and soon returned to their regiment. From here, the 28th took part in some minor operations in Orange River County but then trouble began to brew on the other side of the globe. Several battalions, including the 28th, were immediately shipped off to China in August 1900. This eventually came to nothing, so the 28th spent the next few years guarding Boer prisoners of war who had been sent to Ceylon.

Meanwhile, the 61st (South Gloucestershire) Regiment of Foot had arrived in southern Africa from Aldershot earlier in the year. They were immediately installed in the 13th Brigade of the 6th Division and headed to the Modder River where the new Commander in Chief, Lord Roberts, was waiting. On the 13th February 1900, they began their campaign to relieve another siege, that of **Kimberley**. Roberts marched his men on a wide flanking manoeuvre to trap the forces of Boer leader, General Cronje.

Marching sixty-eight miles in three days achieved Robert's goal. He came up in Cronje's rear, leaving him no choice but to lift the siege of Kimberley and prepare for battle at a place called **Paardeberg**, on the shore of the River Modder. It was here that the 61st came upon an enemy with whom they would soon become extremely familiar. Christiaan de Wet was a politician and feared military leader from the previous Anglo-Boer conflict. On the 18th February, de Wet appeared in the rear of 6th Division on a hill called Kitchener's Kop, with his commandoes. They poured on their fire and this caused immense confusion.

General Kitchener's response, for he was now in charge of the British forces, was to order a full frontal charge against the enemy. Despite the protestations of his more experienced subordinates, the attack went ahead with inevitable consequences. The British were cut down in droves, suffering over two hundred dead and a further eight hundred wounded. So bad was the result that back home in Britain it became known as Bloody Sunday.

The next day, Kitchener again ordered the ridge to be cleared and the 61st were the selected men. They were held for a long time during the advance by heavy fire. The supporting regiment never came up and then suddenly the left flank companies of the 61st gave way. The day once again seemed lost but as night began to fall, the remaining men fixed bayonets and ran the Boer from their position.

Christiaan de Wet had also recently attacked a vast British supply column, and so the British found themselves on greatly reduced rations and running short of ammunition. Even so, on the 21st February, de Wet and other Boer forces began to pull back as they saw they were greatly outnumbered. For reasons that are not truly understood, General Cronje decided not to retreat and his men were now themselves besieged within a loop of the Modder River.

For several days, the various regiments took it in turn watching the frontline as a breakout was expected at any moment, but it never occurred. In the early hours of the 26th February, the Royal Canadian Regiment silently crept up to the Boer positions with bayonets fixed. Somehow, they were not spotted and the Boer awakened to find themselves in huge trouble. A slaughter ensued and the next day Cronje officially surrendered his forces.

The 6th Division then began to push eastwards, and successfully engaged the enemy in a small battle at a place called Driefontein. This gave them access to the capital of Orange Free State, Bloemfontein, which they marched into on the 14th March. On the 1st May, the 61st were ordered to Sannahs Post, a water supply station. The area had recently been raided by de Wet and so the men of Gloucestershire were sent to make sure it did not happen again. Meanwhile Lord Roberts, minus 6th Division, pushed on into Pretoria and Mafeking. The 6th Division were left in Orange Free State to deal with the still considerable

Boer forces. Much time was taken with either manning blockhouses in defensive lines (there were almost eight thousand blockhouses stretching over 3500 miles across South Africa) or being in flying columns (rapid reaction forces) who pursued the enemy commandoes.

Reinforcements arrived on the continent in May, to replace the men lost in battle and those who had succumbed to disease. Enteric fever, a form of typhoid, was ripping through the British Army and as is often the case was racking up a higher body count than the conflict itself. In early October 1900, three companies of the 61st were sent to strike fear into the heart of de Wet himself. They moved on de Wet Dorp, which was his home region and an important road junction.

After six weeks, de Wet took the bait and closed on the 61st. The fighting raged intermittently for three days but as always, the Boer fought a different kind of warfare. The Boer commandoes captured the only water source in the area and the 61st had no choice but to lay down their arms. For several days, the 61st were captives of their great foe but prisoners were detrimental to a guerrilla war campaign. Eventually, de Wet let every single man go free, as this was the kind of gentlemanly warfare that the Boer fought.

December 1900 saw the 61st moved to garrison the important town of Bloemfontein. One half would stay and guard the area, whilst the other half would take part in a quite incredible odyssey. They jumped on a train to central Cape Colony where they joined Major Vine's flying column. Their goal was to pin down and destroy General Hertzog's Commando group.

The column set about their task on the 29th December, when the 61st were ordered to accompany a supply train to Carnarvon. They covered the seventy-one miles in just five days. Here, they briefly joined another flying column in an attempt to track down more Boer commandoes. 148 miles were covered in twenty days but all their attempts at engaging the enemy were fruitless. Eventually at Sutherland, they gave up the chase and the 61st spent the next three weeks operating a series of blockhouses.

Supply column duty was once again the order of the day, as the 61st covered 157 miles in eight days and then again marching 68 miles in five days. It should be said that this is often the hottest period in South Africa with temperatures in the mid-30's and a high humidity along with tropical storms. After these travels, the men of Gloucestershire were given a much deserved two week rest.

The 61st were then added to another flying column, that of Colonel Henry, along the Vaal River. On the 1st June 1901, they marched 220 miles in 28 days. This was the first time that British forces would set foot in the Transvaal, paving the way for an eventual vast expansion of Colonial possessions on the southern tip of Africa. During this time, the 61st partook in Kitchener's extremely controversial "clearing of the countryside". Masses of livestock and many prisoners, including women and children, were rounded up. Even then, the wily Boer could not be brought to battle.

Eventually on the 18th October, the 61st ended up back up in Cape Colony. This ten month circular route saw them cover nearly a thousand miles. They reunited with the other half of the battalion who had stayed in Bloemfontein and spent their time on garrison duty or whiling away the hours in blockhouses. This pattern continued for the 61st, but they would not see action against the Boer again with the war ending in May 1902. The next two years were spent on garrison duty at Bloemfontein until eventually they returned to Britain.

# World War I

# 35. Mons

When World War I broke out on 4th August 1914, the Allied and German armies began their march towards each other. They eventually clashed on the border of France and Belgium. The German Schlieffen Plan saw several armies attempt to pin the Allies, whilst several others swung around the right flank to crush the Allies from the rear. It was these flanking armies that were heading straight for the British Expeditionary Force (BEF) and the men of 1st Battalion, the Gloucestershire Regiment.

The neighbouring French armies failed to put up any significant resistance, and the BEF had to quickly switch from an offensive to a defensive footing. The Glosters dug in north and east of a village called Haulchin, Belgium. This was eight miles south of the city of Mons. The Germans needed to cross the river La Haine, so opened up an attack on nearby regiments holding the bridges that crossed this significant obstacle. At 13:00 on the 23rd August, the Glosters saw their first shots of the war fired. 800 yards in front of them the British artillery fired on German positions. The Germans replied in kind but their aim was poor, and this was all the action 1st Battalion saw on the opening day.

Three days later, they were dug in a further 25 miles south of Mons at the village of Landrecies. From their position, they could see German infantry swarming around. A German plane was spotted overhead and it was soon realised that this was an artillery spotter, as German armaments came crashing down on their position. Captain Shipway, the first recognised Gloster fatality of many, was later killed by a sniper and another four men who were holding an advanced post were never seen again.

Not much of the German attack fell upon the Glosters, but elsewhere they had smashed the Mons Salient and by nightfall High Command had decided to pull back. This would begin the great retreat from Mons and see the Glosters marching two hundred miles in just thirteen days.

# 36. Ypres 1914

After the French defeat at Charleroi and British Expeditionary Force defeat at Mons, the Allied armies retreated to the River Marne. Here on the 5th September 1914, the Allies made their stand and eventually stopped the German advance. A short stalemate ensued as each planned their next move.

The Allied plan was to isolate and destroy thirty thousand men in the German 3rd Reserve Corp. To do this they would penetrate through a small gap between them and the main German force, and then push onto the coast. The German plan was to break through on the lines that now extended across Belgium, and roll up the Allied lines whilst simultaneously securing the Channel Ports. Both these plans were feasible, but unfortunately for the Allies there was one piece of vital intelligence missing. The 3rd Reserve Corp were merely a screen for a much larger (14 divisions strong) and fresher 4th German Army, which was forming up in the rear.

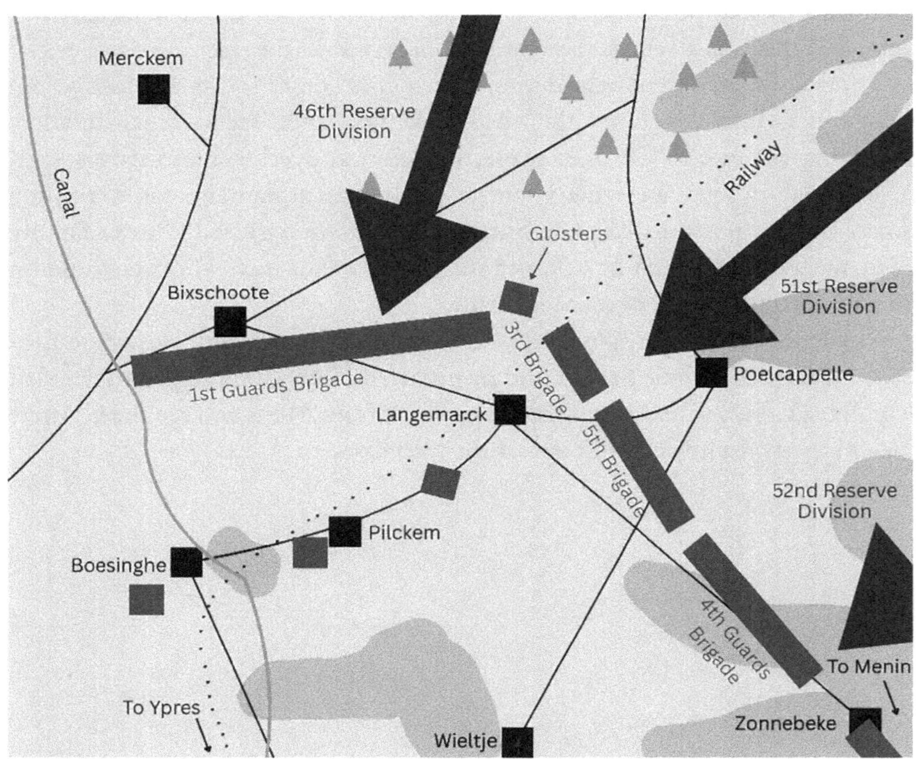

Unaware of the situation the Allies put their plan into play. 1st Battalion, the Gloucestershire Regiment, marched out towards Poperinghe at 01:45 on 21st October 1914. Their destination was a village, which would by the end of the war, firmly take its place in regimental folklore, Langemarck. The Glosters were in 3rd Brigade, along with the Queens (Royal West Surrey) Regiment and South Wales Borderers. Reaching the village of Poelcapelle, they found it held by the Germans. The Glosters remained in reserve, whilst the rest of the brigade attacked the village.

Meanwhile Langemarck, just off to the east, had been earmarked for an attack by the French cavalry, but they were easily driven off. Therefore, 'B' Company, under Captain Radice, moved along the line and occupied Langemarck train station. At 10:00, the rest of the battalion were ordered to reinforce the left flank. So 'C' Company, under Captain Temple, marched straight through Langemarck, whilst 'D' Company plugged the gap between the two companies now in position.

At midday, a hundred Germans attacked Langemarck but they were held by 'C' Company. However, they did lose Captain Temple during the fighting. The bulk of the German attack fell on the Queens who eventually had to pull back. This meant 'D' Company, who were closest, also had to fall back and readjust the line. The French, who were still fighting to the east of Langemarck, now began to retreat and this left the entire flank of 3rd Brigade dangerously exposed.

At 14:00, two hundred Germans attacked but they were once again halted by the men of 'C' Company. The Germans sent more and more men forward, until both flanks of 'C' Company were being harassed. Somehow they held on though, and when reinforcements arrived from 'B' Company, they pushed the Germans back. The Germans were still not done and two hours later machine guns opened up on 'D' Company. These were dealt with, but then columns of German infantry were seen approaching the train station. The Glosters leapt on their adversaries who promptly fled in panic.

By nightfall, literally everyone had fallen back except for the Glosters. These men now held their own personal salient in the lines, and were hugely responsible for the failure of the German counter attack on the opening day. Fifty men had been lost at Langemarck, but thankfully the Germans concentrated their efforts elsewhere on the 22nd. This meant the Glosters were able to reinforce their position.

By contrast, the 23rd October was far from quiet, as at 07:30 smoke came pouring towards the village of Langemarck. The Germans had set fire to haystacks in nearby fields to cover the fact that several columns of men were advancing on the Glosters. Sighting the enemy a hundred yards away, the Glosters opened fire and a terrible battle began. However, yet more trouble was to come.

The Coldstream Guards had now moved up to support the left flank of the Glosters after the French had pulled back. Suddenly, they were attacked in the flanks and rear by Germans who had snuck up a previously unidentified sunken ditch. The Guards immediately fell back, once again, leaving the Glosters left flank exposed to attack. Wave after wave was thrown against the Glosters left, but they valiantly held back the enemy. Eventually by 13:00, the Germans were exhausted and the day's hostilities ended. Fifteen hundred Germans lay dead around the village, whilst another six hundred were made prisoner. General Landon, the Commander of 3rd Brigade, described the action in a letter home:

We had a great fight yesterday and were attacked all day: the Brigade did splendidly and inflicted great loss on the enemy. The Queen's made a most gallant charge and the Gloucesters (100 strong) fired over 500 rounds per man, lost all their officers and many N.C.Os, had the Germans within 50 yards, and not a man retired. Some of their bayonets were shot off their rifles and they had over sixty casualties. A grand performance. The Welch also saw out an attack by numbers of Germans and 'downed them' gallantly.

The following day 'A' Company, who had mostly been in reserve throughout the battle, assisted the Coldstream Guards in reoccupying the trenches they had given up previously. On the night of the 24th/25th, the Glosters were withdrawn from the line. For them, the Battle of Langemarck was over but the conflict raged on. Within hours, any allotted rest had been scuppered and they headed back to the frontline at Hooge.

At 05:30 on the 29th October, the German war machine roared into action. They had soaked up the pressure from the BEF, and the previously hidden 4th German Army now made their way to the front. Two entire British divisions were cut to shreds around the village of Gheluvelt. Unfortunately, the Glosters at this point had actually been broken up to fill various holes in the line. 'C' Company, who had been in support around Gheluvelt, were practically wiped out.

'D' Company had been in support of 1st Brigade who disintegrated around them. Incredibly, once again the Glosters found themselves standing alone. Against overwhelming odds, they held the line and slowly pulled back until linking up with their own men of 'A' Company. These men had experienced their own problems, and had a serious fight on their hands after the collapse of 1st Brigade had exposed their flanks and rear.

Meanwhile 'B' Company fought for, and then held, the high ground in front of Gheluvelt. Finally, after huge pressure and finding themselves isolated, they too had to steadily pull back. Ironically, by pulling back, the 1st Battalion now found themselves reunited as a fighting force. The Queens and South Wales

Borderers now pushed up to the front, and at nightfall 3rd Brigade dug in around the village. Holding the line once again whilst all others retreated had a devastating consequence for the men of Gloucestershire. One hundred and sixty-seven had been killed, wounded or were missing in just twelve hours. Much needed rest was now acquired as the next couple of days saw only light shelling and sniping.

Dawn on the 31st October saw a colossal bombardment open up along the entire line. By 06:00, German infantry were swarming across no man's land. After a furious engagement, the Queens broke and the Germans flooded into Gheluvelt capturing the village. By 14:00, the South Wales Borderers had also broken and all looked lost. Despite the previous few weeks of bravery, holding the line against such awesome numbers was impossible, even for 1st Battalion. Suddenly, even more men were seen pouring out of the woods just to the front of the position.

Identified initially as more Germans, the men in the woods were in fact 2nd Battalion the Worcestershire Regiment, on an unbelievable flanking manoeuvre. The Worcester's sowed great confusion amongst the advancing Germans and although they did not break, it brought enough time for 3rd Brigade to reform and reoccupy their lines. The day had come at great cost for the Glosters with sixty-four men killed.

The next day saw the Glosters barricading Menin Road, the main route into Ypres itself. They were subject to repeated artillery bombardment and infantry probing, but again held their part of the line. At the end of the day they were withdrawn from the front another seventy-six men down. This ended the Battle of Gheluvelt for 1st Battalion, but it did not mean an end to hostilities. Once again, the withdrawal was cancelled and they headed for the trenches at Veldhoek.

Upon arrival, the situation was chaos. Companies of different regiments were positioned in various places all over the line, and nobody was in overall charge. Despite this, the Glosters were almost immediately sent over the top and they found the German trenches empty. They stormed the next line but these were far from unoccupied. A heavy fire opened up, and the men of Gloucestershire had to fall back to the first trench line they had just captured. Thirteen men never made it back, whilst a further forty-seven were wounded. The next five days were spent filling various holes in the British line. However, morale was greatly boosted by the arrival of two hundred reinforcements.

Now occurs the greatest tragedy of the battle. On the 7th November, the Glosters were in the trenches at Zwarteleen, three miles southeast of Ypres. An intelligence report was received stating that the Germans in the trenches opposite had fled. Still no doubt exercising extreme caution, the Glosters crossed no man's land. As they got to within fifty yards of the enemy line, firing broke out. The Glosters were caught between attacking and retreating. Forty-three men were killed and a further forty-seven missing. Regarding the command structure, a captain, two lieutenants and absolutely no sergeants remained throughout the entire battalion. The following morning the men that survived were relieved from the front line.

On the morning of 11th November, a huge German artillery barrage opened up. Masses of infantry came crashing into British lines, including twelve battalions of the elite Prussian Guard. The Glosters though, were still in reserve after the disaster at Zwarteleen. They were soon moving to Polygon Wood, where again they avoided the majority of the attack.

The first of many battles for the city of Ypres was now over, and the infamous Ypres Salient had been firmly established. When they marched towards Poperinghe on 21st October, the battalion was 25 officers and 752 other ranks strong. A month later, despite having received reinforcements, their force had been reduced to two officers and a hundred other ranks. The huge cost in life had at least some small reward. The heroic stand of these men at Langemarck and Gheluvelt had done a vast amount to hold back the German counter offensive, and to save the war for the Britain and its allies.

# 37. Ypres 1915

The Second Battle of Ypres occurred because the Germans needed to cover the fact they were transporting several divisions east to fight the Russians. Eradicating the Ypres Salient would shorten the German front in the west, thus they would need fewer men to hold it. Another sinister reason is that they wanted to test a new deadly and horrifying weapon, poisonous gas. This was used against the French at 17:00 on the 22nd April 1915. Although it opened up a huge hole in the Allied lines, the German soldiers themselves were too scared to advance and the lines were reinforced before they could take advantage.

Only one battalion of the Gloucestershire Regiment took part in this battle, 2nd Battalion, at Frezenburg Ridge. Their battle began with two weeks in supporting trenches, where they experienced heavy shelling and fighting off small combat patrols. On the 8th May, with the Glosters now in the frontline trenches, the shelling was dramatically increased for a period of three hours. The following day at 06:30, another devastating bombardment was aimed at the Glosters. The British had no reply to these barrages as they had already expended all their ammunition.

'D' Company, led by Lieutenant Grazebrook, held the right hand section of trenches whilst 'B' Company, commanded by Major Nisbet, held the left hand portion. The other two companies were in a close reserve. Ten minutes after the second heavy artillery barrage had been dropped on the Glosters, the German infantry came flooding into no man's land and attacked 'B' Company. Another heavy barrage then occurred followed by another infantry attack. This was then repeated once more, resulting in 'B' Company becoming almost completely cut off.

By 07:15, the Germans had infiltrated the defensive system of the much depleted 'B' Company, and chaos ensued. The Germans were everywhere, yet 'B' Company continued to hold onto a tiny slither of trench. The attack was at a mounting cost for the Germans though, as during a very brief pause, over 350 Germans were counted dead around the perimeter. The situation was now clearly serious, so Battalion Headquarters sent 'A' Company to the frontline and 'C' Company into position just behind the surviving men of 'B' Company. A further two companies from the Leinster's were also sent forward to give aid.

Despite the disarray, it was decided the best form of defence was attack. So 'A' Company, led by Captain Vicary, crashed into the enemy right flank. Somehow, the few remaining men of 'B' Company also rallied and pushed upon the left flank. The attack chased the Germans all the way back across no man's land but upon reaching the enemy trenches, the Glosters were devastated by a mass grenade attack.

More support was now ordered up to allow another attack, with the 9th Royal Scots and 2nd Cameron's joining the fray. These men managed to get within twenty yards of the German lines despite heavy resistance, and established a firing line. This should have been followed up by a second and third wave but, as was so often the case, they became bogged down in the mud of no man's land and never reached their comrades. A much reduced and dejected attacking party eventually had to retire back to their own lines.

The 9th May had cost 2nd Battalion dearly. Their Commanding Officer, Lieutenant Colonel Tulloch was dead, along with another 145 men. All that remained from the officer corps were one captain, one lieutenant and three junior subalterns. A significant casualty on the day was future Victoria Cross recipient Dan Burges. One small victory was obtained during the night though. Captain Vicary, commanding officer of 'A' Company, crept forward after dark looking for his old friend, Major Nisbet, commanding officer of 'B' Company. He was found alive and well after he, and a few men, had hidden themselves inside a telephone dugout.

At 01:00 the following morning, the Glosters were relieved by the 1st Royal Scots and at 06:15 on the 11th May, were ordered into the rear for a much deserved rest and resupply. However, just an hour later emergency orders came through. The Germans had broken through the line at Sanctuary Wood and 2nd Battalion were desperately needed to plug the gap.

Upon arrival 'B' Company were thrown straight into the action. They pushed the Germans back, and were ordered to hold a small hill. For twelve strenuous hours, they held the hill despite being under a heavy artillery and machine gun attack. The already greatly depleted 'B' Company lost a further thirty men, and so at 04:45 on the 12th May, 'C' Company headed out to replace them. As is often excruciatingly the case in WWI, it was then decided the hill did not need to be held after all and the Glosters were called back to a position of relative safety. They would play no more part in the Second Battle of Ypres.

On the 20th May, Sir John French, Commander-in Chief of the British Expeditionary Force came to inspect 2nd Battalion. He requested to address the men personally:

Your Colours have many famous names emblazoned on them, but none will be more famous or more well deserved than that of the Second Battle of Ypres. I want you one and all to understand how thoroughly I realize and appreciate what you have done. I wish to thank you, each officer, non-commissioned officer and man, for the services you have rendered by doing your duty so magnificently, and I am sure your country will thank you too.

# 38. Sari Bair

The action for the men of Gloucestershire now turned to the east. The invasion of the Gallipoli peninsula was an attempt to put a stranglehold on the Ottomans, a key German ally. Within four months of the landings, it was clear that something had gone drastically wrong. The Allies were penned in their two beachheads. They had practically given up any hope of breaking out of Cape Helles, on the southern tip. A final roll of the dice was put in place for the August Offensive to break out of the other beachhead, ANZAC Cove. This battle featured just one battalion of the Gloucestershire Regiment, the 7th Battalion, and would gain the regiment its battle honour of Sari Bair.

The plan was for an initial diversion with the Australian troops attacking a place called Lone Pine. Whilst this happened, two columns of men would advance up Sari Bair, a high ridgeline that dominated the central peninsula and overlooked the ANZAC front. Firstly, some key high points in the foothills including Chunuk Bair, Hill Q and Hill 971, would be captured during the night. Then at dawn a further ANZAC assault would consolidate the ridge.

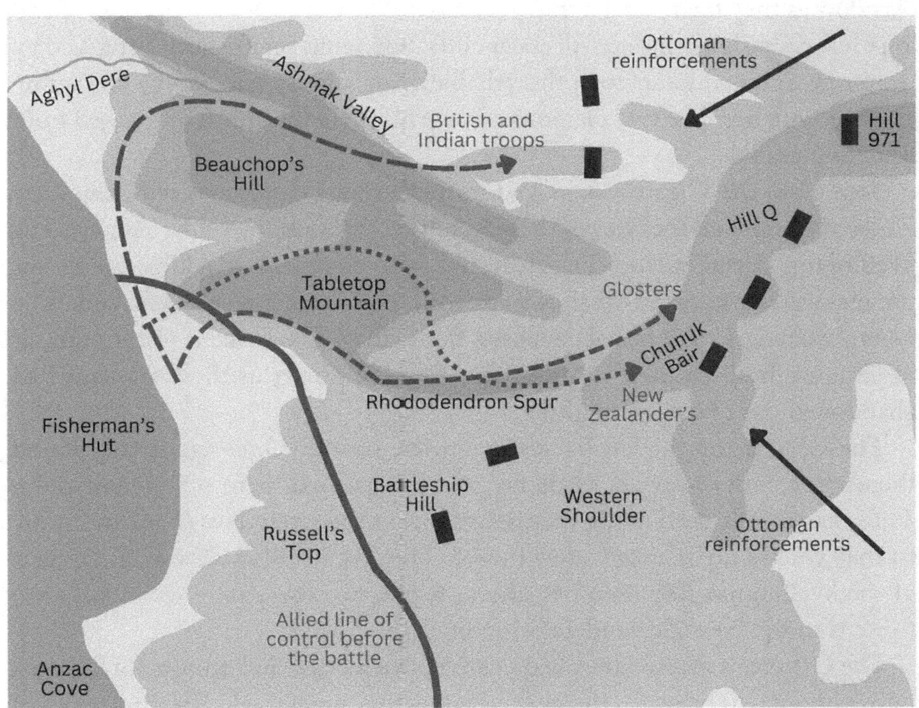

The Australian diversion, launched on 6th August 1915, was actually a success of some sort. After four days of fighting, they managed to capture the area known as Lone Pine. However, the whole reason for launching this diversion was ironically jeopardised. To cover off the assault by the Australians, the Ottomans actually moved more men up to the front and left them in reserve. The place they chose to station their reserves was right on top of Sari Bair, the true target of the offensive.

The main assault, which began at 22:30 on the 7th August, initially went well with the New Zealanders managing to capture the foothills. It was not long until everything began to unravel though. The left assault column of British and Indian troops got lost in the darkness and their attack petered out immediately. The right column never even got going as once the New Zealanders had gotten a foothold in the lower hills, they were supposed to be joined by more Indian troops. These never materialised, so only after a two-hour delay were the New Zealanders ordered to push on regardless.

At this point 7th Battalion entered the fray. They had landed at ANZAC Cove on the 4th August before moving to Aghyl Dere to support the assault. At 03:00 on the 8th August, the order came through for the Glosters, along with 8th Battalion of the Welch Regiment, to support the New Zealand Wellington Battalion in their assault on Chunuk Bair. The advance to join their brethren was slow as they filed along a thin goat track. The terrain was steep, rugged and at points rode along the edge of sheer cliffs. Suddenly, yet not surprising as they were now in enemy territory, the 7th Battalion came under heavy enfilading machine gun fire. The two platoons nearest to where the attack originated from were obliterated.

Somehow, the Glosters managed to make their rendezvous with the New Zealand troops and they began their assault on the morning of 8th August. The Wellington Battalion and the 7th would form the main attacking parties for the renewed assault, and off they went with the Glosters on the left flank. The New Zealanders took heavy casualties but managed to make it to the summit of Chunuk Bair. To their surprise, they found it empty as the Ottomans had abandoned their post overnight.

The Glosters on the left flank did not fare so well. Once again, they found themselves under heavy enfilade fire and this pushed them off to their right. They desperately tried to dig themselves in, but the ground was hard and stony so they could only manage a few inches. They were still some way in the rear of the Wellington Battalion but after a while, two companies did manage to make it to the New Zealanders firing line.

The Ottomans realised they had made a huge mistake in letting go of Chunuk Bair without a fight, so for the next 24 hours they unleashed a dreadful series of counter attacks. Again, the Glosters found the terrain to be rough and so their defensive trenches were barely a few inches deep. This was highly unsatisfactory as the Ottomans unleashed a punishing artillery bombardment. It was hot, dry and there was no food or water.

The 7th Battalion and the Wellingtons managed to hold their line though, and finally when reinforcements arrived they were overjoyed and began to pull back for some much deserved recuperation. However, they were astonished to be informed that these newly arrived men were not their relief and that they would have to stay in the front for an unspecified period. Finally at dusk, they were relieved and the few remaining men pulled back to relative safety. The campaign for the Gallipoli peninsula petered out, and eventually the remaining men were transferred to the Middle East.

# 39. Loos

Back on the Western Front, a fresh Allied offensive was ordered in September 1915, with the idea of decisively splitting the German forces and knocking them out of the war completely. The British would attack the Germans at Artois, whilst the French did so at Champagne. The prelude to the Battle of Loos saw huge numbers of men, including those of the 1st and 10th Battalions of the Gloucestershire Regiment, carting cylinders of gas to the front line. The Allies had decided to avenge the gas attack at Ypres.

After several days of an artillery barrage, the attack was ordered for 06:30 on the 25th September 1915. Brigadier Reddie, in charge of 1st Brigade, decided to test out some of his New Army battalions. These were all volunteer units recruited in 1914 who had only arrived in France six weeks earlier. 10th Glosters and 8th Royal Berkshires, two New Army battalions, would be the assaulting parties. 10th Battalion, attacking Bois Carre, ran into immediate problems. The wind had now stagnated and in some cases completely changed direction. This meant that the recently unleashed Allied poisoned gas attack was blowing right into their faces. Nearly three thousand Allied casualties were reported as a result of this unfortunate blunder.

Despite the early setback, the Glosters charged across the four hundred yards of no man's land and secured the first German lines promptly, but with quite a few casualties. The assault was now ordered onwards and the men charged towards the second German line. Here though, they came upon unbroken barbed wire and had no choice but to cut their way through. One company of Glosters had every single officer killed before they got going again. Still more trouble awaited, as once through the wire a murderous fire of rifles and machine guns opened up on 10th Battalion.

The assault on the second German line had been a disaster, and the men had to scramble into the German communication trenches and flee back to the first line they had captured. High Command ordered the 10th Battalion over the top once again, but it soon became clear that only sixty of the original eight hundred men were left fit for duty. Four hundred and fifty-nine brave souls of Gloucestershire lay dead. Perhaps with the exception of the Battle of Fromelles (a diversionary attack for the Somme), there is no other time in history when so many of the regiment were mercilessly cut down in such a short period.

1st Battalion of the Gloucestershire Regiment had been in reserve for this attack and they were supposed to be supporting the assault on the second line of German trenches. Perhaps luckily for them, they had been delayed by overcrowding and extreme flooding in the Allied trenches. By now, 10th Battalion had been decimated at Bois Carre, and so 1st Battalion were ordered on a flanking manoeuvre. By the time they arrived, their target had already surrendered.

The situation did not improve for 1st Battalion, as they were then ordered to clear the trenches at Chalk Pit Wood. En-route they were hit by such a devastating German barrage that they had to dig in on the spot. Finally, they were tasked with taking over the trenches where 10th Battalion were based, a duty they did until 29th September. The 1st Battalion were then relieved and headed to the rear.

Returning to the front line on the 5th October, 1st Battalion were once again ordered to hold the trenches around Chalk Pit Wood. Three days later a massive German counter attack began. This opened up with a four-hour artillery barrage that caused many casualties. The Germans then sent in two entire regiments who descended upon the Glosters. The men fought ferociously and after just fifteen minutes, the Germans were scrambling back to their own lines having suffered many casualties of their own.

On the 8th October, 1st Battalion had twenty men killed and a further ninety-six wounded. One man that would distinguish himself for the first time was Sergeant Biddle. He would finish the war with a Military Cross, Distinguished Conduct Medal plus bar and a Military Medal plus bar. At 23:00 1st Battalion were relieved and so ended the tragic Battle of Loos. Overall, British casualties in this rather short period would amount to nearly sixty thousand. Although there were some local successes, the operation was a complete failure.

Despite much debate amongst historians, the goal of the Somme was simply to relieve pressure on allies fighting elsewhere. Specifically the French at Verdun, but also the Russians at Galicia and the Italians at Trentino. Nine battalions of the Gloucestershire Regiment would see action at the Somme but only two of them, the 1st and the 10th, had seen significant fighting before. The Battle of the Somme is so vast that it actually ended up being multiple battles in one campaign. The ensuing pages are broken up to allow us to best follow the path of the regiment.

The opening attacks of the Somme were committed at the **Battle of Albert** from the 1st until 13th July 1916. Five battalions of the regiment were present here: 1st, 1/4th, 1/5th, 1/6th and 10th. Their participation was extremely limited except for casualties caused by German artillery. The first real involvement of the Glosters was through 8th Battalion at **La Boiselle**.

During an attack on the village of La Boiselle on the 3rd July, the 8th Battalion were in reserve to the attacking parties of three other battalions. Whilst crossing no man's land the British troops were shredded by a heavy German artillery bombardment. The German infantry then came pouring out of their trenches and the attackers fled back through the Glosters line.

This quick turnaround from attack to defence could have been a real disaster so early in the Somme Offensive. Thankfully though, the 8th Battalion were

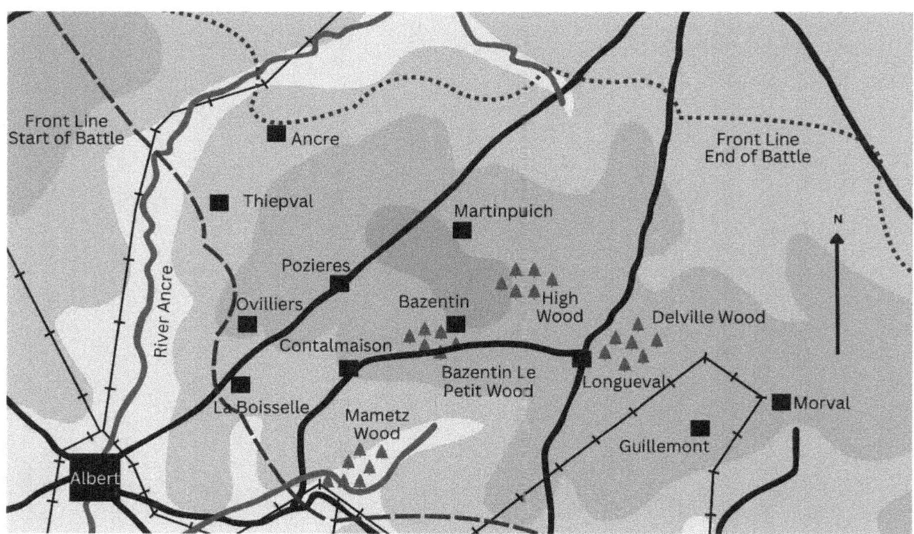

being led by one of its true heroes, Lieutenant Colonel Adrian Carton de Wiart. Realising the desperation of the predicament that the British found themselves in, de Wiart immediately threw 8th Battalion at the advancing Germans. They pushed the enemy all the way back to their own lines, and then on to capture La Boiselle itself and even the German trench system beyond. For this incredible action, de Wiart was awarded the Victoria Cross:

> For most conspicuous bravery, coolness and determination during severe operations of a prolonged nature. It was owing in a great measure to his dauntless courage and inspiring example that a serious reverse was averted. He displayed the utmost energy and courage in forcing our attack home. After three other battalion Commanders had become casualties, he controlled their commands, and ensured that the ground won was maintained at all costs. He frequently exposed himself in the organisation of positions and of supplies, passing unflinchingly through fire barrage of the most intense nature. His gallantry was inspiring to all.

The counter offensive by the Glosters had come at a heavy price though, and ninety-four men were killed along with another 198 wounded. The Somme Offensive now moved on to the **Battle of Bazentin Ridge**. Up to this point, the British offensive was going rather well and this next phase was an organised attack on the second line of German trenches by seven divisions. Four battalions of the Gloucestershire Regiment were involved: 1st, 1/4th, 10th and 14th.

The 10th and 14th Battalions actually saw little fighting and spent most of this period holding the secondary trenches or consolidating gains. However, as a testament to the fearsome power of the German artillery, 14th Battalion would suffer 119 casualties in just a three-day period. Meanwhile, 1st Battalion moved up to the front line on the 14th July. Upon arrival, the fighting had already been so intense and confused that nobody could actually tell them where the frontline was.

Finally arriving at the front, the Glosters quickly realised that the lines opposite them at Cantalmaison Villa were empty so they cautiously moved across the 250 yards of no man's land and occupied them. Later in the day, they attacked the German lines at midnight during a terrible storm. The Germans had little stomach for this fight and soon fled. The order to attack again was given at 02:00 on the 15th July and the Glosters smashed through the German lines. Moving a further three hundred yards, they came under heavy fire and retired back to the previously captured trench system. They quickly created strongpoints and dug communication trenches giving this area the moniker 'Gloster Alley' for the rest of the war.

By now, the Germans in the Somme area were on high alert, as it was obvious that this was a massive pre-planned offensive by the British. Needing to change tactics, 1st Battalion snuck out of their trenches during the night of the 16th July. Somehow the entire battalion, along with 2nd Welch Fusiliers and the Royal Munster Fusiliers on their flanks, reached to within a hundred yards of the enemy line and at midnight, they launched their attack. 'B' and 'D' Company were the main attack parties but there was little fighting as the surprised and confused Germans fled the line. A pinpoint barrage then put up a wall of fire to prevent any counter attack. This textbook attack saw the Glosters lose just three men killed and have twenty-five wounded for significant gains.

Later on the same day, 1/4th saw their first action at the Battle of Bazentin Ridge. At 16:00, Lieutenant Colonel Dobbin led his men to attack trenches near the village of Ovillers. This was achieved in conjunction with 7th Worcester's. The following morning at 01:50, a huge British bombardment opened up. Ten minutes later, 1/4th were going over the top and attacking further German trenches. 'B' and 'D' Company secured the objective within half an hour, yet by 07:00 they were being attacked on both flanks. 'C' Company moved up and began bombing their way along the German trenches. Eventually they linked up again with 7th Worcester's and the flank was secured.

On the 18th July, 1/4th attacked once again but now their momentum began to stall. The first line was easily overcome, however upon reaching the second German trench system they were pushed back with heavy casualties. Yet another attack was ordered for the 19th where the Glosters met with horrendous machine gun fire whilst crossing no man's land and the attack stalled. These four operations had taken much ground although they cost 1/4th thirty-seven men killed, 211 wounded and twenty-seven missing.

The Somme Offensive could now not proceed any further until three prominent features in the centre of the battlefield had been reduced. They formed a small salient and threatened both flanks of the entire British force. The first of these was at **Delville Woods** on the right and the opening attacks took place on the 14th July. 12th Battalion (Bristol's Own), did not move into the front line at Longueval until the 23rd July. They instantly began to take casualties from the relentless German artillery.

On the afternoon of the 28th July, 12th Battalion were ordered over the top and they successfully held the line. The following day, along with the 1st East Surrey's, they again attacked. Preceded by a half hour artillery bombardment, this attack was equally successful as they managed to occupy a five hundred yard sector of German lines. Two days later Bristol's Own were relieved and fell back to the rear of the British lines.

The feature at the centre of the British salient was **High Wood**. Three battalions of the Gloucestershire Regiment were involved here: 1st, 8th and 10th. They would become bogged down in a horrendous two-month campaign. 1st Battalion moved into the front line on 20th July, whilst two days later 10th Battalion attacked and held an important German observation post. For this action, Lieutenant Brewis was awarded a Military Cross. 8th Battalion saw their first action on the same day but an attempt to raid German trenches was viciously beaten back.

On the 23rd July, 10th Glosters along with 1st Cameron Highlanders attacked the Switch Line 1.5 miles east of Pozieres. As the British crossed no man's land, they were suddenly enfiladed by heavy machine gun fire from several positions that had been hidden in long grass. The men pushed on but huge shell craters around the German line made the attack untenable, meaning they had to pull back with significant losses.

On the flank of this attack, 8th Glosters also went over the top with battalions from the Worcestershire and Warwickshire Regiments. The attack was met with furious machine gun fire from within High Wood itself and it bogged down. A hundred and eighty-six casualties were recorded; amongst them were Carton de Wiart who had received a gunshot wound to the neck. Thankfully for the Glosters and British forces as a whole, this hero was now obtaining a reputation as near indestructible. He was soon back with his men pushing the battalion ever onwards.

A week later de Wiart was leading 8th Battalion on another attack, this time shielded by a thick smoke screen. This new tactic did not work as well as hoped though, and heavy machine gun fire along with snipers saw the attack fail. The battalion were then withdrawn from the line not seeing action again until the 17th August. Here they were providing bombing support for an attack on Martinpuich resulting in seventy-two casualties. Two days later, they again attacked Martinpuich and once again, seventy-two men were recorded as casualties.

1st Battalion meanwhile had spent the final week of August holding front line trenches near to High Wood. They experienced a terrifying three-day artillery bombardment by the end of which their trench system had ceased to exist. When the Glosters were pulled from the line on the 28th August, they had seen forty-six men killed and further 141 wounded.

Just a few days later on the 3rd September, 1st Battalion were thrown back into the line and ordered to attack. A mine with 3000lb of explosives was detonated under German positions before the attack began, and some men were armed for the first time with flamethrowers. Despite this, the main British attack was thrown back by a German counter attack. However, 1st Battalion somehow managed to cling onto the vital south west face of High Wood itself.

The British now had a foothold in the woods and this meant the fighting would intensify yet further. On the 8th September, 1st Battalion were in the assembly area ready to attack when their own artillery, falling hundreds of yards short, caused vast casualties. Yet they pressed on and covered the 150 yards of no man's land. Their initial objective, a machine gun nest and artillery cluster was secured. From here, they pushed on to the German second line. This attack was nowhere near as successful though, as many men fell before reaching the enemy. 'C' and 'D' Company coming up in support were hit by a German barrage and they too suffered huge casualties.

By early evening, the heavy German bombardment continued and British High Command had no reinforcements to send up. Therefore, by 22:00 the Glosters were back in their own trenches where they had started the assault. The following day, a vast German counter offensive was launched but was held off. These twenty-four hours of action had cost the men of Gloucestershire dearly. Eighty-nine men were dead, along with a further 130 wounded. Amongst the wounded was the stout Commanding Officer of 1st Battalion, Lieutenant Colonel Patsy Pagan, who received two shots to the stomach. Much like de Wiart though, it would take more than a double gunshot wound to the abdomen to keep Pagan out of the war.

Elsewhere on the 9th September saw a huge mine being exploded under German lines, and 10th Battalion being hurriedly pushed into combat. 'C' and 'D' Company rushed across no man's land and used the confusion caused by the mine explosion to take the western edge of High Wood. The glory would be short lived though. A massive artillery bombardment was unleashed upon them followed by machine gun fire pouring down from all angles. The Glosters soon had to pull back, but this short and sharp action had cost 122 casualties. Finally, on the 21st September, 10th Battalion discovered that the German trenches opposite them had been abandoned. High Wood had fallen.

The final feature that had to be conquered to break out of the British salient was **Pozieres Ridge**. The high ground was a strongpoint in the entire German line, it was also an excellent observation post. Its capture was absolutely essential to British victory. Amongst those who faced this daunting task were the Territorial battalions 1/4th, 1/5th and 1/6th. The village of Pozieres would actually be captured by the ANZAC's within twenty-four hours, yet the battle for the ridge raged for a further seven weeks.

The first to try to take the ridge were 1/5th, but their assault was unsuccessful resulting in 114 casualties. On the 21st July, 1/6th went over the top north of Ovillers and the various companies met with mixed success. 'A' Company reached their objective twice but on both occasions, a German counter attack saw them pulling back. 'B' Company were enfiladed by machine gun fire on both flanks whilst crossing no man's land, high casualties resulted in their gaining no ground. 'C' Company meanwhile managed to penetrate the German defences and actually beat off several counter attacks. The losses during this action were eleven killed and ninety-two wounded.

Two days later, 1/5th were back attacking the main railroad running through Pozieres Ridge alongside 4th Oxs and Bucks Light Infantry. 'A' and 'C' Company were the assaulting parties, but a heavy artillery bombardment followed by machine gun fire pinned them. 'B' Company then moved up through the line and continued the assault, yet this too was a failure. One hundred and fifty-six men were lost on the 23rd July for absolutely no gain.

To the left of 1/5th the other two Territorial battalions were also in action. 1/4th attacked at dawn with 'C' and 'D' Companies in the advanced party but they were mercilessly mown down by machine gun fire seventy yards from their objective. Of the entire two companies, only six men reached the German trenches. 'A' Company then advanced to lend support but they too received the same treatment. By the time they had pulled back, only one officer remained throughout all three companies. Further to the left, 1/6th attacked the German line but this was called off when 1/4th failed in their own endeavour. Five gallantry medals were awarded to 1/6th on the 23rd July, all for going into no man's land under heavy fire to bring back wounded comrades.

The following day a colossal enemy counter attack was launched against 1/4th, with the Germans now suffering their own high casualty count after mortars and artillery hit their advance. That morning also saw 1st Battalion arrive at the front line and they too had to hold off repeated German attacks. Later in the day, the three Territorial battalions were withdrawn from the front line to rest and be reinforced. They would not return to the front until the 13th August.

By this point, the British assault had reached the peak of Pozieres Ridge but much fighting remained. Skylight Trench was the next target, as it was a strong German line that also held several sections of the all important railroad. 1/6th immediately attacked the southern end of the trench system but it was unsuccessful. 1/4th and 1/6th along with the 1st Bucks attacked again at nightfall and found some success. However, a devastating German artillery barrage saw them having to return to their start positions.

Three days later, 1/4th would once again be sent into attack but they were pushed back after encountering fierce resistance and suffering seventy casualties. On the 18th August they supported another attack, which met with great success, 1/4th capturing four hundred prisoners. 1/6th then attacked northeast of the

German trenches with a bombing attack, however this bogged down. They repeated the attack the following day but this also found no gains.

A small salient had now developed in German lines just south of Thiepval, based on the strongly fortified Leipzig Redoubt. On the 21st August, 1/4th and 11th Cheshire's were tasked with clearing the German lines leading up to the redoubt. At 18:00, 'B' and 'C' Companies advanced and quickly took the first trenches. Behind an accurate Allied barrage, they then occupied the second German lines. The next day at 20:00, the Germans launched the first of three brutal counter attacks. Each was repulsed by the Glosters and they consolidated their position. On the 22nd August, 1/4th with 1/6th on their right flank assaulted the redoubt itself. A shattering mortar barrage from the Germans helped blunt the attack. The next day the Germans launched another four waves of counter attacks but again, the men from Gloucestershire held their position.

On the 27th August, the Territorial battalions would launch their final assault at the Battle of Pozieres Ridge. 1/5th, along with the 4th Royal Berkshires, attacked through Nab Valley on the left flank of the Leipzig Redoubt. The battalion made it across no man's land and then evicted the Germans from their own trenches. Two hundred of the enemy were killed along with another fifty prisoners taken. This was for the loss of 114 casualties to 1/5th. By the 3rd September, Pozieres Ridge had been captured and the Somme Offensive began to rage in other sectors.

12th Battalion found themselves fighting outside the strongly held village of **Guillemont**. The area had previously beaten back many British attacks but on the 3rd September, the village received a near four-hour artillery bombardment. At midday, the Glosters began their advance towards a series of dugouts positioned behind a sunken lane. These were found to be unoccupied, but 12th Battalion were subject to a violent machine gun enfilading ambush after the brigade on their right flank had failed to move up. The next German line was then stormed, resulting in few casualties. The third objective was another sunken lane. Unfortunately, the Glosters became lost and wandered straight into their own artillery barrage. Finally though, the lines were located, occupied and consolidated.

The 12th Battalion next found themselves at the **Battle of Morval** at the head of the British offensive. In support of the main attack, they moved through the line and attacked the village of Morval alongside the Kings Own Scottish Borderers. The southern part of the village was taken in under an hour and this would almost be the furthest the British reached on the Somme. By now, the autumn weather had kicked in, and after snows fell and then thawed, the battlefield turned into a morass. There remained one final objective of the offensive, **Ancre Heights.**

On the 18th November, the last official day of the Somme Offensive, 8th Battalion followed a creeping barrage through heavy snow. The advanced parties had been cut off, yet the Glosters moved through the lines and mopped up all resistance west of Grandcourt. A German counter attack the following day saw all gains given up at the loss of 295 casualties. The Somme Offensive was now over with the British having 125,000 men killed, 1813 of them from the Gloucestershire Regiment. Alongside those who gave their lives there were roughly another 300,000 wounded.

# 41. Baghdad

7th Battalion the Gloucestershire Regiment arrived in Basra, Iraq, in March 1916 straight from Gallipoli (see Battle Honour 38). The war in the Middle East was not going well for the Allies and the Ottoman forces had surrounded the town of Kut. Here, almost thirteen thousand British and Allied troops were desperately hanging on. The Glosters would take part in an attempt to lift the siege but on the 29th April, the garrison surrendered in what was a massive humiliation for the British. For the rest of 1916 an uneasy stalemate remained in place.

The British made the most of the impasse, firstly with the arrival of the enigmatic Lieutenant-General Sir Frederick Maude. Thousands of troops were shipped from India, whilst a supply railway was constructed heading north from Basra. Finally in December 1916, the Mesopotamian Expeditionary Force were

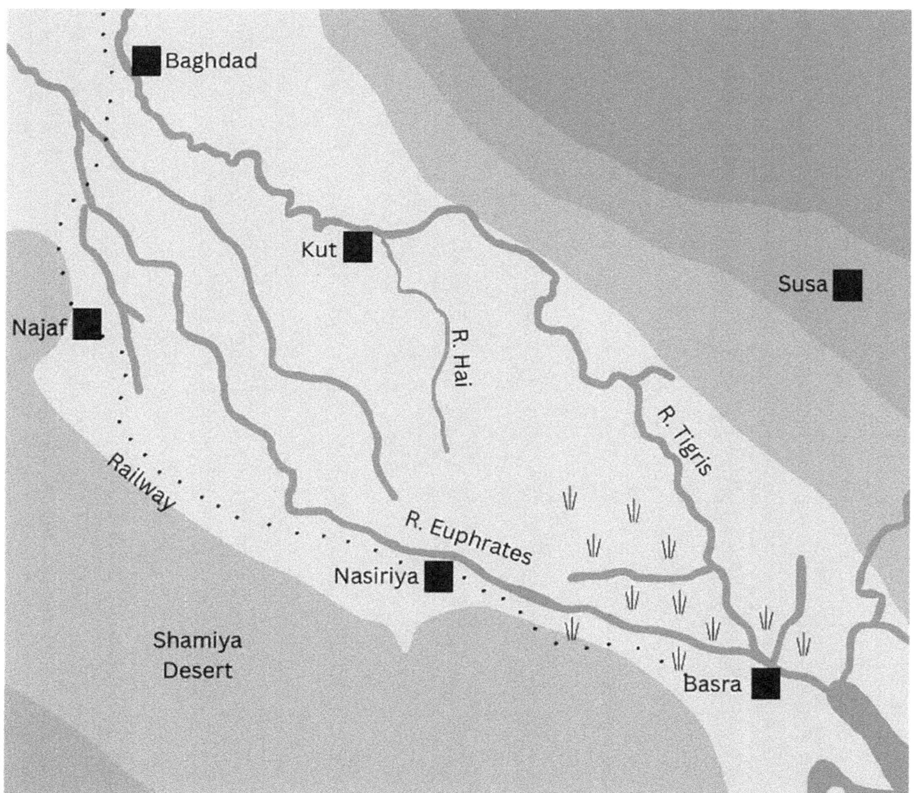

ready to begin their campaign. The 792 men of 7th Battalion, led by Lieutenant Colonel Jordan, were in the rear-guard for one of the two columns that advanced either side of the river Tigris.

On 15th December 1916, two days into the campaign, the Expeditionary Force came upon their first resistance. 7th Battalion, along with the rest of 39th Brigade, were ordered to advance across the eight hundred yards of no man's land. They came under a heavy bombardment and had to dig in where they were. By 15:00, a second push was ordered and a further thousand yards had to be covered. This time the Glosters came under fire from artillery, machine guns and rifles. The men managed to dig in and after a brief exchange of fire, the day was won. Twenty men would be killed in this first battle along with another ninety wounded.

The next obstacle for the British forces were two trench lines that the Ottomans had fortified. This was in a turn on the Tigris called the Khadairi Bend. Heavy fighting was experienced here after the British mined under the Ottoman position. The Glosters though, mostly found themselves in reserve and casualties were light.

The British advance continued along the River Hai, with the 9th Worcester's leading on the eastern bank and 7th Battalion on the right. However, the British now came up against their next major hindrance as further up the river; the Ottomans had constructed strong defensive lines. At 09:40 on the 25th January 1917, the Glosters attacked these positions. The first line was easily taken, but then the Ottomans brought their howitzers into play and launched several fierce counter attacks. Eventually, after the Warwick's had been forced back, the Glosters, including Lieutenant Bazeley who was attached to the Machine Gun Corp, also had to pull back to their own lines:

Turning westwards, our division performed that hazardous military manoeuvre – movement to a flank in the face of an enemy. From our new positions east of the Hai we advanced at dawn over 2000 yards of flat ground, under rapid fire from the Turks, entrenched in the angle between the two rivers. I clearly recall that long march with my teams on either side, carrying our four guns and about 4,000 rounds for each.

It was a hair raising experience but – incredible as it may seem – nearly all of us arrived at the enemy lines 'in one piece'. In my pocket was a prayer book which our padre had given us the night before with his blessing.

Continuing their rapid advance, the Glosters experienced strong Turkish resistance on the night of 2nd/3rd February. 'C' Company particularly suffered high losses whilst they tried to establish a new line. Nineteen men of the company were killed, along with forty-eight being wounded. On 10th February, the Glosters attacked Ottoman lines during a vicious dust storm. Their target was strongly fortified and seventy-three men were casualties before they managed to return to their own lines.

The British would now have the opportunity to avenge the humiliating defeat suffered at Kut in April 1916. The Ottomans had established themselves along a series of canals outside of the town. The fighting began at midday, but the main assault did not start until 17:30. The Glosters, Stafford's and Worcester's charged across 1500 yards of no man's land under heavy artillery fire. The first two Ottoman trenches were captured; however, a huge enemy counter attack whilst assaulting the third line forced them to consolidate. 7th Battalion were the worst hit of all the Mesopotamian Expeditionary Force, having over a hundred casualties on the day.

Kut would fall and the Glosters marched through nearly sixty miles of desert at the beginning of March, as their pursuit of the Ottomans continued. The enemy halted just thirty-five miles south of Baghdad. Maude decided to shift his army north and attempt to outflank the Ottomans. This move was mirrored by Kalil Pasha, the Ottoman Commander, who left just one regiment defending his original position. On 10th March, this regiment was crushed and it sent the Ottomans into a panic. At 08:00 the same day, the authorities ordered the evacuation of Baghdad and it fell the following day. Nine thousand enemy troops were taken prisoner during the confusion and the offensive to capture Baghdad was over.

# 42. Doiran

In autumn of 1915, the Allies landed in Macedonia to help Serbia in their conflict with Bulgaria, who by now had been officially incorporated into the Central Powers alliance. The Allied strategy was to break through an area, west of Lake Doiran, and then press on to Sofia thus knocking the Bulgarians out of the war. Allied inactivity had allowed the Bulgarians, with the help of German engineers, to strongly fortify the Salonika Front where the Allied push would take place. It was already a rough and rugged mountain range of up to 600 metres high and the Bulgarians added trenches, fortifications and gun emplacements.

The proceeding winter had been harsh for 9th Battalion of the Gloucestershire Regiment. The weather was extremely cold and it rained incessantly. The mountainous terrain also made keeping the men well supplied with appropriate clothing, food, water and ammunition a real difficulty. By spring, the warm weather had come yet this brought issues of its own. Mosquitos descended upon the area in huge numbers, and malaria would actually cause more casualties in this location for the duration of WWI than the fighting itself.

The battle began, much like on the Western Front, with a devastating artillery barrage. The British fired over a hundred thousand shells in the space of four days, yet it had little effect upon the well-entrenched Bulgarians. In reply to this barrage, the Bulgarians fired one of their own. They offloaded ten thousand shells in just an hour before the infantry attacks began.

Unfortunately, the men of 11th Battalion the Worcestershire Regiment were just forming up ready to attack Jemeaux Ridge, in the centre of the British assault. One of the heavy Bulgarian bombardments fell right upon them and the results were devastating. 'A' Company of 9th Battalion the Gloucestershire Regiment, were ordered up to the line to reinforce them. Again, with deadly accuracy, the Bulgarians dished out exactly the same treatment. Men of 'B' Company were now ordered up to the front and the infantry attack could finally start.

In the early hours of 25th April 1917, the British attack began and at first, they took a host of enemy positions. Things were not so positive for the Glosters though as 'B' Company commander, Captain Griffiths, messaged back to HQ that his men were stuck in a ravine. They had been pinned down by heavy fire from both machine guns and rifles. Eventually, the men of the 9th Battalion were ordered to return to their lines. Meanwhile, the Bulgarians had launched a devastating counter attack and almost all British gains on the day had been reversed.

The Bulgarian counter attack made its way right up to the original British lines and at 20:00, the Glosters received news that a neighbouring unit was coming under heavy assault. They left their trenches and hit the Bulgarians in the flank causing them to retreat. For two more days, the British went over the top and the results were much the same. High Command were extremely critical of the way in which the battle had been handled and so after a lull in the action another attack was ordered.

On the 8th May 1917, the British opened up another huge bombardment of the enemies positions. The 9th Battalion were held in reserve on this occasion, yet it was not long until they were called up at midnight to take their place at the front. The Black Watch were to consolidate a line of Bulgarian trenches that had been taken and the Glosters would support them. By the time the Glosters had made their way to the frontline though, the Bulgarians had counter attacked and retaken the position.

At 02:00 on the 9th May, the Glosters, along with the Royal Scots Fusiliers, were ordered over the top. Due to confusion in organisation, the attack never actually began until 05:30 and by now, the sun shone brightly overhead. Nevertheless, the men began the assault and the results were somewhat predictable. The artillery barrage had actually destroyed the barbed wire and so the Glosters got in amongst the trenches. The Bulgarians had cleverly built their fortifications to be mutually supporting though, so the men were hit by a violent attack from both flanks.

The Glosters made it back to their own trenches, but not before fifteen men had lost their lives and a further fifty men had been wounded. This pales in comparison to the overall failure of this British assault though. Throughout the Battle of Doiran, the British suffered well over ten thousand casualties whilst the Bulgarians had barely two thousand. The Salonika Front would remain stagnant for almost a year and a half, as both sides further entrenched and fortified their positions.

# 43. Ypres 1917

Like many of the larger operations in WWI Ypres 1917, perhaps better known today as Passchendaele, was actually multiple battles bundled together. The overall Allied plan was to break out of the Ypres Salient and drive to the coast neutralising the German U-boat threat. The French Army had begun to mutiny after the disastrous Battle of Aisne, therefore the British would have to go this one alone. Eleven battalions of the Gloucestershire Regiment took part in Ypres 1917 and the battle will be deconstructed as best allows us to follow their path.

The Glosters involvement started quite late, with only the 13th (Pioneer) Battalion taking part in the opening stages as they created the assembly points and fire trenches ready for the main assault. Once the battle started, they cleared roads just behind the front line so that supplies and artillery could move forward. The pioneer battalions did incredibly important work during WWI and their lack of actual direct combat should not be held against them. For example, in their three days at the **Battle of Pilckem Ridge**, 13th Battalion suffered ninety-six casualties.

The action then moved onto **Langemarck,** an area with which the Glosters were well acquainted (see Battle Honour 36). 48th Division, containing 1/4th, 1/5th and 1/6th of the Gloucestershire Regiment, moved up to the front line on the 5th August. 1/5th were positioned in the advanced trenches and received several days of heavy shelling. At 04:45 on the 16th August, the entire 48th Division attacked with 1/5th as one of the assaulting parties. They advanced steadily behind a creeping barrage and captured trenches on either side of the important St. Julian-Winnipeg road. The creeping barrage then got too far ahead of the Glosters and left them at the mercy of the German machine guns. The men frantically dug in where they were and managed to form something of a defensive line. At 10:00, the Germans launched a counter attack but this was repulsed. The action on the 16th August cost 1/5th 217 casualties.

The day before had seen the 61st Division move up into the Ypres Salient. This saw 2/4th, 2/5th and 2/6th of the Gloucestershire Regiment coming into the front. Opposite them was Pond Farm Galleries, which was a brutal fortress manned by fifty Germans and five machine guns. Five divisions had attacked this obstacle previously and all had been repulsed. Now it was the turn of the men from Gloucestershire. On the 17th August 2/4th went over the top but on reaching the German lines, they found the preparatory artillery barrage

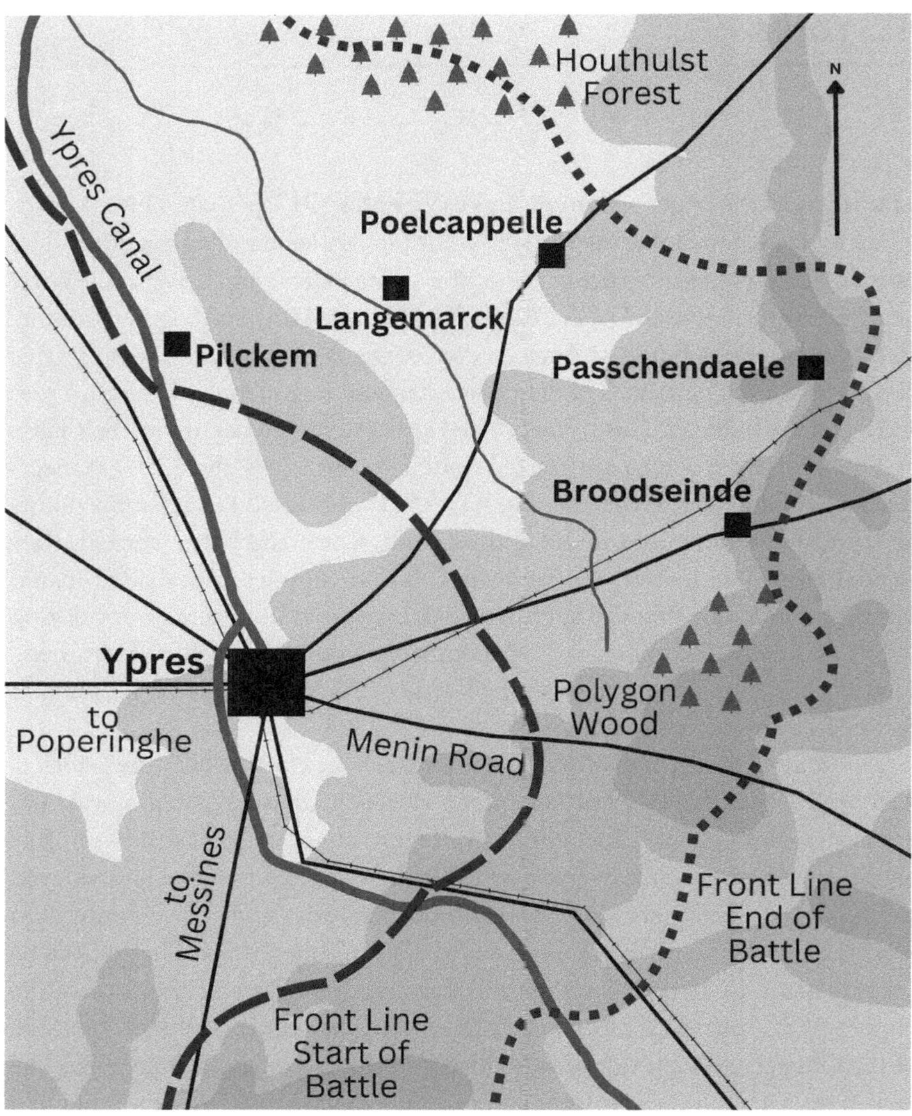



had failed to dislodge the barbed wire defences. They quickly had to return to their own lines.

Next in line to attempt a defeat of this formidable foe were 184 Brigade. This consisted of 2/5th Glosters, 2/4th Ox's and 2/1st Bucks. The Glosters were in reserve for the main assault, but the other two battalions were torn to pieces on approaching the fortress. At midday, the British launched a hurricane bombardment, a quick but vast shelling of the fort. 2/5th then stormed into the German lines and slaughtered all the Germans who were in the fort. This operation cost them eighteen men killed and fifty-one wounded. The following day they were relieved by 2/6th.

During mid-August 14th Battalion, who had just arrived from the Somme, found themselves holding the front line around Epehy. Suddenly, during the night of 20th/21st August, Germans appeared and attacked an advanced bombing post. All the men fled except for Second Lieutenant Hardy Falconer Parsons, who would be awarded the Victoria Cross:

For most conspicuous bravery during a night attack by a strong party of the enemy on a bombing post held by his command. The bombers holding the block were forced back, but Second Lieutenant Parsons remained at his post, and, single-handed, and although severely scorched and burnt by liquid fire, he continued to hold up the enemy with bombs until severely wounded. This very gallant act of self-sacrifice and devotion to duty undoubtedly delayed the enemy long enough to allow of the organisation of a bombing party, which succeeded in driving back the enemy before they could enter any portion of the trenches. The gallant officer succumbed to his wounds.

On the 27th August, 2/4th were ordered over the top but whilst forming up they were hit by an accurate artillery barrage causing vast casualties. Nevertheless, they continued on their mission to attack Scholer Galleries but found no man's land to be its typical morass. Wading through knee high mud, the men were easy targets for German machine gunners. Many fell before reaching the German lines and the entire operation was a disaster.

The action then moved onto the 8th Glosters who were at **Menin Road.** This was possibly the most vital area along the whole front as it was the main route into Ypres. Hundreds of thousands of men and supplies flooded along this road during the four years of war, and the Menin Gate stands today in honour of this. A successful attack saw 8th Battalion go over the top on the 20th September at 05:40. The first German lines were reached with surprising ease and then consolidated. The assault then continued onto the second line and the Glosters had to take several strongpoints, all the while under heavy sniper fire. An enemy barrage on the support lines caused considerable casualties, with the day costing eleven killed, 128 wounded and twenty-five missing.

The next considerable events occurred at **Polygon Wood,** which saw the Glosters merely holding the line. Yet even this task was fraught with danger. 1/5th were heavily shelled on the 27th September, resulting in sixteen men being killed. 8th Battalion then moved into the front lines for just under a week but saw little action. Finally, 12th Battalion moved up on the 1st October but as they did, the Germans launched a gas attack. This saw nineteen men killed and a further hundred and thirty-four wounded.

The action then moved to **Broodseinde** when 1/5th attacked Adler Farm, Inch Houses and Vacher Farm at 05:00. The ground in no man's land was treacherous and the creeping barrage soon got too far ahead of the Glosters. This all too familiar story (the same had happened to them at Langemarck a few weeks earlier) saw the German machine guns picking targets at will. The men had to furiously dig themselves in, three hundred yards into no man's land. Twenty-five men were killed with a further 106 wounded. 12th Battalion, who we have previously seen being gassed on arrival at the front line, held the area for a further twelve days. Repeated shelling and the gas attack saw them withdraw from the line with 359 men less than they had started with.

Up to the point of Menin Road, Polygon Wood and Broodseinde, Ypres 1917 was actually going fairly well for the British. Although many men had been lost, the front line was edging forward. In fact, the Germans even held high-level discussions about pulling out of the sector altogether. One issue we have seen throughout was that no man's land was hard to cross due to being waterlogged, and of course covered with craters. The heavens now opened and the whole battlefield became impenetrable. All the proceeding battles would go terribly and Ypres 1917 quickly unravelled for the British.

The battle had now moved on to **Poelcapelle**, with four Gloucestershire battalions involved. 1/5th spent most of this period carrying supplies and acting as stretcher-bearers for the wounded. A plan was put in place on the 9th October that 1/6th and 1/4th, with 7th Worcester's on their right flank, would attack at Poelcapelle Spur. Specialists who were familiar with no man's land would guide the men through the night to their attack positions. As it was, the promised guides never materialised for 1/4th and they got lost in the darkness. As the sun rose, the attack began but 1/4th found themselves barely able to wade through the mud. The creeping barrage was soon far off into the distance, and German machine guns and snipers forced the men to dig in still a hundred yards shy of enemy lines. Sixty-nine men were dead and a further 108 wounded.

1/6th meanwhile found more success, as for starters their guide had turned up. The ground they had to traverse had also drained better and they charged towards the German lines. The first trench was captured despite heavy machine gun fire. Seventy enemy were taken prisoner and twelve deadly machine guns captured. The Germans counter attacked three times, yet on each occasion they were driven back. 1/6th had eighty-seven men killed and another 105 wounded for their successes.

Finally the battle moved to **Passchendaele**, which was the furthest the British would advance. 8th Glosters held the front line for three days but saw little action. 14th Battalion meanwhile, were thrown straight into the assault on 22nd October. They went over the top at 05:35 behind a creeping barrage. This assault met with great success as the German trenches were captured along with forty prisoners. However, the Glosters suffered seventy-five men killed and an unknown number wounded. The German artillery, admittedly this was quite a rare occurrence, had targeted the First Aid post behind the lines with the help of aerial reconnaissance. Sadly, this is where the majority of deaths happened.

The 12th Battalion held the front line for four days and suffered several casualties from sporadic shelling. 1st Battalion then moved up for the final stages of the battle. They arrived on the 9th November and were in reserve for an attack by 1st South Wales Borderers and 2nd Royal Muster Fusiliers. The attacking parties bogged down and so Patsy Pagan, who was now Brigade Commander, went forward to see what the holdup was. He received a serious wound to his eye, and upon reaching the hospital, was told his war was over. This enigmatic leader would be sent back to England. The 1st Battalion moved up during the night to relieve their beleaguered colleagues and hold the entire line.

The following morning Patsy Pagan arrived at the frontline, wearing nothing but a dressing gown, canvas slippers and a huge bandage over his eye! The only person who was going to take Patsy Pagan out of the war, was Patsy Pagan. Morale skyrocketed amongst the men and Ypres 1917 was over. Almost Fifteen hundred men of Gloucestershire had been killed in this three-month conflict.

The Second Battle of the Somme fills an interim period between the German Spring Offensive and the great hundred day advance to ultimate victory by the Allies. Like many of the vast WWI battles, this is actually several larger conflicts rolled into one. The Gloucestershire Regiment only featured briefly in the form of Bristol's Own 12th Battalion.

The Glosters arrived at Hebuterne on the Somme front on the 19th August 1918. The following morning they moved into the front lines near Boix de Biex as a reserve to the 95th Brigade. An attack was ordered on the 21st August with the 1st Devon's and 1st East Surreys being the attacking parties, with the Glosters in reserve. To their right lay the New Zealand Division. Tanks were supposed to support this attack but they immediately became lost in the thick morning fog.

By midday it was completely unclear what was happening, as there had been little or no communication from the attacking parties. It was decided to push the Glosters forward to get a clearer picture, so 'B' and 'D' Companies set off with 'A' and 'C' in reserve. They pushed through under increasingly heavy machine gun and artillery fire, before linking up with the 1st Easy Surreys. They had taken the first objective, however after another mile of advancing, both battalions became pinned down by German forces on some high ground. This is how the day's activities finished with 12th Battalion having eleven men killed and a hundred wounded.

The following morning the Glosters found themselves holding nearly the entire brigade front. Even worse was that their right flank was wide open, as the New Zealand Division were still at their starting positions. As was often the case, High Command were not flexible enough. They decided that the right flank would not move until the attacking parties had moved three miles. Clearly the attack had bogged down, yet they were still determined to throw the New Zealander's on a wide flanking manoeuvre. As it happened, the Germans did not take advantage and the Glosters spent the day consolidating their position.

At dawn the next morning, a huge artillery barrage opened up on 12th Battalions position. The Germans would not fail to take the opportunity for a second day. At 17:30 a mass of enemy came storming down the right flank, yet there was a somewhat ironic sting in the tail. So large was the gap in Allied lines that the Germans completely bypassed 12th Battalion, thus exposing their own right flank. Two platoons of 'A' Company were ordered to smash into the enemy flank and they did so with gusto. The first three enemy attacking waves were obliterated, with 380 prisoners taken and a further six machine guns captured.

Later on the 23rd August, the Glosters along with the 1st East Surreys, were ordered on towards what was the final objective, the village of Irles. The attack stalled almost immediately, as a deep railway cutting on the Arras to Albert line meant that the creeping barrage got too far ahead of the men. German machine guns built into the railway embankment started to pick off their targets at will. A desperate flanking attack by the Glosters eventually got the advance moving again.

The Glosters now reached the outskirts of Irles but it was far more heavily defended than intelligence had reported. For six hours heavy machine gun, rifle and mortar fire poured down upon Bristol's Own. Finally, the Glosters decided to call up reinforcements but before they arrived Lieutenant Colonel Colt, Battalion Commanding Officer, led his men forward and charged the village at bayonet point. The day was won and for this act of outstanding courage, Colt was awarded the Distinguished Service Order medal.

The battalion was then relieved, but the Glosters were furious when they got back behind the line to discover the 1st West Kent's had the audacity to announce, it was they who had carried Irles. After much argument, it was decided that the Glosters had in fact, arrived at the village centre ten minutes before their rivals. Either way, Irles had cost the battalion thirty-three men killed and 281 wounded. This would end the Gloucestershire Regiments involvement at the Second Battle of the Somme.

# 45. Lys

The Germans launched their second offensive of spring 1918 along a sixty-mile front around Ypres. Although there are claims of the usual goals, such as driving to the Channel coast, it is more likely that there were more limited targets. Capturing a key supply railroad and high ground surrounding Ypres were probably the true objectives. The initial assault by a hundred thousand men was a great success as they concentrated on a sector of the line held by a weak Portuguese force.

The offensive began on 7th April 1918 and 1st Battalion were the initial Glosters to see combat. They held several bridges over the La Bassee Canal but at first, their lines were surprisingly quiet given that they were in the epicentre of the attacking sector. On 9th April, the Germans attacked, appearing out of a thick fog that would be a feature of the entire campaign. The assault was limited though as it was soon driven off, and during a three-day period of holding the line, the Glosters only had one man killed and a further six wounded.

The action then switched to the area of Messines, just south of Ypres. On 10th April, the Germans launched a five-hour bombardment of 8th Battalion and then sent their infantry over the top. They managed to penetrate around the flanks of the Glosters. This meant that 8th Battalion were forced in to an orderly withdrawal to the secondary lines. The following day the entire division counter attacked with limited success, after which 8th Battalion were relieved to the rear.

The Germans then began to concentrate on reaching the supply depot of Hazebrouck. The initial assault was successful with the Germans penetrating several miles. In their way now stood 2/5th and 12th Battalions of the Gloucestershire Regiment. On 13th April, a huge German assault was launched with the enemy, once again, appearing out of the fog and heading straight for 'B' Company of 2/5th. The Germans then moved their heavy guns to within 300 yards of 'B' Company and began a devastating artillery fire. Thankfully, this threat was quickly neutralised by British counter strikes.

The Germans now attacked along the entire line and 'C' Company were not heard from for several hours. They had been assaulted three times, yet had managed to hold their ground. During this period, heavy machine guns had penetrated their flanks meaning they were isolated. Eventually the assault subsided, and incredibly, the cost had only been three men killed and sixteen wounded. Later that evening they were moved to the Bethune area.

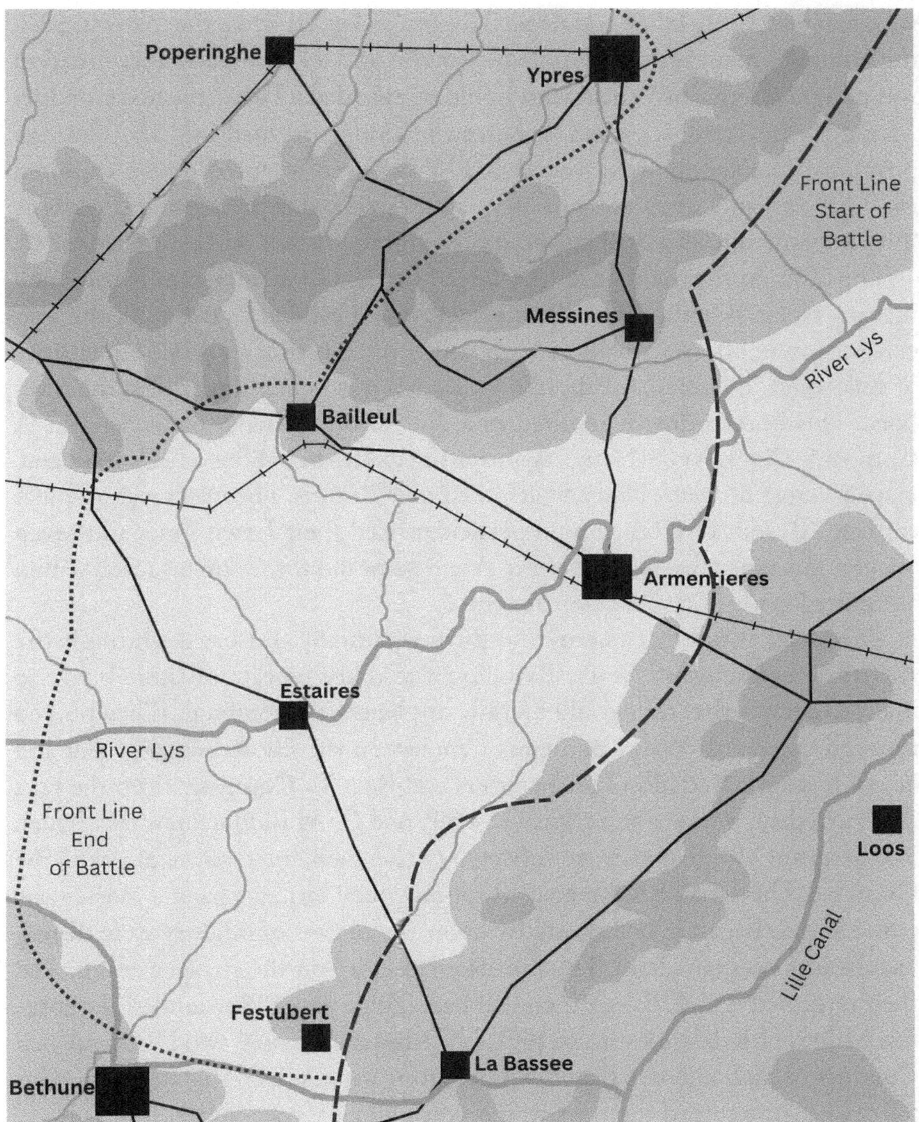


12th Battalion, who unbelievably just ten days previous had been fighting in Italy, were also hit by this same German assault. They too withstood the attack with the loss of sixteen men and fifty-eight wounded. They continued to hold the lines and were heavily shelled and probed by infantry for several days having one man killed and eleven wounded during this time.

Unfortunately for 2/5th, their recent move meant no respite as the next German attack would fall directly on their sector at Bethune. On 18th April, a position to the Glosters east was taken and a counter attack by 'D' Company failed with two men being killed and twenty-five wounded. At dawn the following day, the Germans managed to infiltrate between 'A' and 'D' Company. The situation was perilous. Sergeant White, who would be awarded a Distinguished Conduct Medal for his actions, picked seventeen men and stormed into the German positions. The enemy were routed and White even returned with a captured machine gun and seventeen prisoners. Later in the day, the advanced posts of 'B' Company were assaulted resulting in twelve men killed and eleven wounded.

The 18th April would become a fabled day in Gloucestershire Regimental history as 1st Battalion were also attacked at Festubert. At 04:00, the rear echelons were hit by an artillery bombardment featuring enormous quantities of yellow gas. By 06:30, this horrendous salvo was falling directly on the front lines. This bombardment resulted in a 200-yard gap being opened up in 'A' Companies lines. At 08:15 an awe-inspiring twelve battalions of infantry came tearing across no man's land and attacked the Glosters. The result was absolute carnage. 'B' and 'D' Company in particular used their Lewis guns and seven Vickers machine guns to great effect. At no point did the Germans reach within a hundred yards of the Gloster trenches.

The sheer weight of enemy numbers eventually did break through the British lines though. The 1st Battalion war diary reports of there being so many Germans that they could literally not be shot fast enough. They poured through the South Wales Borderers trenches on the Glosters right flank and began to attack Battalion Headquarters and then 'D' Company from the rear. At 11:00, the battle was at a critical juncture and CSM Biddle knew this. Much like Sergeant White earlier, he collected twelve men and counter attacked the Germans. This small band managed to force the Germans back and then the entire assault began to bog down. By noon, the masses of infantry were fleeing back across no man's land. The Glosters stood up on the parapet and picked their targets at will. Fifty-six men had been killed and 128 wounded. Twenty-five Military Medals, a bar to a DSO, four Military Crosses, two Distinguished Conduct Medals and two bars to DCM's were awarded. To this day, it remains a British Army record for any battalion on a single days combat.

In the final act of the Battle of Lys, 2/5th attacked German lines on 23rd April at 04:33. Within an hour, they had captured the enemy trenches but were countered with a five-hour artillery bombardment. The Germans then sent over three waves of counter attacking infantry all of which were beaten back. 2/5th saw much action during the offensive and by the end of April, 108 men had been killed and another 142 wounded.

# 46. Selle

After breaking through the Hindenburg defensive line the month previously, Allied progress began to slow in October 1918. The Germans took up defensive lines behind the River Selle, twelve miles east of Cambrai. To break a possible deadlock, the Allies threw the 4th Army across the Selle during the night of the 17th October. Despite determined German resistance, the push was a success. During this period, 5th Battalion the Gloucestershire Regiment found themselves in reserve, along with the rest of 75th Brigade.

The following day 5th Battalion moved up to the front line, assisting in capturing the village of Bazuel and then clearing high ground to the east of Le Cateau in the centre of the attack. Despite a heavy artillery bombardment, they took their objectives but were then pinned by machine guns. The next day, 5th Battalion were ordered to attack the German line around Richemont stream. Here they again came up against heavy machine gun fire. They tried once again the next day and this time the attack succeeded. The 4th Army needed a few days to reorganise but the Germans were well on the run by now and so on the 22nd October the assault was renewed. The rest of the battle, more than any other on these pages, can be told through the actions of just one hero.

The next area that needed to be cleared was that of the Bois l'Eveque on the right flank of the operation. Here lay the Foret de Mormal, a thickly wooded area with masses of barbed wire and hidden German machine gun nests. On the 23rd October, 5th Battalion headed out to attack this area in reserve to the 7th Brigade. Arriving at 01:20, they were immediately in the fight and five hours of deadly combat saw little result. A thick mist had descended on the battlefield and this was greatly to the advantage of the defenders. 'C' Company of 5th Battalion became the main assault party but after advancing 500 yards, they too became bogged down after being hit by machine guns positioned in a sunken road. Enter Private Francis George Miles.

Understanding the situation, Miles leapt out of cover and tore across open ground with almost all German fire directed at him. Somehow he made it to the German line and launched himself at the nearest enemy machine gun team. He killed the gunner, kicked over the weapon and then took the other six men in his vicinity prisoner. Yet he was nowhere near finished. Spotting another machine gun he again advanced, completely alone, killed the gunner and then took another eight Germans prisoner. Up to this point, Miles comrades from

'C' Company had been watching on in amazement and awe. He now stood up and signalled for the rest of his brethren to join him.

'C' Company advanced en-masse and captured a further sixteen machine guns and took fifty-one prisoners. For this quite incredible act of heroism, Francis George Miles, from Clearwell in Gloucestershire, was awarded the Victoria Cross. He would be the only private soldier in regimental history to obtain this honour.

> Private Miles alone, and on his own initiative, went forward under exceptionally heavy fire, located a machine-gun, shot the gunner, and put the gun out of action. Observing another gun nearby, he again advanced alone, shot the gunner, rushed the gun, and captured the team of eight. Finally, he stood up and beckoned to his company who, acting on his signals, were enabled to work round the rear of the line and to capture 16 machine-guns, one officer and 50 other ranks. It was due to the courage, initiative and entire disregard of personal safety shown by this very gallant soldier that the company was enabled to advance at a time when any delay would have jeopardised seriously the whole operation.

The following evening 74th Brigade passed through the line, and further captured Malgarni and Fontaine-aux-Bois, before the entire division was relieved from the line later that night. 1st Battalion of the Gloucestershire Regiment would also see their last action of World War One at the River Selle. They spent most of the time in reserve but on the 19th and 20th October, helped in the push towards Canal de la Sambre resulting in nine men killed.

# 47. Vittorio Veneto

We now turn to the Italian Front, with this battle being one of the harder to analyse amongst the Gloucestershire Regiment's many battle honours. The reason for this is twofold. Firstly, the Austrian Hapsburg monarchy was already in great trouble by October 1918 with the Empire falling apart. It is often claimed that the Battle of Vittorio Veneto was actually just one mass retreat. The second reason is that the Italians have made this a prominent battle in their story of independence. This means that any foreign units, such as the Glosters, are given a much-reduced role in the narrative.

Nevertheless, after just managing to hold on at the Second Battle of Piave River, the last major Austro-Hungarian offensive of WWI, the cautious Italian leadership would not launch its own campaign until it could be fully certain of victory. This moment arrived on the 24th October 1918, as three armies crashed into seventy-seven miles of Austrian lines from Monte Grappa on the southern edge of the Alps, right across to the Adriatic.

1/4th and 1/6th of the Gloucestershire Regiment were based with the 144th Brigade, alongside two battalions from the Worcestershire Regiment, in the 48th (South Midland) Division. At first, these troops were not even meant to take part in the battle. However, a trench raid by the neighbouring Ox and Bucks found the lines opposite them to be empty. Orders were soon received for the entire 48th Division to push forwards until it had contact with the enemy. 144th Brigade began their advance during the night but it was less than two miles before they stumbled across the enemy at Camporovere and had to dig in.

Things now began to unravel very swiftly for the Austrians. On the 27th October, the Italian Army broke through at Sacile, sixty miles east of the British division. The Austro-Hungarians were ordered into an immediate counter attack but they refused. This localised insurrection quickly turned into a full-blown mutiny and the Austro-Hungarian troops began a mass retreat. On the 31st October, Hungary officially withdrew from their half-century long union with Austria.

On the 1st November, intelligence reported that the Austrian retreat was along the entire line and the Glosters were ordered to join a general advance. Yet still the Austrians resisted and the breakthrough could not be achieved at Camporovere. Finally, when the neighbouring 145th Brigade penetrated the line, this stubborn defence relented and the 144th Brigade pushed on another three miles the next day.

Advancing another eight miles found the 48th Division at Osteria del Termine early on the 3rd November. This was on the Italian-Austrian border, meaning that these men were the first to set foot in western enemy territory (i.e. land that officially belonged to a Central Power) during the entirety of World War I. Later that day, 300,000 Austrians capitulated and, on the 4th November 1918, the Austrians officially surrendered. A week later, the armistice was signed and WWI officially came to an end.

Almost 40,000 men served in the Gloucestershire Regiment throughout WWI, with 8100 losing their lives and many thousands more being wounded. Seventy-two battle honours were won during the duration of the war however, only thirteen of these can be displayed on the colours.

# 48. West Europe 1940, 49. Escaut, 50. Cassel

The men of 2nd Battalion, the Gloucestershire Regiment, arrived in France 641 men strong on 2nd October 1939 during the period of the phoney war. This does not mean they did not see action though, as there would have been various aggressive patrols and raids as well as defending against the Germans who carried out similar work. As an example of the type of acts being undertaken, the second Military Cross of the entire war was awarded to a Gloucestershire Regiment officer. Lieutenant J.A. Mackenzie, along with two others, ambushed a night patrol of thirty Germans. Mackenzie and his tommy gun sent the much larger German forces scattering for the wind.

The probing and patrolling would all soon change though, as on 10th May 1940 the Germans launched their blitzkrieg invasion of Western Europe. The 2nd Battalion were ordered to move out from Landas in France and into Belgium on 14th May, arriving close to the historic battlefield of Waterloo on 16th May. The Allies had little or no response to these fresh German tactics and so 2nd Battalion almost immediately received the order to retreat back towards France.

By the following day, the Glosters were on their way to a town called Terlinden. Whilst en-route they were attacked by eighteen Stuka dive bombers but luckily no casualties were recorded. They arrived at their destination and looked forward to an evening of rest. Unfortunately though, just an hour and a half later the order to further retreat was given, with the battalion heading for the village of Cocquaine.

An early casualty of the retreat was 2nd Lieutenant Way, who was out on a night patrol when he was felled by a sniper. It was unlikely to be a German soldier this far advanced but fifth columnists were a constant issue for the retreating British Expeditionary Force. At 09:00, the battalion set off again. All towns on the march were completely deserted but heavy shelling was still experienced as they marched through Enghien.

By the evening of the 18th May, the battalion had arrived in the town of Ath and grabbed some sleep in nearby woods. The German Air Force and artillery were now far too frequent and deadly to be sleeping out in the open. Upon arrival in Ath, the Glosters were ordered to blow some nearby bridges over the Dendre Canal. Yet when they got there, the bridges were being staunchly held by some French troops so they left again. This incident highlights the chaos that was ensuing and general lack of a clear overall picture during the retreat.

'A' Company were given the job of holding the west bank of the Dendre Canal along with a nearby bridge. At 21:00, the order came through to blow the bridge, which this time they did achieve. At 04:40 some motor transport appeared and the battalion were loaded up, with the retreat continuing towards a town called Bruyelle and then towards Lesdain.

The retreat now began to run into difficulty, with heavy traffic caused particularly by retreating French horse artillery and soldiers on stolen bicycles. The next issue was that the Glosters narrowly avoided being stranded when they reached the bridge over to Tournai, thirty seconds before it was due to be blown. Matters were soon to become much worse though. Just on the other side of Tournai, the retreating convoy was attacked by Stukas. Reports of numbers vary wildly, with some accounts stating nine aircraft whilst others claim two hundred. Lieutenant Fane was one of the lucky ones who escape the aerial assault:

Low flying German bombing planes flew over and bombed and machine gunned the column. One bomb scored a direct hit on an artillery ammo carrying lorry which was jammed between the lorries containing men of A and C Coys. The explosion of the bomb and the ammunition and the machine gun fire from the planes caused casualties amounting to 94 killed, wounded and missing.

No matter how many aircraft attacked the column, the results were devastating. Seventy men were eventually confirmed killed. The battered and weakened Glosters then made their way to Escaut Canal later that evening.

On the 20th May at the Escaut Canal, it was decided the Glosters would make a stand. They protected a thousand yard stretch of the line. To their right were the 4th Ox & Bucks and to their left a battalion of French Moroccans. There were light German patrols at first and Battalion Headquarters experienced heavy shelling upon the chateau where they were situated.

Suddenly though, the German infantry came flooding across the canal to the battalions left where the Moroccans had been. 'A' Company, severely depleted after Tournai along with elements of the Ox and Bucks, had to push them back in a furious fight. A little later, the Moroccans reappeared. They had not retreated as first thought. In fact, they had not been on the line at all having strolled into town to do a little plundering!

Soon the fighting was intense; the gallant Glosters could not even lift their heads above the hastily erected defences due to heavy German machine gun fire. Fighting would be hard for several days, with the Germans even reaching Battalion Headquarters at one point, but they were soon thrown back across the canal. Eventually 'A' Company had to relieve 'D' Company, as they had borne the brunt of the German assaults and heavy shelling. The Glosters had gone nearly sixty hours under constant heavy artillery bombardment with little or no cover.

On the 23rd May, the order was again given to retreat. This time the destination was the Gort Line, a series of pillboxes and bunkers built by the British Expeditionary Force a year earlier. However, no sooner had the Glosters arrived, did the French take over. The following day the retreat continued and the battered and bruised battalion made their way up to a hilltop town called Cassel. The Glosters had experienced almost a hundred miles of retreat under constant attack from land and air with many casualties, yet their biggest battle was only just beginning.

The Germans now had the British Expeditionary Force trapped in a gradually decreasing pocket at Dunkirk. Their plan of attack was simple. The elite western divisions would need to capture the road from Cassel to Dunkirk and this would leave absolutely no access onto the beaches. The British Expeditionary Force would have to surrender or be destroyed. These elite Germans however, had not yet had a real taste of British vigour. The men of Gloucestershire had no intention of letting the Germans parade down the Dunkirk road.

Arriving at Mont Cassel on the 25th May, the overall picture was still unclear. However, it was obvious the Glosters would be making a stand here. Cassel is a

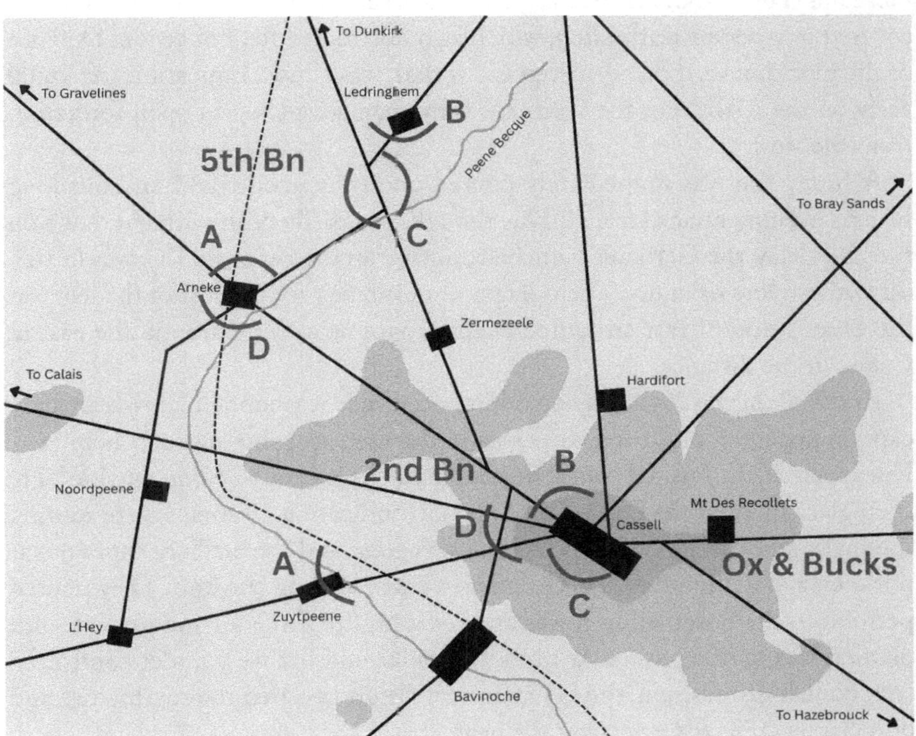

natural fortress, being the only high point (577ft) for many miles around. A plan was put in place to form a tight circular defence of the town. 'B' Company would hold the north west flank covering the main road to Calais. 'C' Company set up in the south east to neighbour the Ox and Bucks. 'D' Company overlooked the wooded area to the south west, whilst the badly mauled 'A' Company remained in reserve.

The evening of the 25th/26th May actually proved to be relatively quiet. At daybreak, a small patrol was sent out from Cassel with an 18-pounder anti-tank gun. They returned a few hours later without the useful weapon. They had destroyed two heavy German tanks in an ambush, but then took a direct hit from a third. So valuable were such weapons that another patrol was organised to retrieve the 18-pounder but it was indeed beyond repair.

A short digression is now required as we explore the heroic actions of a single platoon of 2nd Battalion. At 14:00 on the 26th May, a message came through from Brigade HQ for a blockhouse a few miles north of Cassel at the village of Hardifort, to be manned. The only choice was for 'A' Company, 8th platoon, to leave the reserve and carry out this order.

An earlier recce had shown the blockhouse had no doors, no proper slits and no observation potential. It was also full of refugees escaping the advancing Germans. The blockhouse was very much in a state of being constructed and still covered in wooden scaffolding, which also obstructed field of vision. Defence of the blockhouse, if one can even call it that, was almost impossible. At 18:00 early on the 27th May, the Germans were seen advancing in open formation from the west.

A heavy fire was immediately poured upon the enemy and an hour long furious evening attack ensued. This though, was easily dealt with. At dawn on the 28th May, the Germans launched another attack, yet again this was beaten off without loss or injury. The only point of interest for the rest of the day was the observation of vast armoured enemy columns moving around the east of Cassel in the distance.

At 09:00 on the 29th May an oddity occurred. A wounded British artillery captain appeared and tried to persuade the men to come out and help him. Unexpectedly in hushed tones, he then told them "not to come outside". He then glanced up at the bunker roof possibly indicating Germans were waiting there. As quick as he had appeared he was gone and the artillery captain was not seen again. However, the Germans were indeed on the roof. They poured petrol into the observation tower and set it on fire using a hand grenade. 8th platoon had to don gas masks until the smoke and fire were under control. In true British grit fashion, the Glosters actually appreciated the roaring fire and boiled a few pillaged eggs over the heat.

Towards the evening of the 29th and next morning, several German cars were fired upon whilst heading along the Dunkirk road. These were put out of action and the occupants killed. By the afternoon, a concerted attack developed with a fire being set to the west as a distraction and then an attack from the east. The Glosters withstood the initial assault, but then heavy and accurate automatic fire came pouring through every gun slit. The men persevered but heavier weapons were then brought into the assault. It was time to lay down arms after three days of fighting.

Back in the present (26th May), as if losing 8th platoon was not bad enough, the rest of 'A' Company were now ordered off on their own mission. Forces at Cassel now had no reserve. Running along the south east perimeter of Cassel was a train line. This was deemed, by Brigade HQ, as an excellent forward post at which to stop the Germans. Therefore, 'A' Company were marched off to Zuytpeene, whilst the reserve of the Ox & Bucks went to Bavinoche, further east along the railway line. Upon initial inspection, a handful of French were positioned in the west but the east of the village offered the best defensive opportunity with a thick railway embankment, three houses and a cross roads.

The morning of the 26th May saw the French approach Percy Hardman, Commanding Officer of 'A' Company, to discuss the best position for the anti-tank weapons at their disposal. The French suggested a far from desirable plan, which the Glosters declined, and so the allies parted ways. On his way out, the French officer mentioned that it did not really matter as they were only "armed" with dummy practise shells. All of this was elementary anyway, as very soon nine Stuka dive bombers swooped down on Zuytpeene and dropped twenty-seven bombs on the towns western end and the French fled. The French soil here would only be defended with British blood.

Less than an hour later (10:00), Zuytpeene was attacked by twenty tanks and in excess of a hundred infantry. Immediately following this, mortars and machine gun fire poured down upon their position. With the French abandonment, 'A' Company had been forced to tighten their perimeter, making any attempt to reach Battalion Headquarters fruitless.

Just an hour and a half into the German onslaught, word was received that the Ox & Bucks had been pushed out of Bavinoche. In a reflection on how poorly the situation across the board was understood, Brigade HQ gave the order for 'A' Company to advance down the railway line and smash into the German flank. In a bittersweet moment, 'A' Company were so cut off they luckily never received this suicidal order. By midday, 'A' Company were ordered back to Cassel but sadly this message did not reach them either.

The heavy German attack on Zuytpeene continued when the enemy began to penetrate along the railway embankment. Sergeant Gallagher moved his 7th platoon to the top of the exposed embankment. This was a very risky manoeuvre but his bold plan came off as the enemy retreated once again. Relentless shelling, mortaring and machine gun fire raked the remaining few men of 'A' Company for the rest of the day.

By 17:00, Sergeant Gallagher and what was left of 7th platoon, were the only ones at their post. The few other able-bodied men were entrenched in one of the houses tending to the many wounded. At 19:00 two privates arrived in Cassel, they had somehow fought their way through and reported themselves as the only survivors. However, they were wrong. Their comrades continued to fight late into the evening. 'A' Company had barricaded themselves in the house where the casualties were being treated, and were fighting room to room. Eventually, the few remaining survivors found themselves in the basement with hand grenades rolling through the windows and nearly eighty enemy infantry swarming through the rest of the house. It was time to lower their weapons.

Back on Mont Cassel itself, the night of the 26th/27th May also proved to be another quiet one for the defenders but this was soon to change at daybreak. Like at Zuytpeene, the attack began at 10:00, with the Glosters being heavily attacked by mortar, aircraft, armoured vehicles of all description, infantry and machine guns.

'C' and 'D' Companies certainly seemed to be the target for the initial phase of softening up. 'C' Company reported a barrage of mortar fire gradually creeping towards their position. The mortar barrage grew heavier and heavier, whilst a report of enemy armoured fighting vehicles massing in front of their position was also received.

'D' Company reported tanks rolling up the road towards Company HQ. These had come from the Bavinchove area, as by now, the Ox & Bucks there had been overrun. Enemy infantry were also seen coming out of the wooded area in their sector. The roadblocks were improved and artillery shelled enemy mortar positions that had been located. Unfortunately, these had been incredibly well positioned in the hillside and little damage could be brought upon the enemy.

By early afternoon, 'C' Company had destroyed four German tanks. Communications were near impossible though, as the Glosters were constantly pinned down by accurate sniper, machine gun and mortar fire. This meant that already the companies were fighting as individual units instead of as a unified fighting force.

'D' Company were not faring so well and a major turning point in the battle was taking place. A German Panzer rolled right into the middle of 'D' Company sector and broke down. The enemy could not be shifted and the tank promptly became its own mini fortress right in the heart of the Glosters. Throughout the afternoon every time they tried to outflank or destroy the tank, mortar fire dropped precisely upon 'D' Company and caused huge casualties. Fifth columnists actions, which had plagued the Glosters throughout the retreat, were once again at play.

Men of 'B' Company were brought in to dislodge the tank and eventually by 17:00, it had been destroyed. 'D' Company requested reinforcements but of course, there were none to be had. German infantry was then reported to have established themselves in cottages on the southern perimeter of 'D' Company position. A brisk bayonet charge was ordered and the Germans fled. This was the final significant action of the day and the Germans were reported to be pulling back on all fronts by 19:00.

That evening and then into the daytime of the 28th May, proved to be eerily quiet compared to the previous twenty-four hours. The Germans though, were not dormant and constructed a series of machine gun nests as close to the Glosters perimeter as they could, under the cover of darkness. Half rations also managed to reach the defenders of Cassel, although this would be the last delivery of the ordeal.

Sniper and artillery fire continued with great accuracy whilst aircraft intermittently attacked fortress Cassel but mostly did battle with the remaining few anti-air defences. The Germans began to intensely probe 'B' Company sector for the first time with tanks and infantry. These were easily driven off by anti-tank guns and machine gun fire. Meanwhile the central square of the town was reinforced and turned into a keep ahead of the final battle that was clearly coming.

Brigade Headquarters had a different view though. A message was sent telling 2nd Battalion to pull out and head towards Dunkirk. This message would not reach Cassel for another vital twenty-four hours. Much to the men's amusement, a rather desperate runner did arrive with news that the 1st French Motorised Division were on their way to relieve them. Plainly, they were not. Yet another highlight of how confused the overall picture remained.

The 29th May saw another quiet start except for sporadic aerial assault and light mortar fire. The previous day's rest had the Glosters back into some form of fighting shape. So the decision was made to start attacking heavy German traffic moving towards Dunkirk. Although they did not know the overall picture, from their lofty perch 2nd Battalion could see something big was happening in that direction. Huge plumes of smoke had now been hanging over the area for several days. A section of a T.A. Artillery Regiment took the remaining 18-pounders and opened fire on the Germans.

The next German attack began with heavy tanks and infantry rolling up the steep slopes of Cassel, but they were once again repelled by the Glosters of 'B' and 'D' Companies. 'B' Company, 10th Platoon held a few farm buildings that sat on the border of their sector and dominated the surrounding area. Unfortunately for them, they were the main target of the German aggression this day. A colossal heavy and accurate artillery bombardment smashed into the farm compound. The few survivors tried to fall back to safe ground but were cut off from the rest of 'B' Company by accurate machine gun fire.

At 17:45, the Brigade liaison officer finally arrived with the verbal order to withdraw. 'A' Company had been destroyed at Zuytpeene, 'B' Company suffered huge casualties at the farmhouse and 'D' Company never recovered from the tank that crept into their sector midway through the battle. This meant that 'C' Company made up the bulk of the fighting men left in 2nd Battalion. As such, they formed the rear guard for the initial escape. Orders were confused though, and order followed counter order. The Glosters decided to ignore all "advice" from Brigade from here on in and travelled roughly north east by compass.

The battle of Cassel had now officially come to an end and the desperate, yet ultimately fruitless push to be evacuated from the Dunkirk beaches had begun. The Glosters had 132 men killed, with 60 wounded and 475 captured to remain POW's for the duration of the war. A reformed 2nd Battalion would return to France in June 1944 to avenge their brethren at Cassel.

5th Battalion of the Gloucestershire Regiment arrived at Le Havre on the 16th January 1940. They immediately jumped on a train and travelled the thirty-five miles to Caudebec, a mining village that sits on the Seine. Here they spent two months training for the certain conflict with Nazi Germany. Their next destination was Saar where they took over a section of the Maginot Line.

On the evening of 3rd April, 'A' Company took out a strong patrol into German territory around the village of Grindorff. They soon encountered 150 Germans heading straight for Battalion Headquarters. A Bren gun was set up on high ground to defend the area but the gunner was quickly wounded and his weapon fell over a parapet. Without a second thought, Sergeant Adlam jumped over the parapet, picked up the weapon and began unloading into the enemy. They fled and Adlam became the first Territorial soldier of WWII to receive a Military Medal.

5th Battalion then moved three miles north to Douai and here on the night of 9th May, they were awakened by a disturbing noise. Vast numbers of aircraft flew overhead and the sound of distant bombing could be heard. The German Blitzkrieg into France and the Low Countries had begun. A few days later the entire battalion jumped into motor transports and headed, like comrades from 2nd Battalion, to the historic battlefield of Waterloo. En-route they were machine gunned by enemy planes but arrived unscathed on the 15th May.

The following day 5th Battalion were sent to relieve a French unit who were holding the line. However upon arrival, it was discovered that the French had already fled. As it was, the Glosters were ordered to turn around anyway but as they did so, they had their first sighting of German armour. A hard rear guard action had to be fought to allow them to disengage. The retreat of the British Expeditionary Force had begun, and 5th Battalion would cover thirty miles over the next twenty-four hours with no sleep and little food.

They reached the town of Wannebecq after marching a further twenty-five miles the following day, and were ordered to hold a series of canals whilst 1st and 2nd Division withdrew. When it came time for the Glosters to pull out they were once again harassed by German armour and only by breaking into smaller groups did they succeed in escaping. On the 19th May, 5th Battalion arrived at Buissenal with the promise of warm billets and some hot food. Yet upon arrival, it was reported that German tanks were still on their tail and so the retreat continued.

At Escaut Canal, the Glosters were once again ordered to hold the line whilst others pulled back. With 2nd Warwickshire's on their right and 8th Worcester's on their left, the defensive lines were constructed. At 11:00 on the 20th mortaring began, followed by heavy rifle fire from across the canal. The Germans were specifically targeting 'D' Company on the left flank, and by days end fifty men lay dead or wounded. The next day the fighting continued and the line was so overstretched that repeated incursions occurred on both flanks. These were beaten back and on the 22nd May, the Glosters were relieved. They had suffered 158 casualties at Escaut Canal.

Two days later, a rumour began to fly around that 5th Battalion were heading for Dunkirk and indeed, they were. On the 25th May, they reached the beaches and could see things were being organised to save the BEF. Surprisingly though, the next day they were ordered to march back into France and hold the villages of Arneke and Ledringhem for twenty-four hours. This was just north-west of 2nd Battalion who were making their stand at Cassel.

Upon arrival at the given destination on the 27th May, 'B' Company occupied Ledringhem whilst 'A' and 'D' Company pushed on to Arneke just down the road. 'C' Company held the road between the two villages. Three 25mm anti-tank guns, along with two 2-pounders, were moved up to Arneke to provide support against the expected armoured attack. Engineers also arrived to fit roadblocks of iron rails to the main thoroughfares. That morning the Glosters also had their first glimpse of the enemy as huge convoys of armour and infantry were spotted heading northeast.

A spotter aircraft now began to circle over the Glosters and its position was followed by a direct mortar barrage. At 18:00, the barrage became more general and started dropping all over the village. Tanks and infantry now attacked Arneke from the north and the east. The assault was intense, with one tank even reaching the front door of 'A' Company Headquarters before being destroyed. The Glosters though, were well prepared for the fight and the Germans had to withdraw. One of the 2-pounders alone accounted for five tanks, four armoured cars and masses of infantry.

A carrier section, which had transported 5th Battalion to Ledringhem, was now sent forward under Sergeant Brown. These men managed to ambush several parties of Germans and stunted any attack. For this bravery, Sergeant Brown was awarded the Military Medal. The rest of the battalion transport had been well camouflaged and hidden in an orchard. Surprisingly though, it was one of the Germans first targets and was completely destroyed. This was probably located through fifth columnist action that had blighted both battalions on their retreat from Waterloo.

Despite this early victory, it was clear that the Glosters faced overwhelming numbers and a big difference in quality of weaponry. As such, it was decided to pull 'A' and 'D' Companies out of Arneke and back towards Ledringhem. At this point, a message also arrived stating that Ledringhem would have to be held for a further twenty-four hours and so pulling out of Arneke became a necessity.

At 04:00 on the 28th May, the German infantry were spotted massing in the distance for another attack. In cooperation with artillery in the rear, the assembly area was bombarded and the Germans suffered huge numbers of casualties. In the afternoon, it was decided to form a circular defence of Ledringhem as it was suspected that the Glosters were surrounded. This soon became clear when a German truck full of machine gun belts accidentally ran the roadblock in 5th Battalions rear. The truck was captured and the driver shot whilst attempting to flee.

At dusk, another messenger arrived telling the battalion to pull out after dark. The Glosters though, realised the importance of their mission and chose to ignore these orders. They had decided to stand and fight a few more hours to give the flotilla at Dunkirk more time to get men off the beaches. The Germans, now also realising the battle was at a critical stage, ramped up their attack. Short infantry attacks on both flanks were interchanged with heavy mortar and machine gun fire pouring upon Ledringhem. Despite determined resistance, the Germans began to establish themselves in houses in the village outskirts.

What occurred next was arguably one of the most fearsome, iconic and brave moments in regimental history. Realising the tide of battle was turning against them, the Glosters assembled in the village churchyard. Here they attached bayonets, turned towards their foe and began charging down the main street of the village under heavy fire. This terrifying sight of bloodthirsty warriors tearing through the fog of war was enough for the Germans, and they abandoned their positions and fled for their lives. The scene, painted below by Captain Hauting, was repeated several times and each time, the enemy ran in fear.

> The orders [to pull back] were consequently cancelled and all of our efforts concentrated on keeping the enemy out of the village. His method appeared to be a short and intense mortar bombardment alternating with an infantry attack accompanied by as many noise producing fireworks as possible.
>
> Each time the enemy appeared to be establishing himself at one end of the village a counter attack up the main village street drove him out at the point of bayonet and was successful on every occasion.

Despite this heroic resistance, it was now clear the Glosters could barely hold on much longer. All carriers and anti-tank weapons had been destroyed and the Germans had them surrounded. The enemy continued to hit the village with mortar and machine gun. Once this died down, German infantry flooded the village armed with stick grenades and flamethrowers (luckily the latter failed to ever ignite). Again and again, the Germans came and each time they were somehow held back.

At midnight, it was decided the Glosters could hold on no longer. The remaining men assembled in an orchard at the east of the village and prepared to withdraw. In single file, they crept through hedgerows and then followed a stream northwards. After the stream dissipated, they headed north by compass but came right up on German batteries aiming at Dunkirk. Luckily for 5th Battalion, every one of the enemy were asleep and this is how they were left.

The next obstacle to be reached was the village of Rietveld and it was heavily held by German infantry. Incredibly though, once again, the enemy were caught literally napping and 5th Battalion continued to push north. Reaching the village of Bambecque, they saw shadows in the distance. These figures turned out to be men of the 8th Worcester's. Further to the delight of the Glosters, these brethren also had ample motor transport.

On the 30th May, this convoy to safety passed along roads so heavily congested they could barely make progress. Abandoned vehicles, heavy guns and horses added to the carnage. At 04:30 though, they reached Bray Sands on the coast. The men of 5th Battalion got into the waiting rowing boats and made their way to the destroyer waiting half a mile off shore. So ended 5th Battalions campaign but they would return to haunt the Germans as the 143rd Reconnaissance Regiment in June 1944 (See Battle Honour 56).

# 51. Burma 1942, 52. Taukkyan, 53. Paungde

When war was declared with Japan on 7th December 1941, the only men available for defence in Burma were 1st Battalion of the Gloucestershire Regiment. They were based at the airfield of Mingalodon, which was twelve miles south of Burma's capital, Rangoon. The battalion were well below strength and ill equipped for war. Forty men alone were listed as permanently unfit for duty. Despite this, they had to jump into action and prepare for the forthcoming Japanese invasion.

The battalion quickly found itself dispersed over a large expanse, as the list of areas they had to protect was vast. Firstly, they had to carry on defending the airfield at Mingalodon. The coast had to be watched for any seaborne invasion and the important oil refineries at Syriam had to be guarded. The Christmas period was spent under attack from the Japanese air force. On the 23rd December, fifty bombers smashed Mingalodon airfield and all the native workers fled. This meant the Glosters now had the additional task of keeping the airfield operational. Two days later, a hundred bombers unleashed their deadly payload on the airfield and Rangoon.

During the opening months of 1942, the Glosters had yet another duty. Vast amounts of men, munitions and supplies were flooding into the country through the docks. The Glosters were the only men available to help offload the ships. This in addition to the tasks already listed above. A further thirty-seven times the Japanese bombed Mingalodon airfield during January and February, each time 1st Battalion were on hand to repair the runway.

By now, the Japanese had penetrated deep into the country, and so on the 2nd February, the regimental silver was sent to Maymyo for safekeeping. Ten days later, it became clear that the enemy were making straight for Rangoon. Here, the Glosters were also tasked with putting up and operating roadblocks leading to the capital. By the end of February, holding Mingalodon airfield had become untenable and it was abandoned. However, much useful weaponry such as anti-tank rifles and mortars were salvaged.

By the beginning of March, the battalion had become fully motorised. Through rescue, borrowing and stealing they had obtained 115 vehicles from lorries to scout cars. Many of the weapons salvaged from Mingalodon were mounted onto these vehicles, and several days were spent testing and training on these innovations.

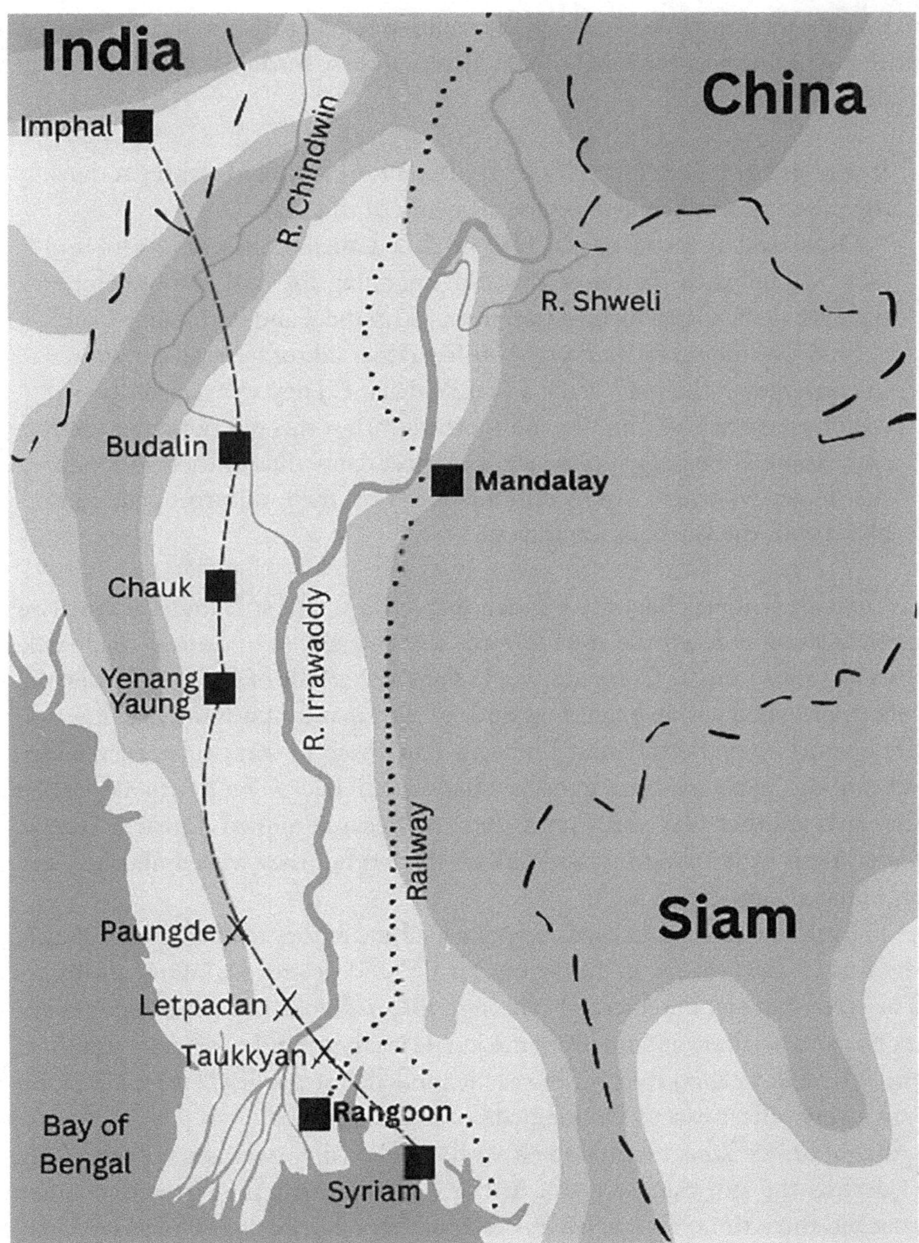


On the 7th March, the battalion, now pretty much reunited, were ordered to the village of **Taukkyan** twenty-four miles from Rangoon. The Japanese were known to be in the area and upon arrival, the Glosters were sent to investigate reports of an enemy roadblock. The roadblock was keeping the quickly, and recently, formed British Burma Army from escaping. The operation was supposed to be supported by tanks; however, they refused to budge due to recent Japanese tactics of hiding anti-tank guns on the flanks of these roadblocks. Staff Sergeant Hale sets the scene:

> It was left to Col Bagot [CO of 1st Battalion] and his Infantry to have the proud position of getting the army out of this trap…
>
> On arrival at his [Bagot's] HQ he called all the officers to him and said "to Hell with the tanks, the 28th are going forward and remember the 28th does not know how to retreat, go up there and don't come back".
>
> So B Coy moved forward in the bush at either side of the road and started to converge on the road block a ½ mile distant. They were instantly met with heavy machine gun fire and mortar fire, but this did not deter them and casualties became very heavy. The most dangerous of their foes were the snipers who were strapped in the trees with their uniforms painted to blend with the surrounding leaves.

Lieutenant Colonel Bagot, Commanding Officer of 1st Battalion, sent two carriers straight down the road towards the now sighted Japanese roadblock. Two platoons from 'B' Company would flank either side of the road. When the infantry reached within a hundred yards of the Japanese position, machine gun fire opened up on both flanks. The right flank tried to manoeuvre even wider, yet ran into more machine guns and had to pull back. The left flank pushed forwards another fifty yards until they too became pinned down. A reserve platoon was sent forward to outflank on the left but they were ambushed and annihilated almost to a man.

The carriers meanwhile, sped down the road and as they reached the roadblock, the first carrier was hit by heavy mortar fire and destroyed, killing all inside. The second carrier burst straight through the roadblock but came under heavy mortar and machine gun fire from the jungle just beyond the Japanese frontline. An anti-tank weapon then hit the carrier and all but the driver were killed. By now, every officer except for one had become casualties.

Bagot ordered the infantry on either flank to push forwards and particularly to destroy the anti-tank weapon. At this exact moment, the Japanese counter attacked three times and on each occasion, only a liberal use of hand grenades saved the day. Finally, a surprise Japanese attack from the east forced the Glosters back. Heavy sniper fire then struck up all over the battlefield and the Glosters had to pull back right onto the road to stay out of range.

It was now clear that this was no mere roadblock and that in excess of five hundred Japanese held the position. Clearing the road remained absolutely vital, so Bagot now threw in the rest of his battalion. 'C' Company, who had just arrived, were pushed up the left flank to try to make contact with any survivors. An intelligence gathering patrol was sent out, made up of members of the sanitary squad, pioneer and intelligence teams. These men were ambushed by a machine gun in a tree and suffered heavy casualties, yet they managed to return with vital information on enemy positions.

Bagot then brought his eight mortars up and as soon as the men on the right flank had withdrawn, the area was flattened. So intense was the mortar attack that the jungle actually caught alight and a huge fire blazed. The right flank was now attacked once again, supported by another two carriers. These men managed to push all the way through the Japanese position and out to the other side of the jungle. As they emerged from the dense jungle, an awesome attack was launched upon them and they quickly found themselves back at their starting positions.

The Japanese now brought up their mortars and the fire caused several casualties. 'A' and 'D' Companies were now pushed down the left flank and they managed to establish a defensive line, which they held until nightfall. The fighting died down but several Japanese patrols had to be beaten back during the night. As dawn approached, it quickly became clear that the Japanese had fallen back and the Battle of Taukkyan was over. The Glosters had suffered sixteen men killed, twenty-eight wounded and a further three were missing.

With the road now clear, the Glosters travelled a little further to reconnoitre and then allowed the Burma Army columns to march through their lines. An exhausting fifteen-mile night march was then ordered, as the retreat from Burma began in earnest. 1st Battalion were given the honour of becoming the Divisional Reconnaissance Regiment. This meant that they would permanently be in the rear-guard of the retreating forces trying to hold back the Japanese hoards. Bagot took this position to heart and molested the Japanese at every possible moment. At one point, he even had to be called and told that he was doing a fantastic job, but to be careful. The Glosters were operating so far from the main column they were almost functioning as an independent unit.

On the 14th March, the Glosters headed to the village of Letpadan to cover various brigades who were pulling out of the area. Bagot realised that he had a two-day march on the enemy and saw his opportunity to set a trap. The first item on the agenda was dealing with the natives. The Burmese locals had little love for the British and made no effort to hide their delight at the Japanese approach. Bagot imposed a curfew on the villagers so his devious plans could not be exposed.

Three days later, the Japanese finally began to arrive at Letpadan. This was now earlier than expected and the ambush looked set to fail. Luckily, 'D' Company Commanding Officer, Captain Johnson, was the first to receive the news and without awaiting orders, he decided immediately to spring the trap. He sent a platoon in motorised transports straight into the heart of the village and they opened up on the enemy. Meanwhile, the rest of 'D' Company swung around to the east and west of the village, whilst mortars set up to cover the western approaches.

At 07:30, the eastern flankers rode straight into two Japanese patrols. The Glosters attached bayonets and chased the enemy into the jungle. Unfortunately, they went too far and nine men were never seen again. The attack on the western flank was much more successful though. No enemy patrols were encountered and they moved straight into the village. Most of the Japanese were assembling in the schoolhouse and they were mown down with Thompson submachine guns. The entire Japanese force now began to panic and fled the village.

The retreating enemy were chased by men in carriers and few escaped. Contact with the enemy was then broken off at 18:00 and the Glosters vanished into the jungle. Apart from the nine men who were missing, only one man was wounded. Within a few days, the victory of Letpadan had become global news. The Japanese tiger had received its first real wound and was, perhaps, not so indestructible as first thought. The famed warriors of Gloucestershire would soon appear all over the Western World on "Smash Japanese Aggression!" propaganda posters.

The 21st March is of course Back Badge Day (See Battle Honour 8), when the Glosters celebrate the Battle of Alexandria. Bagot was desperate to mark the occasion and they sped towards reports of fifty Japanese slightly ahead of their advancing armies. The entire battalion were dismayed when they arrived to find they had missed the opportunity by only a matter of minutes. Four days later, it was reported that a police checkpoint had been wiped out by over two hundred Japanese, so the Glosters made their way to the village of **Paungde**.

Upon arrival, 'D' Company set up a defensive perimeter two hundred yards to the north of Paungde, whilst Company Headquarters held the main road leading into town. Despite wide ranging patrols having no contact with the enemy, Bagot was uneasy when he dropped off to sleep in the early hours of 27th March, feeling not all was right. Within an hour he was justified, as Bagot was awakened to be informed that the Japanese were advancing in great strength from the west.

Bagot was confident though, as he believed that after months of fighting the same enemy he had identified their key weakness. An inability to react quickly to sudden troop movements. With this in mind, he immediately threw the battalion into action and Bagot himself advanced to the outposts with the mortar platoon. At 08:00, a car was seen speeding towards the Glosters position. Once it was identified as flying a Japanese flag, three machines guns instantly disabled it.

Covered by mortars and machine guns, 'A' and 'B' Companies then advanced into the village. The fighting soon became intense and 1st Battalion were fighting house to house. The Glosters had a distinct advantage though with their liberal use of grenades and Molotov cocktails. Japanese light aircraft then appeared in the skies above and started dropping anti-personnel bombs. Corporal Candle fired his Bren gun skywards and that was the last of Japanese air cover. Attacking the village was merely to allow Bagot to determine the size of the force against them. Able to predict that they faced two battalions in Paungde and a further three thousand men arriving from the east, Bagot withdrew his men to a more defensive position.

The entire battalion now withdrew a further five miles to a railway crossing, due to being hugely outnumbered. The much promised tank support never arrived but they held the line nonetheless. Throughout the night, the Glosters were heavily attacked, yet once again, managed to withdraw and the retreat continued.

The 2nd April found 1st Battalion patrolling a wooded area. A sudden heavy artillery attack caused three deaths along with another five wounded. Three days later a heavy air raid caused five further casualties. The Glosters were then directed to Yenang Yaung and Chauk to cover the oilfields whilst they were demolished. On the 13th April, many men of the battalion were engaged with driving oil trucks north to keep supplies out of Japanese hands. The Glosters had relieved Kings Own Yorkshire Light Infantry Regiment and begrudgingly, had to hand over all their machine guns and mortars to this under equipped unit.

On the 15th April, with the oilfield demolition complete, the men of Gloucestershire were back on the retreat. They came upon an allied Chinese roadblock but only at the last moment did they realise their mistake. They were actually Japanese dressed in Chinese uniforms and the leading platoon were badly shot up. Bagot sent out two patrols but these too were heavily attacked by the Japanese. Only one man managed to return from one of the patrols. Frustratingly, clearing the roadblock needed mortars and machine guns. The Glosters had of course been ordered to give all theirs away a few days earlier.

Eventually bypassing the Japanese roadblock, yet another was encountered and the Glosters had no choice but to fight their way through. The lack of mortars and machine guns was now having deadly consequences, as nine men were missing, one killed and four wounded on this day. The battalion finally reached Mandalay on the 23rd April, with a strength of just seven officers and 170 other ranks. The men were much cheered when Bagot, who had previously been wounded at Paungde, arrived with a reinforcement of a hundred men from India. On the 26th April, the regimental silver was buried in a jungle graveyard to prevent it from falling into enemy hands. Sadly, this would never be recovered.

On the 1st May, the battalion were clearing air raid wreckage on the banks of the River Monywa. The Japanese snuck up the river and began their attack, preceded by heavy mortaring and artillery fire. This was one of the most critical points in the entire retreat. The Burma Army was yet to reach this juncture and if the Japanese took it, the retreat to India would be near impossible. An assortment of units who were in the area, were collected up and became 'Bagot Force'. They headed to Budalin, where they hoped they could stifle the Japanese advance.

Enemy tanks appeared on the battlefield for the first time on the 3rd May. They destroyed two Allied tanks just before nightfall. The Glosters positioned themselves in a small area of jungle just south of the village of Budalin. Beyond this point, the Japanese would have to cross a single bridge to make their attack. The Glosters erected a large tank obstacle so no assault could be made with ease.

At 04:30 on the 4th May, the Japanese attacked with three more tanks, a small infantry force and some mortars. The Glosters held their fire until the last possible moment. The enemy never actually arrived at the firing line, possibly getting lost in the dark. Three hours later, Bagot Force was ordered to fall back as the main units of the Burma Army had now bypassed their position. Disaster had been averted.

On the 10th May, the Glosters crossed the River Chindwin and then five days later they arrived at Imphal, India. The final slog through jungles and across mountains must have been a torturous experience. Lieutenant Cumming was in the rear guard and one of the last British soldiers to cross into India:

The serious climbing began, and, believe me, it took everything one had. You can get some idea of the amount of effort which we put in when I tell you that 60 odd British troops marched mile upon mile without uttering a word. At halts an occasional jest came out and faces lightened, but once on the move faces set grim and determined- a fight against time. Can we make it before the monsoon? Sometimes we went uphill on hands and knees, or rather hands and toes, digging into cracks in rocks. Up, up, up, only to come down and start all over again. By Sunday, 17th, we had done only 182 miles. It was terribly cold at night at those high altitudes…

Sometimes no water for 24 hours. Up, up; well, we must get there some time, and just think what we would do when we got to Calcutta. We kept ourselves alive and the will to live alive in us with thoughts of England, home, food. It was a battle of wills. Along the paths we saw many poor corpses, death from exhaustion, mostly natives, but not all. In the morning of the 18th was our great performance. We climbed up 3,000 ft. of altitude in under two miles. It was just tooth and nail. Water very scarce, a trickle out of a rock, and still another mountain in front of us to climb. On the 19th the rains started. Thank God they did not start the day before. That day we marched on and on. We did not dare stop for long for fear of pneumonia, as we were soaked through. We did 24 miles, slipping, climbing, the prospect before us a damp night's sleep with damp wood to make fires with.

The next few months were spent resting and refitting whilst being on constant guard for the, much anticipated, Japanese invasion of India. As it happened, the already vastly overstretched Japanese had little intention of attacking India and the battalion would spent the rest of the war fairly inactive.

The men of 2nd Battalion the Gloucestershire Regiment went ashore on the second wave of D-Day, 6th June 1944. They were expecting heavy resistance from the Germans that held Gold beaches around the town of Le Hamel. Much to 2nd Battalions surprise though, when the ramps dropped on their landing craft the scene was rather calm. The first wave had failed to secure the beachhead at Le Hamel and so, unknown to them, the Glosters had been directed two miles further east to the beach at Hable de Heurtot. The only Germans here were POW's who had already been captured by the advanced parties. Lieutenant Colonel Biddle had the honour of commanding 2nd Battalion on D-Day:

As we moved in we began to see evidence of the fighting for the beaches. There were some wrecked landing craft, drowned vehicles, the odd disabled tank, floating pieces of equipment, but not on the scale I think most of us had expected. Inland there were traces of more recent action, shattered houses and columns of smoke. What shocked us the most was the general appearance of the countryside – it bore no resemblance to the Le Hamel area we had studied so carefully. However, it did not take long to discover that the beach we were making our way for was some way to the east of Le Hamel and we soon had the reason. Le Hamel was still occupied by a

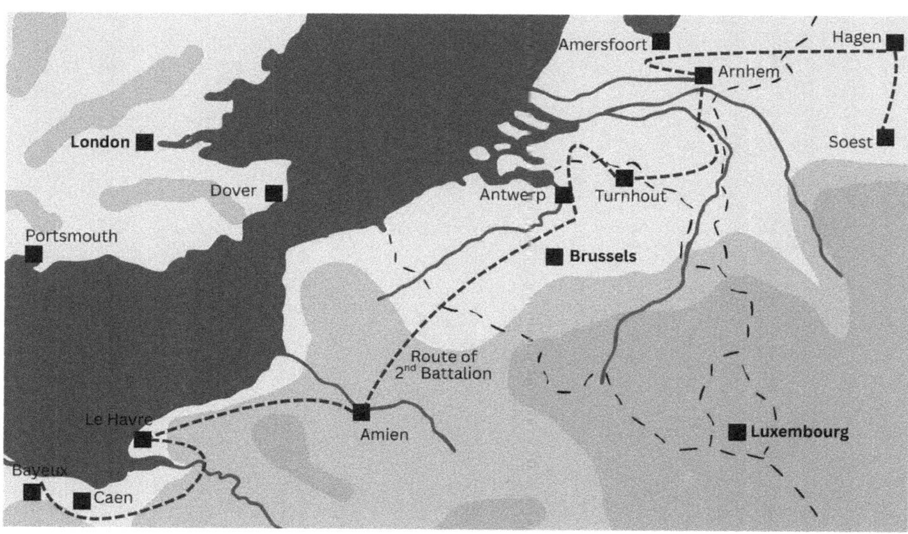

party of Boche who could not be dislodged and our L.C.I.s had been re-rerouted to come in at Hable de Heurtot, about two miles east of Le Hamel.

The Glosters landed alongside the men of the South Wales Borderers and the Essex Regiment. Together they marched in land through the clearly marked minefields and barbed wire. Their target was the village of Buhot but it was not long until the advancing troops were fired upon by the feared 88mm. This weapon was originally developed as an anti-aircraft gun but the Germans soon realised that its awesome power could rip through almost any armoured vehicle and sow chaos amongst massed infantry. Eventually the 88mm was knocked out by a Sherman tank but not before 2nd Battalion had suffered their first two casualties of D-Day, Sergeant Price and Private Cresswell of 'B' Company.

The men finally reached Buhot at 15:30, and their next objective was to reach high ground southwest of the town of Bayeux. The delay with the 88mm had cost them much daylight, so it was decided to dig in for the night at the nearby village of Magny. Throughout the journey, they were constantly hassled by German snipers, which would very much become a feature of the near future for the Glosters. The overall situation was still unclear and so extensive night patrolling had to be undertaken. Sporadic fighting, Germans fleeing and the capture of POW's (thirty-one in all) kept the men busy this first night.

As dawn rose over the village of Magny, the Glosters suddenly found themselves under heavy sniper fire. It soon became clear that three Germans had secreted themselves in the church tower that evening and now opened fire. Various methods were used to fire at the tower but no weapon had the available angle. The Glosters made the decision to merely leave them where they were. So at 08:30 they headed for the town of Bayeux, arriving at midday. Here they were mobbed by hundreds of happy and drunken civilians, overjoyed that Nazi occupation was finally over.

The time for revelling was short as reports of German armour massing to the south were reported and once again, the Glosters made for high ground. The tanks never materialised but 2nd Battalion were ambushed by a party of ten Germans. As soon as the Glosters warmed up their Bren gun's, the white flag came out and the war was over for this plucky bunch. The next several days were spent billeted back in Bayeux, with heavy patrolling and frequent contact with snipers the flavour of the times.

On the 9th June, 2nd Battalion moved out and linked up with 7th Armoured Division, the famous Desert Rats. They headed towards the town of Jerusalem but as usual the only contact en-route came from snipers trying their luck. Upon reaching their destination at 19:00, the Glosters immediately cleared the surrounding woodland coming up against light opposition. That night a patrol from 'B' Company managed to capture a German tank after they caught the occupants outside having a rest.

On the 11th June, the Glosters cleared the town of Buceels, again only experiencing light opposition. They could be forgiven for starting to think that the invasion of Europe was not so daunting a task as they had imagined. However, reality would soon hit home at the village of Tilly. Reconnaissance told the men that the village was lightly defended but they still proceeded with caution.

'D' Company took the lead and went down the left flank, experiencing no opposition or even signs of enemy activity. 'A' Company pushed down the right side of the village and as they approached the picturesque French orchards, heavy machine gun and rifle fire opened up on them. 'B' and 'C' Company then pushed into the village itself and laid down a base of covering fire. This allowed 'A' Company to join them but as they moved in a German tank suddenly opened fire from a hidden position. This was quickly followed by more machine guns and then mortar fire. Lance Corporal Rhodes helped to even the odds somewhat, when he leapt out of cover with a PIAT (portable anti-tank gun) and knocked out a German armoured vehicle. For this act, he was later awarded a Military Medal.

The fighting now flared up all over the village and the Glosters found themselves embroiled in their first heavy combat of the liberation. From the evidence of enemy casualties, it was clear that they were engaged against the elite SS Panzer Lehr Division. Finally though, the men were joyful to hear the sounds of tanks rumbling into action. The Desert Rats had arrived to win the day. Alas not. Trundling around the corner came a Panzer Mark IV with a whole section of infantry accompanying it. The tank pounded the Glosters and they had no choice but to readjust their lines. After nearly five hours of combat, night began to fall. It was decided that 2nd Battalions position was untenable in the dark and so they pulled back. Despite being under heavy fire, they managed to retreat a thousand yards north and here they dug in for the night. For them the battle for Tilly was over.

On the 14th June, 2nd Battalion were ordered to head towards the village of Lingevres, where the Durham Light Infantry had been heavily attacked. 'B' Company took the lead and headed off on the bicycles they had been given. They arrived at Lingevres just in time to find a small party of Durham's surrounded by fifty Germans, demanding their surrender. The Glosters immediately opened fire, the Germans fled and the Durham's lived to fight another day. The rest of the battalion then arrived and they moved into the village completely unopposed, despite the signs everywhere of the heavy fighting that had only just taken place.

At 14:00, the Glosters moved off again towards the village of Ellon three and a half miles away. The Desert Rats had accidentally crushed 'B' Companies bicycles upon arrival at Lingevres and so they begrudgingly joined their comrades on foot. An order was then received to return to the town of Bayeux, where the men would be rewarded with several days' relaxation. The majority of them did not actually enjoy it though, as every drunken soldier in Normandy also seemed to be on leave there.

On the 28th June, word came through that 2nd Battalion would move out to Parfouru l'Eclin. Here they remained for two weeks aggressively patrolling the area and experiencing heavy shelling and mortaring. The Glosters eventually moved off to conduct more patrolling elsewhere until, on the 29th July, they found themselves preparing to attack St. Germain d'Ectot.

Whilst forming up at 05:00 the battalion were bombed from the air. 'C' Company took many casualties but still the attack preceded. 'D' Company formed the assault lead but upon setting off at 06:00, immediately found themselves embroiled in a minefield. Heavy rifle fire soon started up so the rest of the battalion had to advance to provide assistance. After slowly edging forward throughout the day, the Glosters finally penetrated orchards on the right flank with the assistance of Sherman tanks. This was the primary target of the assault and so the fighting died down but at a cost of twenty killed and a further forty-five wounded. This ended the Glosters experience in the Bocage region and they moved to Buceels for a rest.

On the 9th August, 2nd Battalion established a bridgehead over the River Orne. This was important as it saw the Glosters crossing a potentially big obstacle on the extreme left flank of the Allied advance. They pushed onwards towards Courmeron, which they reached at midnight. The village was cleared of light opposition. The next day at 06:50, the Germans unleashed a heavy shelling upon the village. One of the casualties was Lieutenant Colonel Biddle, Commanding Officer of the Battalion. The men took this as a huge loss, for they saw him as personally responsible for turning them from the green recruits of the 6th June, into the deadly fighting force they now were.

The 11th August found the Glosters at the village of Espins but a heavy German counter attack saw them pulling back. On the following day, 2nd Battalion approached the key town of Thury-Harcourt. This had several main roads, including those to **Falaise** and Caen, running right through it. The town was something of a natural fortress as it sat on top of a hill. The Orne protected its east flank, whilst other higher hills surrounded the area and the approaches were thickly wooded. The plan of attack was a simple one though. 'B' Company down the right flank and 'A' Company down the left in a pincer move. 'D' and 'C' Companies would follow up with a squadron of tanks from 34th Armoured Brigade.

The plan started smoothly enough until 'A' Company became pinned down by small arms fire. Finding the undergrowth impenetrable, they had to fight in the open, which only increased casualties. 'B' Company on the other flank took their first objective, they then became caught by heavy machine gun fire whilst approaching another of the Orne bridges. Two large buildings, a mill and then a chateau, had to be cleared of the enemy with some hand-to-hand combat.

Suddenly all hell broke loose, the fearsome 88mm along with some mortar batteries opened fire from the surrounding hills. The tanks of 34th Armoured could not come to assist as they were still at their start positions, hampered by the thick terrain. Artillery was desperately needed yet on request, the Glosters were told it was being used on more important areas. Ammunition began to run low and it was realised the area would not be taken on this day. 2nd Battalion pulled out at 19:00, leaving the village in flames. Forty-eight men had been either killed or badly wounded in the days fighting. Captain Nash describes the fury of the fighting at Thury:

Thury- Harcourt, for sheer noise and stonking, was one of the worst battles we had through- out the campaign, and that "A," "B" and "D" Companies got as far as they did in this death-trap says a great deal for the leadership of all commanders and for the grit and determination of the men. After the battle the squadron commander of the 34th Armoured Brigade summed up the efforts of the 61st by saying that never before had he seen men fight with such bravery and determination against such fearful odds.

We were all very depressed after this battle, and our morale was not improved by hearing on the B.B.C. an eye-witness account of how our troops captured Thury- Harcourt. That really was the last straw.

The next day, a strong patrol moved into the Thury-Harcourt but they found it abandoned. This ended the Glosters involvement in the Allied advance for a period of time. They rested and experienced some light, sporadic combat. Major Butterworth also arrived to take over the battalion as Commanding Officer.

The River Risle was the next destination for the Glosters and they headed off early on the 25th August. Very soon though, they came under heavy fire from the village of Epaignes. 'D' Company advanced but they were pinned down by machine guns, artillery and mortar. They slowly edged closer to the enemy, drawing within enough distance to exchange hand grenades. At 13:00, 'A' Company flanked the village and found a path to the rear with no opposition. Soon they too were engaged and what was supposed to be a day of marching developed into a serious battle.

At 17:00, Butterworth threw in the rest of his battalion along with a few tanks that had arrived on the scene. By 19:30, the Germans had surrendered but this interruption on the day's activities had cost the Glosters twelve killed and forty-one wounded. Later that evening, forty-eight German bodies were counted littering the area. The next morning Major Arengo-Jones, who would become something of a character in Glosters history, arrived to become Butterworth's second in command.

The 29th and 30th of August were spent clearing the forest of Foret de Brotonne. Hidden away they found huge quantities of abandoned German equipment. Clearly, the forest had been used as something of a supply dump, hidden from the RAF. 2nd Battalion now found themselves moving on the all-important port of Le Havre. The Allies needed the facilities to be captured so that this could become a major resupply centre for their armies.

Heavy bombers began softening up the ports defences on the 9th September. The next day, the attack began with the Glosters playing a central role throughout. The plan saw 'D' Company lead the way, with their objective being a ridge in the German position. 'A' Company would then flank left with 'D' Company heading right, both supported by two troops of tanks each. 'C' Company would then pass through them all and capture the final objective.

The attack was a total success. A mortar attack at the opening of hostilities landed on 'A' Company, which caused the majority of casualties. Importantly though, the Germans had been so scared of the Lancaster bombers circling overhead, that they were all hidden underground. When they poked their heads out of their shelters, entire groups were mopped up. On the 11th September, the entire battalion mounted up on Churchill tanks and rode into the centre of Le Havre. Here they encountered the main fortress and had to cease fighting for the night.

On the 13th September, 'D' Company once again mounted their Churchill's and entered the fort, prepared for a harsh fight. What awaited them was even more shocking. Hundreds of Germans were lined up in the courtyard, luggage and all, ready to be carted off into captivity. So much for Hitler's order to hold Le Havre to the last man. A well-stocked cellar was liberated that night and the battalion celebrated well. Casualties for the Glosters at Le Havre were just three killed and fifty wounded. The battalion then swept along the coast mopping up more POW's. By the time they had finished, sixty-seven officers and 1760 other ranks had surrendered to them.

On the 22nd September, the Glosters set off for Belgium to join the rapidly advancing front line there. Here they spent the next few weeks putting down light German resistance and forcing a path across various canals in the region. During this time, they faced elements of the Hermann Goring Division who exposed the Gloucestershire Regiment to heavy shelling and a continuous mortar attack. From the 23rd to 26th of October, the Glosters attacked the urban areas of Esschen and then Nispen. Again, the mortaring and artillery was very heavy but actual resistance on the ground was light. Casualties during this period were at a minimum.

The 2nd Battalion were the first to experience a new German tactic, flooding. They attacked Stampersgat on the 31st October but found all the ground before them unexpectedly impassable. That night loud explosions alluded to the fact that the Germans were blowing up dykes and dams all over Holland. On the 2nd November, the Glosters were ordered again to attack Stampersgat. Just before setting off, a German shell landed right in the heart of Battalion Headquarters killing Commanding Officer, Major Buttersworth.

Despite the loss, the attack went ahead with 'A' Company silently rushing the advanced posts before they could get a shot off. 'B' Company then passed through and advanced into the west of the village. 'C' Company had the task of clearing one of the largest sugar factories in Europe. The various buildings made the task confusing in darkness. At daylight Lieutenant Cough and twelve men, found themselves surrounded and were taken prisoner. They were discovered five days later, locked in an underground shelter by the river Maas and re-joined the battalion.

Early in the new year of 1945, the battalion were ordered back to Nijmengen for some well-deserved rest. This was rudely interrupted on the 18th January, when the Germans launched a huge counter attack on the village of Zetten. 'D' Company and then 'B' Company were thrown into the front line to help comrades of the Leicestershire Regiment. Despite this, they were pushed back as heavy snow and a hard frost made conditions especially difficult. A day later the rest of battalion arrived and several objectives were taken after fierce fighting.

The fighting for Zetten now became house-to-house, with heavy casualties being sustained for the gain of only a few homes. On the 21st January, the German counter attack was finally halted and the village was once again occupied. The next day, the battalion were attacked for the first time by a new technology, the V1 Flying Bomb or Doodlebug. Casualties at Zetten accounted for ten men killed and a further forty wounded. The Germans by contrast, lost eight hundred men killed and had two hundred and fifty taken as prisoners of war.

The Glosters spent the next few weeks patrolling close to the front line at a place called Haalderen, they then moved to high ground west of Arnhem. At one point, an aggressive patrol of forty Germans was beaten back by the outposts of 'A' Company, leaving seven Germans dead with only one man wounded in the Glosters. Early April saw a platoon from 'D' Company take three landing craft down the river Neder Rijn. These men became the first Allied troops to set foot on the far bank since the failure of Operation Market Garden.

An attack on Arnhem was now necessary and the Glosters were called up to be in the main assault force. On the 12th April, they would cross the River Ijssel and form a bridgehead, which allowed the rest of their Division to assault Arnhem itself. At the top of the peninsula (the planned landing location) were 'B' Company who would storm across in Buffalo assault craft and then set up a defensive perimeter in an orchard. 'A' Company, also in Buffalo's, would attack the old Dutch fortress, Scheisprong. 'C' Company were tasked with taking the prominent silk factory, whilst 'D' Company would land on the base of the peninsula and clear up any resistance.

The landing area was softened up by an air and artillery attack. Despite some delays with the Buffalo's and light German resistance, the attack was a complete success. High Command predicted a hundred casualties but the Glosters only had three men killed and twenty-seven wounded. The South Wales Borderers and Essex then passed through the bridgehead and assaulted the city. This would be the last major action of the war that 2nd Battalion would see. Within a month, the German forces had surrendered and World War II in Europe was over.

# 56. Mont Pincon

After their escape from the beaches of Dunkirk in 1940 (see Battle Honour 50), 5th Battalion became a reconnaissance battalion. In 1942, all reconnaissance battalions became regiments in their own right but the attachment to the Glosters remained strong. 5th Battalion became the 43rd Reconnaissance Regiment and they headed off for the Normandy beachhead in late June 1944. They anchored off Sword Beach in Seine Bay on the 23rd June.

The previous night the Germans, who were now in no doubt that this was the much-feared Allied invasion of France, dropped mines off the Normandy coast. The Derrycunihy transport ship, with the 43rd Reconnaissance Regiment aboard, turned its engines over in preparation of receiving landing craft to transport the men ashore. Within seconds, the noise detonated an acoustic 'oyster' mine and a huge explosion ripped the ship in half. Lieutenant Groves was one of those lucky enough to escape the disaster:

> As on all nights during the voyage I was fully dressed except for my boots, battle dress blouse and my revolver…Reveille was to be at 8.30 and most of the men were still sleeping in the holds on the wooden floor that had been installed above the vehicles. The ship's engines started and ran for what could only have been a few seconds. There was a tremendous explosion aft of the boat deck. I was aware of the force of the explosion but I have no recollection of the noise it must have made. I jumped up and had a glimpse of the aft mast slowing tipping backwards…the stern of the Derrycunihy had been sliced off and was sliding into the sea taking our men and vehicles with it.

One hundred and eighty men would perish in this terrible episode along with another 150 wounded, representing the single largest loss of life on or off the Normandy beaches. The survivors were brought ashore and it took weeks to bring the regiment back up to full strength.

Finally, on the 28th July, 'B' and 'C' squadrons moved into the assembly area as part of 2nd Army. The next day 'A' squadron, who were mostly made up of Green Howards, arrived fresh from Britain. The goal was a significant one; the Glosters would reconnoitre the German held routes, which would be used to break out of the Normandy bridgehead.

On the 3rd August, 43rd Reconnaissance Regiment who were mostly in Humber Armoured Cars, moved towards Jurques ready for the advance. Already ahead of them to the northeast was the significant Mont Pincon, one of the final bastions of the German defences. The following day they arrived at Jurques but found the village littered with hundreds of dead Germans. There were flaming tanks, German Panzer IV's and British Sherman's, plus huge craters. A substantial battle had recently taken place here; more importantly to the Glosters it made their route impassable.

The same day, the regiment suffered their first casualties of this campaign. Being a reconnaissance regiment meant that they would travel at speed to certain locations, then two men would get out and survey the way ahead through binoculars. Arriving at Brequessard, Sergeant Midgeley and Trooper McAllister did just this but they were ambushed by concealed German machine guns. Being in the actual warzone was very different to training and it soon transpired that all reconnaissance would have to be done from within the armoured vehicles.

It was then reported that the route the Glosters had selected to continue their advance was lined with the deadly 88's. Changing their plans, it was further reported that Tiger tanks were also dead ahead and so a wide flanking manoeuvre was initiated. Being so far out in front of the main force had many disadvantages, including being clearly identified by your own side. As they continued the advance, the regiment were attacked with rockets by a group of RAF Hawker Typhoons. Luckily, no casualties were reported from the attack.

Throughout the advance, the Glosters were almost constantly peppered with mortar fire. Much of the 5th August was spent trying to locate and destroy these mortars but not one could be found. 'B' squadron also had the task of clearing a heavily mined bridge during which they tangled with a German patrol.

On the 6th August, the Glosters learnt that ahead of them were heavily defended crossroads at the town of Duval. Being a reconnaissance force meant the Glosters could move at pace. Surprise and speed would be their friends when attacking. The men charged into battle at around 40mph and then opened fire on the enemy. The Germans were caught completely off-guard by this sudden assault, several casualties were inflicted and many prisoners rounded up.

Later in the day, the regiment arrived at Ondefontaine, yet had to rapidly pull out as they ran straight into a host of German tanks. During the afternoon, several vehicles were sent to investigate another crossroads. Covering the last few metres on foot, they heard the rumbling of tank tracks and dived into nearby bushes just before elements of the Panzer Lehr Division rode by. The men were luckily not spotted and dusted themselves off. Then suddenly, two Panther tanks came trundling around the corner and the men fled, abandoning their vehicles. Again, luck was on their side as the enemies turrets were facing the opposite direction so they had time to escape.

On the 7th August, a vital bridge on the lower slopes of Mont Pincon was taken, despite being defended by machine guns. The Glosters then had to carefully probe their way through a minefield. As their advance continued, they rode straight into what had clearly been setup by the Germans as a defensive zone. A hard fight began with the assault squadron proceeding on foot. They fought the Germans hand-to-hand, whilst clearing several houses, and had the unenviable task of storming multiple machine gun nests. Resistance was finally subdued and a good amount of prisoners rounded up.

Elements of the 8th Armoured Brigade captured the peak of Mont Pincon on the 8th August. All that remained was to mop up the rest of the enemy in the area. The 43rd Reconnaissance Regiment pushed on towards the village of St. Jean, where they came into heavy contact with the Germans. After a brief firefight, it was clear they would have to pull back. This marked their last combat at the battle for Mont Pincon. By now, the American forces were on a near unstoppable drive into central France and the war in Western Europe had decisively turned.

For their brave actions, often being well in advance of any friendly units, the Glosters were awarded five Military Crosses and five Military Medals in the space of just a few days. 43rd Reconnaissance Regiment would become the first Allied troops to reach the Seine and the Rhine rivers. By the wars end, 219 men would have laid down their lives.

Throughout the early years of WWII, 10th Battalion had been a home defence unit and then converted to a tank regiment in 1942. In October they sailed out for India, stopping at Brazil on the way. As is often the case in warfare, the last year of intense training was rendered obsolete as the 10th converted back to an infantry battalion. However, they would put their experience with vehicles to good use in the coming campaign. Of course, absolutely no jungle warfare training, which would have proven useful, had been received.

In February 1944, the Glosters arrived at Calcutta and then moved to Chittagong in Bangladesh. They then finally landed at Coxs Bazaar, Burma, on a river steamer on 26th February. They had been assigned to the 72nd Brigade in 36th Division and the goal was clear. Push the Japanese out of Burma and, on a personal note, avenge 1st Battalion for what had occurred in 1942 (see Battle Honour 51).

The start of the campaign was a quiet one for the Glosters as they patrolled the Arakan Front and then headed eighty-five miles south to the Mayu Range of mountains. Here they extensively patrolled the "Jap Pass" area for many days but the only sign of the enemy was the odd document and abandoned equipment. On the 20th March, the 10th Battalion moved further south and were now in the absolute peaks of the Mayu Range. Three days later, they had their first successful encounter during a patrol, accounting for several of the enemy.

The Japanese were now entrenched in these peaks and on the 26th March 72nd Brigade were ordered to attack four prominent features. Battalions of the South Wales Borderers and Royal Sussex would form the assault. Meanwhile, 'A' Company of the Glosters provided direct fire support with mortars and machine guns. The attack was a resounding success and the Japanese were seen running away over two features called "Hambone North" and "Hambone South". The men of 10th Battalion would soon become extremely familiar with this landscape.

On the 29th March, a patrol was sent out to see if both of the Hambones were clear. On the northern feature, there was no sign of enemy activity. Approaching the southern Hambone though, the patrol came under extremely heavy fire and had to pull back. They dug in a little way south but came into repeated contact with Japanese patrols throughout the night. It was now clear that the enemy intended to hold this feature and they would have to be removed.

The following day, 'B' Company were sent forward but they received the same treatment as their comrades. They were able to identify a number of

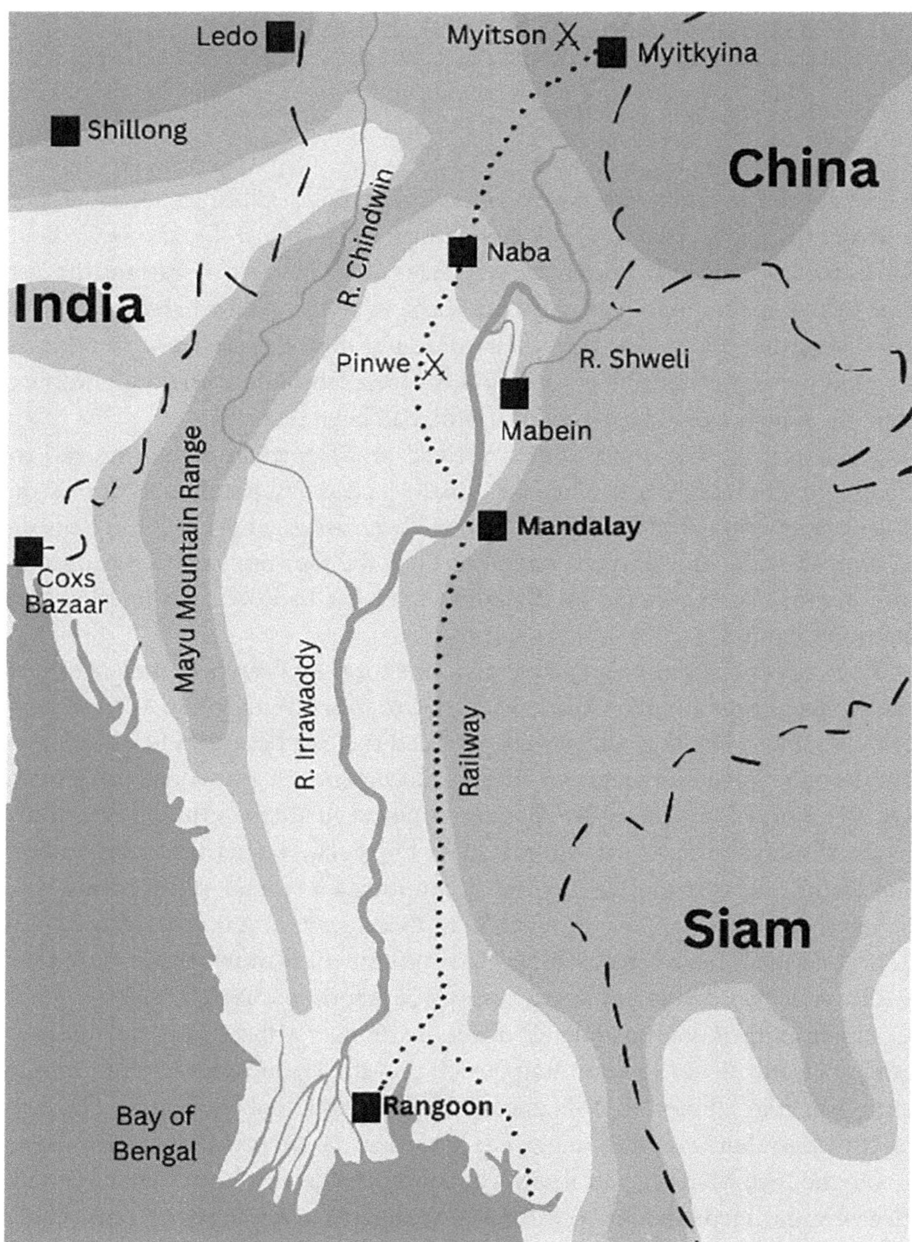


well-camouflaged Japanese bunkers, where heavy machine gun fire was coming from. On the 1st April, 'D' Company were sent in and their spirits were buoyed by the promise of a heavy aerial assault to precede their attack. As it happened, only three bombers took part in the raid and so once again, the Glosters were beaten back.

Finally realising how well dug in the Japanese were, High Command launched a devastating artillery attack throughout the 2nd and 3rd April. In the afternoon, a patrol was sent out and they discovered that the Japanese had abandoned their position. After holding the position for several days, the Glosters were relieved and their first serious combat had come to a close. Twelve men were killed on South Hambone whilst another thirty were wounded.

Next, 10th Battalion suddenly found themselves back in India in the town of Shillong. Five hundred miles from the action, they underwent a serious period of retraining and it was not until July that they were airlifted to Myitkyina in northern Burma. The Glosters now found themselves under the command of a popular American, "Vinegar" Joe Stillwell, in the Northern Combat Area Command. Stillwell's objective was to keep a supply route open from Ledo in Assam to China.

The 36th Division were ordered to advance down the Myitkynia–Mandalay railway to the area of Naba Junction in Katha. Katha was important to the Japanese supply route up the Irrawaddy River. As they slogged south, the Glosters helped clear and repair the railway line. A terrible ten-day route march through thick jungle, monsoon mud, unbearable heat and torrential rain then took place. Such conditions often brought disease and ten men a day were being emergency evacuated with malaria and dysentery.

Finally, on the 6th August they reached their destination, a stream called Sahmaw Chaung. The Japanese had dug in here and the Glosters flew straight into action. 'A' Company captured an important prominence that overlooked the main road, whilst 'B' Company cleared the right flank. Both these operations only cost one man wounded for 10th Battalion. The following day, 'C' Company went further around the right flank and surprised a Japanese machine gun party. 'D' Company also pushed on but became lost due to an inaccurate map, with which they had been provisioned.

The following days were spent continuing down the railway line capturing small villages and towns on the way. Resistance was light due to the fact that a terrifying Allied aerial bombardment had proceeded them some days earlier. On the 10th August, the Glosters marched into Taungni. This had been Stillwell's original target but the settlement was abandoned. It was clear that 36th Division had the enemy on the run so the advance was ordered to continue.

The very next day though, the Japanese sent the Allies a reminder that they were far from a beaten force. A huge counter attack hit the South Wales Borderers on the Glosters flank. The Glosters moved their mortars into position and used them with devastating effect. Blowing huge holes in the advancing infantry, the Japanese had no choice but to pull back once again. This was followed by several days of shelling, which resulted in a number of casualties.

The Glosters realised how isolated they were, as medically evacuating anyone was now a logistical nightmare.

Early on the 15th August, the advance down the railway line continued. Suddenly, 'D' Company on the right flank were ambushed by multiple Japanese machine guns. They almost instantly suffered fifteen men killed with a further seven wounded and found themselves pinned down. Perhaps luckily, one platoon of 'D' Company had somehow bypassed the machine gun ambush. When they heard the sound of firing, they charged back with bayonets fixed and slaughtered the enemy.

During the preceding period, the 36th Division had taken great pride in the fact that they were the only British division that was entirely supplied by air. They had been accompanied by US Army engineers who repeatedly constructed small airstrips in the middle of the jungle as the advance continued. On the 22nd August, the 10th Battalion were pulled back from the frontline to guard some of these airstrips and drop zones. The lack of action was much welcome though. Endlessly advancing through thick jungle or wading through waist high paddy fields had taken its toll. Dysentery and jungle sores had seen the battalion strength drop to just 286 men.

Further rest and reinforcement now occurred as the men redirected to Mingon for a three week period. Once they headed back into the main advance, route marches and patrolling were the order of the day. Weeks were spent in the thick teak forests where visibility was rarely over thirty yards. In mid-October, further reinforcements arrived to bring the battalion back up to nearly full strength. These would soon be sorely needed.

On the 7th November, two battalions from the Royal Sussex and the South Wales Borderers led the advance, whilst 10th Battalion were in the reserve. Good progress was made until the South Wales Borderers were hit by strong enemy resistance in the **Pinwe** area. A raging battle quickly developed but the Glosters remained in the rear, evacuating casualties and bringing up supplies. On the 15th November, the battalion were called into action and a new plan developed.

The Glosters would go on a wide flanking manoeuvre and come out in the Japanese rear. Things began badly, as forty-one of the hundred mules they used for transport were killed in a Japanese artillery strike. The column moved incredibly slowly due to the thick teak wood, stubborn mules and reliance on poor aerial photography for navigation. Three days later, they finally arrived at their destination but almost immediately ran into a Japanese patrol. The element of surprise was lost and the battalion had to pull back to the village of Tonlon, north of Pinwe, and dig in.

Another plan was now put in place, with the Glosters attacking an area around Gyobin Chaung, a stream that runs between Pinwe and Tonlon. This would then be used as a springboard to attack Pinwe itself. The battalion would move behind a creeping barrage laid down by artillery, which itself was preceded by an aerial bombardment. The only slight flaw in the plan was that the British knew there were Japanese bunkers and strongholds, yet these could not be accurately located due to the dense undergrowth.

At 10:30 on the 22nd November, the men of Gloucestershire launched their assault. Unfortunately, the slight flaw in the plan immediately became a huge problem. 'D' Company followed the barrage closely down the right hand side of the road that led from Tonlon to Pinwe. They managed to come across a group of Japanese returning to their bunker after the artillery assault and cut them down. Instantly though, they were fired on by a bunker on the opposite side of the road. The Glosters returned fire and charged the bunker but their assault was repulsed. 'C' Company then came up in support and attacked the bunker but they too were driven back.

Meanwhile on the other side of the road, 'A' Company came across another bunker but managed to attack this successfully. Once across the stream though, the Japanese opened a heavy fire and the men had to dig in and hold the ground they had so far taken. 'B' Company followed up in support but they were quickly pinned down by machine guns and snipers, meaning they did not even reach the stream. They dug in thirty yards short of the obstacle.

Enemy fire now literally came from every direction getting heavier minute by minute. The Japanese pummelled the Glosters with mortars, machine guns and sniper fire. Despite this, the men bravely held the ground they had gained and they managed to cling on until nightfall. This day of combat had cost the Glosters twenty-two killed and forty-seven wounded.

The next day, as an example of how truly thick and unforgiving the jungle was, 'C' Company launched an attack on the bunker that had pinned the Glosters down on the right side of the road. They simply could not find it again and had to return to their original positions. The battalion then turned their own mortar and machine gun fire upon the enemy. An attack in the afternoon by the South Wales Borderers was well supported but ultimately unsuccessful.

The 24th November was spent aggressively patrolling, when news came through that the Royal Sussex had seized a vital bridge across the stream. Soon after this, the Japanese fire died down, and the next day all the Glosters had to contend with was light sniper fire. On the 26th, the Royal Scots Fusiliers arrived to relieve the battalion and the Battle of Pinwe was at an end.

Days later, 10th Battalion found themselves five miles behind the line at the village of Hpapan. This was a railway station vital for communications and bringing up supplies. Here they spent the next few weeks reorganising and retraining. On the 8th December, the Glosters moved back into Pinwe but the enemy were nowhere to be seen. They pressed onwards and by Christmas Day, they were freely crossing a major obstacle, the Irrawaddy River.

It was now monsoon season and movement for either side became near impossible. The advance continued at a glacial speed, with the only danger coming from sporadic sniper fire. Eventually reports were received that the Japanese were holding the village of Mabein. On the 14th January 1945, half of 'D' Company raided the village but it was so full of enemy that they hurriedly withdrew. An enormous artillery and aerial bombardment was launched upon Mabein. When 'D' Company returned only twenty enemy remained. They were swiftly dealt with and the village was taken.

The next few days were taken up with patrolling and on the 18th January 'B' Company fell in with a Japanese unit, just eight hundred yards into their journey. They fell back and the area was shelled before they moved in once again. Still the numbers of enemy were overwhelming so they pulled back and upon returning the Japanese had vanished. Another patrol later in the day stumbled across what must have been the same enemy force and they suffered heavy casualties.

The next task for the Glosters was to provide support to the 26th Indian Brigade. They made an assault across the River Shweli on the 8th February, occupying the village of **Myitson**. The Japanese believed that this was a mistake and began to launch a counter attack. They thought the entire 36th Division was trapped in a bend of the river and that they could be annihilated.

On the 11th, 'B' and 'D' Company crossed the Shweli to support the 26th Brigade. Together they formed a 'protective box' from where they could guard crossing points of the Shweli and its large tributary, Nameik Chaung. The rest of 10th Battalion then also crossed the river and took up position within the box. Things were going well as the next day much needed reinforcements arrived on the scene. However, any morale boost was soon quelled as reports of vast enemy activity to the northwest were reported.

On the 13th February, the Japanese managed to suddenly infiltrate themselves between 'D' Company and 26th Brigade Headquarters, effectively isolating them. 'B' Company immediately leapt into action and attacked the Japanese in a full frontal charge hoping to reach their comrades. They were hit in the flank by Japanese machine guns, suffering four killed and six wounded, meaning they had to pull back. 'C' Company then tried to reach their stricken comrades later in the afternoon, yet they too were flanked by enemy machine guns and had to retire. The irony of these two attacks was that they could not be supported by artillery or mortars as 'D' Company were considered too nearby.

Meanwhile the Japanese had launched a mass attack against the men of 'D' Company. The enemy were spotted by a perimeter patrol and beaten back. In the attack, the Glosters lost eight men killed and a further three wounded. As an example of the stealth and guile of the Japanese, that evening 'D' Company found an enemy solider dug in just two yards from their forward outpost.

The next plan to reach 'D' Company involved 'A' and 'C' Company moving out into the long grass and forming two "bases". This they managed to do but 'A' Company were so heavily countered by the Japanese that they had to fall back and form up with 'C' Company, who themselves only had forty-five men left. That ended the opening day of hostilities for the Glosters, with 'D' Company still dangerously isolated.

That evening, 'D' Company received heavy mortar and artillery attacks throughout the night but the day remained mostly quiet. The same could not be said for Battalion HQ though, who faced a banzai attack during the afternoon. This suicidal charge by the Japanese resulted in ten dead for zero casualties for the Glosters.

An event now occurred that would later result in a very public falling out between the commander of the 26th Brigade, Brigadier M. B. Jennings, and the 10th Battalion's Commanding Officer, Lieutenant-Colonel Richard Butler. Without the knowledge of the Glosters, the 26th Brigade withdrew, leaving behind all their ammunition and supplies. It was now not just 'D' Company who were cut off, but the entire battalion. Japanese snipers quickly infiltrated behind the Glosters and made any attempt to reach the river crossing far too deadly. The battalion decided to dig in and during the evening, the Japanese put up roadblocks to further isolate the men of Gloucestershire.

Unperturbed by their situation, it was decided that the goal was to remain the same, reach 'D' Company. Early on the 16th February, the entire battalion moved out wading through the tall elephant grass. At 09:30, a welcome sight appeared through the undergrowth as comrades of 'D' Company began to be found. They had been cut off for four days.

The Glosters now created a defensive perimeter at the junction of the two rivers, Shweli and Nameik Chaung. This covered two of their flanks and they then set up a ferry service across the river. This instantly negated being cut off, whilst casualties were evacuated and supplies flooded in. The next day, the Japanese launched a series of heavy artillery barrages and some light probing but probably realising the exceptional defensive position of the Glosters, they did not attack again.

On the 18th, the battalion sent out aggressive patrols but only came into light contact with the enemy. They returned to where 26th Brigade had abandoned their supplies but the Japanese had already taken everything. After several more days of patrolling, it was realised that the Japanese had melted away and the battalion were soon relieved by the Gurkhas. Of the 250 men in 10th Battalion before the battle, 119 of them had been killed or wounded by the time the Japanese withdrew.

It is clear that the Glosters had fought well, however as previously mentioned, bitter recriminations now began as to who was at fault for the poor conduct at the Battle of Myitson. Brigadier Jennings, perhaps because he was the senior man, was deemed to be faultless, and battalion Commanding Officer, Lieutenant Colonel Butler would be sacked.

10th Battalion once again crossed the Nameik Chaung on the 22nd February, immediately coming under heavy machine gun fire. 'A' and 'B' Companies dug in and provided fire support, whilst 'C' Company went on a wide flanking move and positioned themselves deep in the enemy rear. They managed to ambush several fleeing Japanese but the next day the enemy had once again disappeared. The next few days were spent patrolling and keeping the road open and clear of the enemy.

On the 3rd and 4th April, the battalion were flown out of the line and landed in Burma's religious capital, Mandalay. The contrast for these warriors who had spent so much time fighting in the thick jungle must have been overwhelming. On the 8th April, the Glosters were given a 'special mission' to grab a man in a nearby village who had been reported as a member of the Burma Traitor Army. They successfully accomplished this and the man was brought back for interrogation. The rest of the time was now spent protecting stores, bridge building and intelligence gathering.

On the 19th May, the men received their first leave in over a year. A tented camp full of luxuries, such as showers and warm beds, that they had only dreamed of now awaited. From here, the battalion travelled back to India and in December 1945, this battalion of Burma heroes was disbanded. The campaign had cost the men of Gloucestershire 125 lives and countless wounded. Four Military Crosses, two Distinguished Conduct Medals and twelve Military Medals had been awarded.

The Second World War ended on the 2nd September 1945. The Japanese had nothing to defend against this new destroyer of worlds, the atomic bomb. Fighting across Europe, the Middle East and Far East had cost the Gloucestershire Regiment over 1100 men killed and many more wounded.

# Korea

Post World War II the Korean peninsula was split along the 38th parallel into two zones of administration, the Soviet backed communist north and the US backed capitalist south. On the 25th June 1950, North Korean forces came crashing across the 38th parallel in a surprise attack. The assault was a stunning success reaching the southern tip of the peninsula in just two weeks. On 3rd November 1950, the first elements of 29th Independent Infantry Brigade Group began disembarking at Pusan on the south eastern tip of the Korean peninsula. Six days later 1st Battalion of the Gloucestershire Regiment arrived on board H.M.T. Windrush. By this point, the conflict was going well for the UN Forces and they were pushing right up to the Chinese border.

After five days, traveling by train the 29th Brigade arrived at Suwon on 20th November. Here they would have their first enemy contact as the Ulster Rifles fought a brief battle with a guerrilla force. The following day the brigade moved through Seoul and spent nine days patrolling. During this period, the Glosters would have their first enemy contact, also against a guerrilla force. On 26th November 'C' Company were sweeping the countryside when they found a huge crater. It caused so much excitement that even Lieutenant Colonel Carne, Battalion Commanding Officer, came out to view it. He declared it a "fine crater". Moments later fire erupted all around the Glosters. Eighty enemy with seven machine guns poured on their fire. The men quickly found cover and began to return fire. Once the supporting artillery found its range, the ambushers fled. Two men were killed and eight wounded in this first contact.

After the days of patrolling had ended the Glosters jumped into motorised transport and travelled eighty miles to Pyongyang. By now though, the campaign had dramatically changed. The Chinese Army had come flooding across the border and the UN Forces were in a desperate retreat. 29th Brigade were allotted the task of holding bridges north of Pyongyang but on the 6th December, they were ordered to blow these up and pull back south.

On 1st January 1951, 29th Brigade found themselves holding a line on the Imjin River. News soon arrived that the Chinese had smashed through the South Korean troops on their flank and so 29th Brigade were ordered into an immediate counter attack. It soon became clear that the South Koreans had been so resoundingly beaten that any counter moves were useless and so the retreat continued. The brigade then set up defensive lines in front of Seoul with

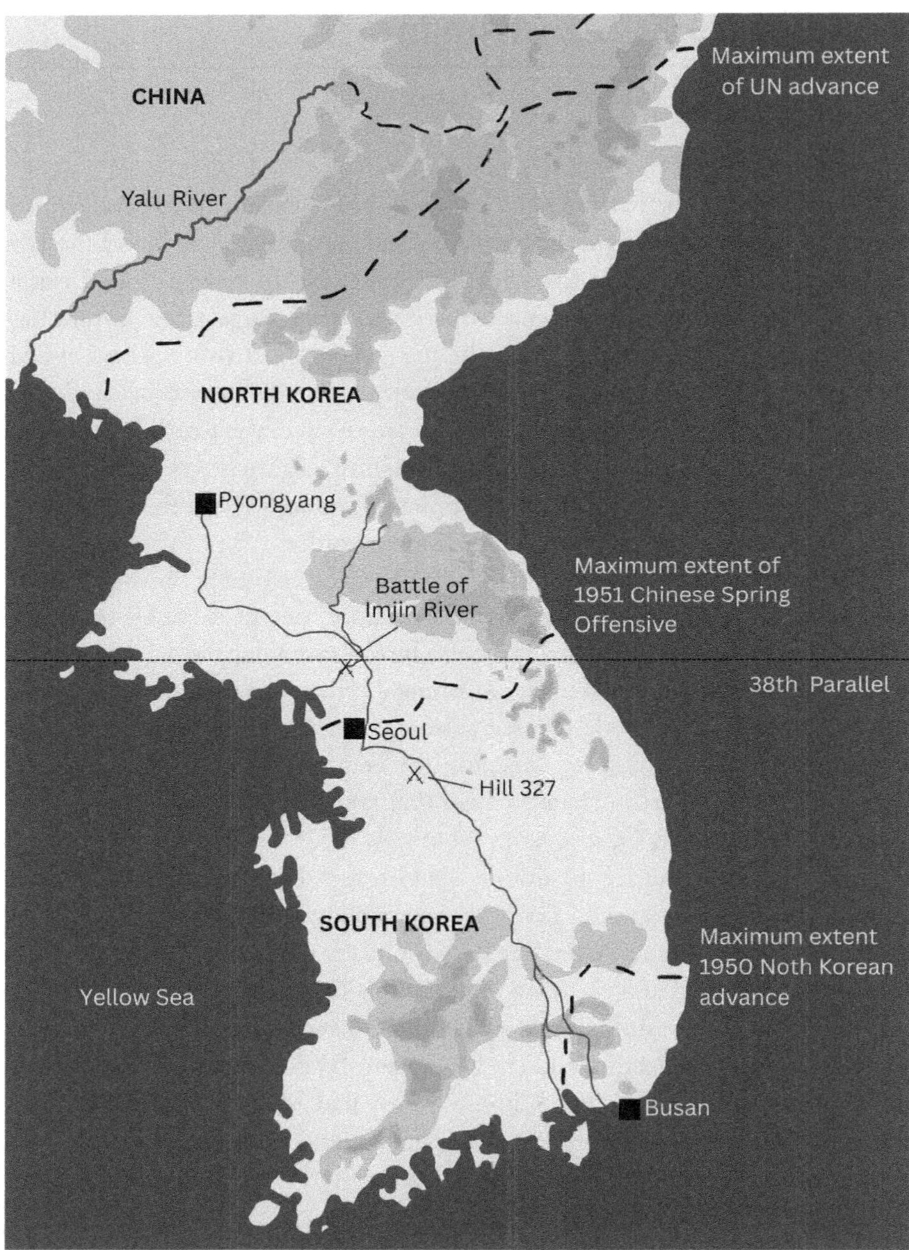


the Ulster's on the left, Northumberland Fusiliers on the right and Glosters in reserve.

The Chinese attacked the defensive line on 3rd January but the Ulster's and Fusiliers held their ground inflicting serious casualties on the enemy. Despite this a further withdraw was ordered as the success had not been reflected elsewhere. However, during the process of pulling back the Ulster's, along with Cromwell tanks of the 45th Field Regiment and reconnaissance troops of the 8th Hussars, were ambushed. They fought heroically throughout the day and managed to breakout but suffered 342 casualties.

By 6th January, the seemingly unstoppable torrent of the Chinese advance was finally checked at Pyongtek. 29th Brigade played no real part in this effort but during the few days in which they held a sector of the line 250,000 South Korean troops retreated through them. For the rest of the month something of a stalemate ensued with the Chinese probing the UN defensive lines looking for a weak spot.

The UN Forces continued to hold the defensive line into February and on the night of 12th/13th February, 'A' Company found themselves on the front line. During a quiet night, the Glosters were suddenly sprayed with rifle fire from very close range. The attack vanished as quickly as it had appeared. The Glosters were now on their guard though and when the enemy returned they waited until they were almost at point blank range and then let all hell loose. The Chinese retreated to forty yards and began returning fire. A short firefight ensued until UN artillery and mortars were unleashed at which point the enemy once again vanished. At daybreak, the Glosters counted eleven dead enemy within ten yards of their slit trenches.

The following day Battalion Headquarters was shelled by artillery but there were no casualties. Finally though, after several months of defence and retreat the Glosters were able to switch to an offensive footing. Before them was Hill 327 and on the 14th February this was softened up by the US 5th Air Force who unleashed a devastating rocket attack. This was in preparation for the hill to be attacked by the Glosters on the 16th February. As the men moved into their start positions at 10:30 the sky was heavy and snow hung in the air.

The men had to charge 200 metres up an extremely steep slope before they could engage the enemy. Carne sent 'D' Company left and 'C' Company right. Artillery, tanks and mortars bombarded the hill as the Glosters advanced but there was no sign of the enemy. Suddenly, 100 metres from their first objective grenades came rolling down the hill. This was quickly followed by rifle fire and then machine guns. Carne had to change tact and ordered 'C' Company to lay a base of fire whilst 'D' Company swung around on a flanking manoeuvre.

The hill was littered with enemy bunkers and 'D' Company soon came upon the first of these. They quickly assaulted the enemy position and by doing so had occupied the western portion of Hill 327. This was the signal for 'C' Company to continue their ascent and they too came upon more bunkers. Each had to be cleared, often in fierce had-to-hand combat, with the Chinese always fighting to the last man. Finally, the two Companies managed to link up again and then they began clearing another series of bunkers.

At this point Carne sent 'B' Company to assault the eastern side of the hill but when they reached the peak, the only sign of the enemy was their food still cooking on small stoves. The Chinese had fled from the scene. The advance continued and on the 21st February, 29th Brigade found themselves at the River Han, just south of Seoul. They soon moved out of the frontline and spent a few weeks resting in Suwon. On 1st April, they moved back to the **Imjin River**. This was part of a new seven-mile defensive effort, the 'Kansas Line'. For several weeks, the Glosters patrolled the opposite bank but little enemy contact was had.

On the 21st April 1951 'A' Company were based on the 148m high Castle Hill. The position was well chosen as it overlooked the main crossing point of the Imjin River (soon to be forever known as "Gloster Crossing"), just 2000 yards to the north. To the southeast were 'D' Company holding a point called 192. 'B' Company held the flank and were the closest unit to the neighbouring

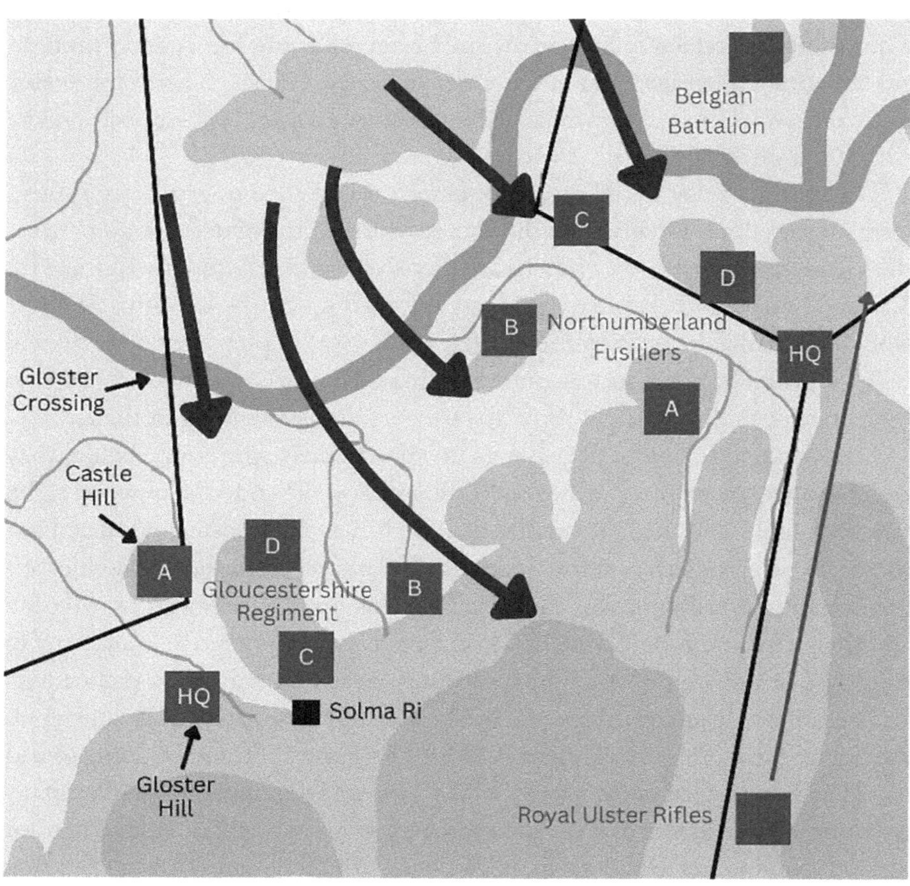

Northumberland Fusiliers. Nevertheless, these allies were positioned two miles away. Finally, 'C' Company was held in reserve whilst Battalion Headquarters was nestled in the river valley with several of the mortar brigades.

At 22:00, Drummer Eagles spotted some movement on the opposite bank of the Imjin River. He radioed back to the Adjutant, Anthony Farrar-Hockley, who proceeded to send up a few flares. They very clearly highlighted fourteen Chinese troops wading across the crossing. Eagles and his two comrades opened fire and the Chinese retreated. The rest of the night passed in silence. A tepid start to the soon to be brutal Chinese Spring Offensive.

Dusk on the 22nd April brought welcome news. Aerial reconnaissance reported that there were no Chinese troops within ten miles of Gloster Crossing. Despite this, Lieutenant Guy Temple of 'C' Company had moved up to an ambush position right on the crossing point. Later in the evening, an entire Chinese battalion began to cross the Imjin and the Glosters opened fire. Combining with UN artillery meant that countless numbers of the enemy fell. Even so, they kept coming and eventually Temple and his men were forced to pull back as they started to run out of ammunition.

Soon after the first contact was made, two Chinese battalions smashed into the flank of 'A' Company. In theory, this should have been impossible. All crossings were well guarded and the Chinese troop positions were all on the other side of the river. What the UN forces had not realised though was that there was an ancient underwater bridge just down river, which appeared on no maps. This error allowed the Chinese to penetrate into the gaping hole between 'B' Company and the Fusiliers, turning their full weight upon the Glosters.

Throughout the night 'A' Company were relentlessly attacked but several well positioned machine gun sections covered both Castle Hills summit and flanks. At times, they were outnumbered by as much as 6–1 but still the Glosters held. At midnight the Chinese captured a bunker forward of 'A' Company's position so Lieutenant Curtis was given the job of recapturing the position. By the end of this episode, Curtis would have paid with his life and been awarded the Victoria Cross:

During the first phase of the Battle of the Imjin River on the night of 22nd/23rd April 1951, "A" Company, 1 Glosters, was heavily attacked by a large enemy force. By dawn on 23rd April, the enemy had secured a footing on the 'Castle Hill' site in very close proximity to No. 2 Platoon's position. The Company Commander ordered No. 1 Platoon, under the command of Lieutenant CURTIS, to carry out a counter-attack with a view to dislodging the enemy from the position. Under the covering of medium machine guns, the counterattack, gallantly led by Lieutenant

CURTIS, gained initial success but was eventually held up by heavy fire and grenades. Enemy from just below the crest of the hill were rushed to reinforce the position and a fierce fire-fight developed, grenades also being freely used by both sides in this close quarter engagement. Lieutenant CURTIS ordered some of his men to give him covering fire while he himself rushed the main position of resistance; in this charge Lieutenant CURTIS was severely wounded by a grenade. Several of his men crawled out and pulled him back under cover but, recovering himself, Lieutenant Curtis insisted on making a second attempt. Breaking free from the men who wished to restrain him, he made another desperate charge, hurling grenades as he went, but was killed by a burst of fire when within a few yards of his objective.

Although the immediate objective of this counter-attack was not achieved, it had yet a great effect on the subsequent course of the battle; for although the enemy had gained a footing on a position vital to the defence of the whole Company area, this success had resulted in such furious reaction that they made no further effort to exploit their success in this immediate area; had they done so, the eventual withdrawal of the Company might well have proved impossible.

Major Angier, 'A' Company Commanding Officer, then decided they could not hold Castle Hill any longer. Ammunition was almost completely depleted and the casualties were rocketing. At this exact moment, Major Angier was killed and one could forgive an element of panic spreading through the company; but this never occurred. The Glosters needed a natural born leader to steady the ship and up stepped CSM Gallagher (a hero of the Regiment who we last saw fighting the Germans at Zuytpeene in Chapter 50). He organised the fifty-four survivors and led them down off Castle Hill to link up with comrades on the eastern slopes of Gloster Hill.

The loss of Castle Hill meant Colonel Carne had to reorganise his forces. The tightening of the perimeter also saw the Glosters flank being turned. This was not such an issue at the current time as it was a tactically sound move but more worrying was the message to HQ that air support was no longer available.

On the morning of the 23rd April, the hostilities greatly decreased. The Chinese and North Koreans rarely fought in daylight due to fear of UN air superiority. This gave the Glosters chance to evacuate the wounded and ferry in supplies from the rear echelons. This would be the last opportunity to carry out such tasks though as by early evening the Chinese had cut off the road. From here on in the Glosters would be surrounded.

During the previous evening, the Glosters had been facing the Chinese 187 Division. So high were their casualties on that first eve that they had to be withdrawn from the line. By 22:30, the offensive was in full swing again with most of the aggression falling upon 'B' and 'C' Companies. At Battalion Headquarters, they found themselves far to exposed to the action and so moved further up the hill.

'B' Company had taken the brunt of the nights attack and had quickly found themselves isolated. At daybreak, they were ordered to break through and re-join the rest of the battalion. Their comrades could only watch on in horror as the retreating 'B' Company were mercilessly cut down by their opponents. Only twenty men would make it back to the line.

At overall UN command, it had become clear that the Glosters were completely cut off. So on the 24th April Centurion tanks of the 8th Hussars and some Filipino light tanks, led by Major Digby Grist who was in charge of the Glosters rear echelons, attempted to reach their beleaguered comrades. The steep sided ravines and valleys of the area were certainly not classic tank country and they soon found themselves ambushed. Once the lead tank was knocked out, it formed a perfect roadblock and there was no way through.

Once news of the failed break through reached Colonel Carne it was clear that the situation was desperate. The warrior quality and battle spirit was clearly not diminished but what was a major issue was the lack of ammunition and radios not to mention water. In a near suicidal mission RSM Hobbs (also a Cassel veteran, see Battle Honour 50) led a small team of men back down into the valley to retrieve supplies the Glosters had been forced to abandon earlier. They somehow returned with batteries, a wireless and much ammunition.

By the early evening of the 24th, Colonel Carne knew he had to tighten his perimeter even further. He moved all his remaining men to the very top of the precipitous slopes of Gloster Hill. This would make relief much less likely but make defending themselves far less dangerous. So here, the remaining heroes of the regiment dug in. Predictably, the Chinese attack once again started at 22:00 and they once again threw their overwhelming numbers of attackers straight at 'A' Company.

At dawn on the 25th April, the enemy continued with their attack. A noticeable sound above the constant din of battle were Chinese trumpets for this is how they communicated on the battlefield. Captain Farrar-Hockley ordered Drum-Major Buss to offer a reply to this. He stood up exposing himself to enemy fire and played every British bugle call he could muster, except of course Retreat. This small moment did a huge amount to raise the men's spirits and fill them full of courage for the final battle.

Unusually, dawn saw no respite for the Glosters and the Chinese continued their onslaught directed at 'A' Company. Now only one officer and twenty-nine men remained. Farrar-Hockley went up see how they were fairing and instantly saw the situation was desperate. He immediately organised and personally led a counter attack to relieve the pressure. Wave after wave was thrown upon 'A' Company and they sent seven enemy attacks scurrying back in the space of just an hour.

At 06:30, word came through for the Glosters to withdraw. However, such an order was easier said than done. The attacks on 'A' Company continue but ammunition was running perilously low. The situation was now desperate with even Battalion Headquarters coming under intense machine gun fire. Finally at 08:30 air support unexpectedly arrived. They laid down a furious carpet of rockets and napalm that no man could survive. For now the Chinese attack subsided. Colonel Carne realised that the dying down of the Chinese assault was a good time to order the withdraw. After 60 hours, the Battle of Imjin River was over.

Only forty-six men managed to return to friendly lines after a terrifying odyssey. Fifty-nine men of Gloucestershire had been killed during the battle and a further 522 became prisoners of war suffering a hellish two and a half years in North Korean captivity. Many accolades would follow including a US Presidential Citation, a George Cross for Lieutenant Waters relating to his care of the wounded and a Victoria Cross awarded to Lieutenant Colonel Carne.

On 22/23 April 1951 near the Imjin River, Korea, Lieutenant Colonel Carne's battalion was heavily and incessantly engaged by vastly superior numbers of the enemy. Throughout this time Colonel Carne moved among the whole battalion under very heavy mortar and machine-gun fire, inspiring the utmost confidence and the will to resist among his troops. On two separate occasions, armed with rifle and grenades, he personally led assault parties which drove back the enemy and saved important situations. His courage, coolness and leadership was felt not only in his own battalion but throughout the whole brigade.

On the 26th April, the 29th Brigade moved onto the left flank of UN Forces on the River Han. Equipment and reinforcements came flooding in and by 4th May, Lieutenant Colonel Grist had the honour of reporting the Glosters as operational once again. By the 23rd May the Brigade were back on the Imjin River holding a much shorter front. Within a month four thousand tonnes of mines, wires and obstacles littered the area, the UN Forces would not make the same mistake again.

The opposite bank of the Imjin River was again extensively patrolled but all they ever found were bundles of North Korean propaganda tied to trees. By mid-July, the Glosters were back up to their full strength and within a month found themselves back on Gloster Hill. A new defensive line, Wyoming, was established a mile and a half north of the river on 12th September. The line was established with no contact from the enemy. Finally, on 1st November the Welch Regiment relieved the Glosters and their Korean campaign was over. The Chinese Spring Offensive was actually the last major operation of the war on either side. The lines would remain stagnant but it would not be for another two years until the ceasefire was signed.

# Acknowledgements

This book would certainly have not been possible if not for the incredible efforts of the Grazebrook family, particularly two brothers. Colonel Robert Grazebrook, OBE, MC (1893–1965) was Commanding Officer of 1st Battalion of the Glosters from 1936 until 1939 and was also Honorary Colonel of 5th Glosters from 1951 until 1956. Brigadier Tom Grazebrook, CBE, DSO, DL (1904–67) was Commanding Officer of the 1st Royal Inniskillings and 159th Infantry Brigade.

Robert was a founding member of the Soldiers of Gloucestershire Museum. He was also the Head Archivist and editor of the regimental magazine, Back Badge. He carried the moniker 'Nap' (for Napoleon), as a tribute to his vast military knowledge. Tom was also an excellent amateur historian and held the post of first Regimental Secretary.

Very much standing on the shoulders of giants, a large amount of knowledge contained within this work was only possible to access through the Grazebrook brothers decade's long effort to bring some sense of order to the mammoth Regimental archive.

A debt is also owed to HRH the Duke of Gloucester who kindly agreed to produce the forward for this work. The patronage of His Royal Highness still means much to the men and as the Colonel-in-Chief, he is still held in the highest regard.

Finally, to the patience of Melissa. Without her help, support and editing skills, this book would certainly not have made it past the first draft stage. I am sure our baby son, Felix, will enjoy the fruits of our combined labour when he reaches an age at which he can appreciate it.

# Bibliography

**Books**

Atteridge, A. H. *Marshal Ney: The Bravest of the Brave*. Barnsley, 2005.

Bryant, Arthur. *Years of Elegance*. London, 1950.

———. *Years of Victory*. London, 1944.

Campbell, Colin. *Memorandum on the Part Taken by the Third Division of the Army of the Punjab at the Battle of Chillianwala*. London, 1851.

Coote, Stephen. *Napoleon and the Hundred Days*. Reading, 2004.

Daniell, David Scott. *Cap of Honour*. Stroud: History Press, 2005.

Esdaille, Charles. *Napoleon's Wars*. St. Edmunds, 2008.

Farrar-Hockley, Anthony. *The Edge of the Sword*. Liverpool, 1955.

Ferguson, Niall. *Empire: How Britain Made the Modern World*. St. Ives, 2004.

Fortescue, J. W. *History of the British Army*, Vols. VI–X. London, 1899–1933.

Grist, Robin. *A Gallant County*. Barnsley, 2018.

Griffith, Kenneth. *Thank God We Kept the Flag Flying*. New York, 1974.

Hamley, Edward. *The War in the Crimea*. London, 1907.

Holmes, Richard. *Marlborough*. St. Ives, 2008.

Keegan, John. *Six Armies in Normandy*. Chatham, 1992.

Marshall, P. J. *Edmund Burke and the British Empire in the West Indies: Wealth, Power, and Slavery*. Oxford, 2019.

Marks, Dean. *Bristol's Own: A History of 12th Bn Glosters*. Dolman Scott, 2011.

McCarthy, Chris. *The Somme: The Day-by-Day Account*. London, 1995.

Meredith, Martin. *Diamonds, Gold and War*. London, 2007.

Moiret, Joseph-Marie. *Memoirs of Napoleon's Egyptian Expedition, 1798–1801*. London, 2001.

Napier, W. F. P. *The War in the Peninsula*. Vols. I–VI. Unknown publisher, 1828–1840.

Oman, Charles. *History of the Peninsular War*. London, 1902.

Pedersen, Peter. *Fromelles – French Flanders*. Barnsley, 2004.

Radice, A. H. *A Subaltern's Recollections of the Boer War*. Unpublished, 1935.

Reid, Stuart. *Quebec 1759: The Battle That Won Canada*. Croydon, 2022.

Reilly, Robin. *Wolfe of Quebec*. London: Cassell, 1960.

Salmon, Andrew. *To the Last Round*. London, 2010.

Tracy, Nicholas, ed. *The Naval Chronicle: Contemporary Views of the War at Sea*, Vol. 3. Chatham, 2003.

Urban, Mark. *The Tank War*. London, 2013.

Wyrall, Everard. *The Gloucestershire Regiment in the Great War 1914–1918*. London, 1931.

**Diaries (Unpublished)**

2nd Battalion War Diary. *The Gloucestershire Regiment, 1943–1945*. Unpublished.

2nd/4th Battalion War Diary. *The Gloucestershire Regiment, 1914–1918*. Unpublished.

2nd/6th Battalion War Diary. *The Gloucestershire Regiment, 1914–1918*. Unpublished. Appendix 3.

Bazeley, Edward. *7th Bn The Gloucestershire Regiment: War of 1914–1918*. Unpublished, pp. 68–99.

Brassington, Captain. *Services during May 1940*. Unpublished.

Fane, 2nd Lt. *Diary, 14th May – 2nd June 1940*. Unpublished.

Gordon, W. A. *Journal of the Siege of Louisburg*. Unknown, pp. 117–152.

Hardman, Percy. *Diary of Percy Hardman, 1940*. Unpublished.

Hauting, L. C. *Diary of Capt. L. C. Hauting, Adjt. 5 Glosters*. Unpublished, pp. 111–115.

Hudson. *Journal, 22nd November 1848 – 21st February 1849*. Unpublished, pp. 5–9.


**Letters (Unpublished)**

Adams, F. Letters to Arthur Adams. March 5, May 4, and June 29, 1855.

Averies, W. Letter to Father and Mother. October 26, 1899.

Cumming, J. A. Letter to Parents. May 24, 1942.

Dunkley, H. Letter to T. N. Grazebrook. Unknown date.

Ladds, G. W. V. Letter. December 9, 1942.

McLeod, A. Letter to William MacLeod. July 28, 1849.

Trescow, H. Letter to Lt. Col. Butterworth. September 13, 1944.

Williams, J. Letters to Sophy Smith. 1854–1856.


**Documents (Unpublished)**

Crenan, Sgt. *Chillianwallah: An Account*. Unpublished.

Grazebrook, T. N. *Egyptian Campaign – 1801*. Unpublished.

——. *Waterloo Campaign – 1815*. Unpublished.

——. *The 61st Foot – 18th Century*. Unpublished.

——. *Peninsula War*. Unpublished.

——. *43rd Recce Bn in North West Europe*. Unpublished.

Groves, John. *Experiences as a Serving Officer in the 43rd Reconnaissance Regiment*. Unpublished.

Halliday, J. P. *Service in the 61st from 1843 to 1857*. Unpublished. pp. 41

Hudson, W.J. *Extracts from a Journal*. Unpublished. pp. 69

Maunsell, Major General. *Captain Maunsell, Some Recollections of Active Service*. Unpublished.

Scarr, Desmond. *Memoirs of 43rd Reconnaissance Regiment*. Unpublished.

Willis, P. F. *Story of 10th Glosters*. [1945]. Unpublished.


**Articles**

Burkart, E. F. "The 2nd Battalion at Arnhem, 1945." *Back Badge Magazine*, [year?].

Chambers, A. H. R. "The Capture of Le Havre." *Back Badge Magazine*, [year?].

Holgate, H. "After Le Havre to Blerick." *Back Badge Magazine*, [year?].

——. "After Thury-Harcourt to Le Havre." *Back Badge Magazine*, June 1951.

——. "The 61st in the Western Europe Campaign, 1944." *Back Badge Magazine*, [year?].

Hitsman, J. MacKay, and C. C. J. Bond. "The Assault Landing, 1758." *The Canadian Historical Review* 35, no. 4 (December 1954): 327.

Nash, R. "Thury-Harcourt." *Back Badge Magazine*, [year?].


**Newsletter**

*2nd Battalion Newsletter*, January 1–April 30, 1945.

# Index